The Comparative Politics of Transnational Climate Governance

Following the 2015 Paris climate agreement, the global politics of climate change depends more than ever on national climate policies and the actions of cities, businesses, and other non-state actors, as well as the transnational governance networks that link them. *The Comparative Politics of Transnational Climate Governance* sheds new light on these critical trends by exploring how domestic political, economic, and social forces systematically shape patterns of non-state actor participation in transnational climate initiatives. The book develops a common conceptual framework and uses a unique data set to explore the interplay between transnational and domestic politics and how these interactions shape the incentives and modalities of participation in transnational governance. The contributing chapters explore the role of cities, non-governmental organizations, companies, carbon markets, and regulations, as well as broader questions of effectiveness and global governance. Bringing together some of the foremost experts in the field of global governance and environmental politics, this book significantly advances our understanding of transnational governance and provides new insights for policymakers seeking to address the problem of climate change.

This book was originally published as a special issue of *International Interactions*.

Liliana B. Andonova is Professor of International Relations and Co-Director of the Center for International Environmental Studies at the Graduate Institute of International and Development Studies, Geneva, Switzerland. Her research focuses on international institutions, transnational governance, public-private partnerships, European integration, and environmental cooperation. Her books include *Governance Entrepreneurs: International Organizations and the Rise of Public-Private Partnerships*; *Transnational Climate Change Governance*; and *Transnational Politics of the Environment*.

Thomas N. Hale is Associate Professor at the Blavatnik School of Government at the University of Oxford, UK. His research seeks to explain how political institutions evolve—or not—to face the challenges of globalization. His books include *Beyond Gridlock, Between Interests and Law: The Politics of Transnational Commercial Disputes* and *Transnational Climate Change Governance*.

Charles B. Roger is an SSHRC Postdoctoral Fellow in the Department of Political Science at the University of Toronto, Canada. His research focuses on processes of informal and transnational governance, and global environmental politics. He is a co-author of *Transnational Climate Change Governance* and co-editor of *Global Governance at Risk*.

The Comparative Politics of Transnational Climate Governance

Edited by
Liliana B. Andonova, Thomas N. Hale and
Charles B. Roger

LONDON AND NEW YORK

First published 2018
by Routledge
2 Park Square, Milton Park, Abingdon, Oxon, OX14 4RN, UK

and by Routledge
711 Third Avenue, New York, NY 10017, USA

Routledge is an imprint of the Taylor & Francis Group, an informa business

© 2018 Taylor & Francis

All rights reserved. No part of this book may be reprinted or reproduced or utilised in any form or by any electronic, mechanical, or other means, now known or hereafter invented, including photocopying and recording, or in any information storage or retrieval system, without permission in writing from the publishers.

Trademark notice: Product or corporate names may be trademarks or registered trademarks, and are used only for identification and explanation without intent to infringe.

British Library Cataloguing in Publication Data
A catalogue record for this book is available from the British Library

ISBN 13: 978-0-8153-5378-2

Typeset in Minion Pro
by RefineCatch Limited, Bungay, Suffolk

Publisher's Note
The publisher accepts responsibility for any inconsistencies that may have arisen during the conversion of this book from journal articles to book chapters, namely the possible inclusion of journal terminology.

Disclaimer
Every effort has been made to contact copyright holders for their permission to reprint material in this book. The publishers would be grateful to hear from any copyright holder who is not here acknowledged and will undertake to rectify any errors or omissions in future editions of this book.

Contents

Citation Information   vii
Notes on Contributors   ix

1. The Comparative Politics of Transnational Climate Governance   1
   Charles B. Roger, Thomas N. Hale, and Liliana B. Andonova

2. Join the Club: How the Domestic NGO Sector Induces Participation in the Covenant of Mayors Program   26
   Nives Dolšak and Aseem Prakash

3. Transnational Climate Governance and the Global 500: Examining Private Actor Participation by Firm-Level Factors and Dynamics   49
   Lily Hsueh

4. Transnational Climate Governance Networks and Domestic Regulatory Action   86
   Xun Cao and Hugh Ward

5. Blurred Lines: Public-Private Interactions in Carbon Regulations   119
   Jessica F. Green

6. Transnational Climate Governance Initiatives: Designed for Effective Climate Change Mitigation?   146
   Katharina Michaelowa and Axel Michaelowa

7. Domestic Sources of Transnational Climate Governance   179
   Miles Kahler

Index   199

Citation Information

The chapters in this book were originally published in *International Interactions*, volume 43, issue 1 (January–March 2017). When citing this material, please use the original page numbering for each article, as follows:

Chapter 1
The Comparative Politics of Transnational Climate Governance
Charles B. Roger, Thomas N. Hale, and Liliana B. Andonova
International Interactions, volume 43, issue 1 (January–March 2017), pp. 1–25

Chapter 2
Join the Club: How the Domestic NGO Sector Induces Participation in the Covenant of Mayors Program
Nives Dolšak and Aseem Prakash
International Interactions, volume 43, issue 1 (January–March 2017), pp. 26–47

Chapter 3
Transnational Climate Governance and the Global 500: Examining Private Actor Participation by Firm-Level Factors and Dynamics
Lily Hsueh
International Interactions, volume 43, issue 1 (January–March 2017), pp. 48–75

Chapter 4
Transnational Climate Governance Networks and Domestic Regulatory Action
Xun Cao and Hugh Ward
International Interactions, volume 43, issue 1 (January–March 2017), pp. 76–102

Chapter 5
Blurred Lines: Public-Private Interactions in Carbon Regulations
Jessica F. Green
International Interactions, volume 43, issue 1 (January–March 2017), pp. 103–128

Chapter 6
Transnational Climate Governance Initiatives: Designed for Effective Climate Change Mitigation?
Katharina Michaelowa and Axel Michaelowa
International Interactions, volume 43, issue 1 (January–March 2017), pp. 129–155

Chapter 7
Domestic Sources of Transnational Climate Governance
Miles Kahler
International Interactions, volume 43, issue 1 (January–March 2017), pp. 156–174

For any permission-related enquiries please visit:
http://www.tandfonline.com/page/help/permissions

Notes on Contributors

Liliana B. Andonova is Professor of International Relations and Co-Director of the Center for International Environmental Studies at the Graduate Institute of International and Development Studies, Geneva, Switzerland.

Xun Cao is Associate Professor at Pennsylvania State University, USA.

Nives Dolšak is Professor and Associate Director of Marine and Environmental Affairs at the University of Washington, Seattle, USA.

Jessica F. Green is Assistant Professor in the Environmental Studies Department at New York University, USA.

Thomas N. Hale is Associate Professor at the Blavatnik School of Government at the University of Oxford, UK.

Lily Hsueh is Associate Professor at the College of Public Service and Community Solutions at Arizona State University, USA.

Miles Kahler is Distinguished Professor in the School of International Service at the American University, USA.

Axel Michaelowa is Senior Researcher at the Department for Political Science, University of Zurich, at the Center for Comparative and International Studies (CIS), University of Zurich and ETH Zurich, Switzerland, and at Perspectives Climate Research, Freiburg, Germany.

Katharina Michaelowa is Professor at the Department for Political Science, University of Zurich, and at the Center for Comparative and International Studies (CIS), University of Zurich and ETH Zurich, Switzerland.

Aseem Prakash is Professor in the Department of Political Science at the University of Washington, USA.

Charles B. Roger is an SSHRC Postdoctoral Fellow in the Department of Political Science at the University of Toronto, Canada.

Hugh Ward is Professor in the Department of Government at the University of Essex, USA.

The Comparative Politics of Transnational Climate Governance

Charles B. Roger, Thomas N. Hale, and Lilian B. Andonova[1]

ABSTRACT
We live in an era of remarkable transformations in how governance is supplied at the global level, as traditional means of intergovernmental institutions are being joined by a growing diversity of transnational arrangements. Yet, at present, we still have only a superficial understanding of what causes actors to adhere to transnational rules, norms, and initiatives once they appear, and especially what role domestic political, economic and social variables play in their decision making. Focusing on climate change as an issue exemplifying the tendency for complex governance interplay, this special issue provides a comparative political economy perspective on the increasing but uneven uptake of transnational climate governance (TCG). This article articulates a conceptual framework for the analysis, highlighting the interplay between transnational and domestic politics and how such interactions shape the incentives, opportunities, and modalities of participation in transnational initiatives. An original data set of participation in transnational governance initiatives is introduced to capture the significance of the phenomenon and to provide a common basis to systematically address, for the first time, questions about the cross-national patterns of involvement we find across different arenas and types of TCG, be they networks of sub- or nonstate actors, private rules, or hybrid arrangements.

Introduction

We live in an era of remarkable transformations in how governance is supplied at the global level. Across nearly all areas of global politics—from climate change, to conflict, to trade, to finance—the traditional means that have been used to govern cross-border issues, such as formal treaties and intergovernmental organizations, are being joined by transnational forms of governance. These new varieties of cross-border governance include transgovernmental networks that link together public actors, such as cities and local governments; private governance schemes involving businesses, civil society groups, and individuals; and a wide variety of hybrid arrangements that bring together combinations of public and private actors to provide collective goods.

---

[1] Authors are listed in reverse alphabetical order, with equal contributions to the article.

Due to the pace of these changes and their potentially vast implications, transnational governance has attracted a great deal of attention from scholars. Much productive research has focused on when and why transnational governance appears, how different kinds of initiatives operate, and the dynamics that lead transnational actors to become global governors (Andonova 2010; Avant, Finnemore, and Sell 2010; Avant and Westerwinter 2016; Bulkeley, Andonova, Betsill, Compagnon, Hale, Hoffmann, Newell, Paterson, Roger, and VanDeveer 2014; Büthe and Mattli 2011; Falkner 2003; Green 2013; Hale and Held 2011; Hall and Biersteker 2002; Haufler 2005; Potoski and Prakash 2009; Roger and Dauvergne Forthcoming). Prevailing explanations largely focus on how markets, norms, and networks motivate the creation and diffusion of initiatives by a variety of substate and nonstate actors. While such theories offer important insights, they tend to abstract from domestic political conditions and neglect their influence on the uptake of transnational governance.[2] However engagement in transnational governance varies enormously across countries, and is fundamentally shaped by the different domestic political contexts that actors are embedded in. If we are to provide a comparative insight on this variable engagement, which is essential for understanding the role of transnational governance in world politics, it is therefore critical to consider the role of domestic interest groups, policies, and institutions in conditioning transnational forces.

This special issue seeks to fill this research gap by focusing on the comparative politics of participation in transnational climate governance across jurisdictions, actors, and types of governance arrangements. The independent variables we are concerned with therefore include the varying domestic policies, institutions, and other national-level economic, social, and political factors that collectively shape the domestic contexts within which sub- and nonstate actors are embedded. The core dependent variable of interest—"participation" in transnational governance—is the act of adhering, or claiming to adhere, to transnational rules. It can include public claims about compliance with transnational rules or membership in a transnational initiative that specifies criteria for admittance. We seek to examine comparatively how domestic political, economic, and social variables can systematically boost or dampen actors' propensities to engage in governance transnationally.

To do so, the special issue uses the domain of climate change as a "laboratory." Within this issue area, a groundswell of transnational climate governance (TCG) initiatives has arisen alongside decades of interstate gridlock (Bulkeley et al. 2014; Victor 2011). Recent research has made significant progress toward mapping this universe of TCG by building data sets of TCG initiatives that allow scholars to move beyond individual case studies to assess broader trends (Bulkeley et al. 2014; Hale and Roger 2014; Hoffmann 2011; Widerberg and Stripple 2016). These data

---

[2]See Bartley (2011) for a discussion of this tendency within the literature on transnational governance as well as several recent studies that emphasize the need to take into account the interplay between domestic politics and transnational regulation.

sets have uncovered a wide variety of TCG schemes, composed of varying combinations of substate and nonstate actors that address different aspects of the underlying problem. Building on these efforts, a new cross-national data set produced by the organizers of the special issue expands our understanding of TCG by showing not only which schemes are active across countries but also what actors in which countries participate in TCG initiatives (Andonova, Hale, and Roger Forthcoming). This allows the articles in this issue to systematically address, for the first time, questions about the cross-national patterns of involvement we find across different arenas and types of TCG, be they networks of public actors, private rules, or hybrid arrangements.

By explaining how country-level factors affect TCG, the special issue also makes an important contribution to a pressing policy question. The climate regime is becoming increasingly complex, with a proliferation of TCG initiatives, intergovernmental clubs, and "unilateral" national actions emerging alongside, and increasingly linked to, the United Nations process (Abbott 2012; Falkner, Stephan, and Vogler 2010; Held, Roger, and Nag 2013; Keohane and Victor 2011). The 2015 Paris Agreement gave unprecedented prominence to sub- and nonstate actors, calling on cities, companies, civil society groups, and others to act on climate change, creating a Web portal to record and track their actions (Hale 2016). Such initiatives are intended to support the new institutional structure of the climate regime, which is centered on a system in which country targets will be determined nationally at regular intervals but then subject to verification and review at the international level. The Paris conference appointed two "High-Level Champions" to actively orchestrate and expand TCG initiatives in critical areas, and created an annual event at UNFCCC summits for sub- and nonstate actors to be recognized (Chan, De Souza, Hale, Lang, McCoy, St John, and Weigum 2014; Hale 2016). In other words, the multilateral components of the climate regime are increasingly complemented by—and intertwined with—both national policies and transnational governance. Understanding the relationship between the domestic and transnational arenas, and how the former constrains, supports, or drives the latter, is thus crucial for understanding the emerging climate regime. Will this shift provide a new way to manage the global commons as suggested, for example, by Elinor Ostrom's (2009) vision for "polycentric" climate governance? Or is transnational governance merely a second-best alternative to, or even a deliberate diversion from, more comprehensive regulatory efforts at the global level, as skeptics charge?

While the special issue focuses on the climate regime, the articles individually and collectively seek to contribute theoretical insights to the broader literature on transnational governance and institutional interaction. Beyond climate change, there are a number of issue areas that have been characterized by multilateral gridlock, institutional pluralism and complexity, and the rise of transnational governance, and these trends are arguably increasing across many realms of world politics. While testing the broader generalizability of the special issue's findings is beyond its scope, the hypotheses and theories are explicitly designed to reach beyond the climate realm.

In what follows, we provide an overview of the empirical and theoretical concerns of the special issue and preview how the findings of the individual articles contribute to our understanding of the domestic politics of transnational governance. We start by discussing the database that is employed by the contributing articles and providing a descriptive overview of trends in the field of TCG to help readers visualize the range of variation in participation in TCG. We then discuss three core theoretical themes addressed in the special issue: determinants of sub- and nonstate actors' motivations and strategies; domestic institutions and their conditioning effects on participation in transnational governance; and how transnational governance relates to the public objectives and policies. We locate the contributions of the special issue within the broader literature on these themes, offering an overview of the individual articles. We then discuss the general findings that emerge across the articles, highlighting insights that may extend to other areas of world politics. We conclude by considering the implications of these findings for the evolving climate regime.

Mapping the world of transnational climate governance

Transnational governance is an increasingly important phenomenon in world politics. It can be said to arise when nonstate or substate actors located in at least two states adhere to a common set of rules aimed at steering their behavior toward shared, public goals (Andonova, Betsill, and Bulkeley 2009; Bulkeley et al. 2014; Roger and Dauvergne Forthcoming). When the objective of such rules is to steer behaviour so as to address some aspect of the problem of climate change, we term this phenomenon *transnational climate governance* (TCG). We refer to a specific instance of transnational climate governance— that is, a particular set of TCG rules—as a "TCG initiative" or "TCG scheme." Participation in TCG is each specific instance in which an actor becomes a member of a TCG initiative or claims to comply with the rules of a TCG scheme. In recent years, a burgeoning number of studies have been concerned with why TCG schemes arise and take the shape that they do. In doing so, they have focused on analyzing individual TCG initiatives, primarily relying on case studies to document the causal processes at work. However, in recent years, several attempts have been made to develop databases of TCG schemes that have helped scholars to systematically map patterns of variation across different initiatives and to move toward a large-N analyses (Andonova et al. Forthcoming; Bulkeley at al. 2014; Hoffmann 2011; Widerberg and Stripple 2016). These have greatly expanded the kinds of questions that can be asked about TCG and provide additional sources of leverage for answering more traditional ones.

This special issue draws on a new data set, which documents the participation of substate and nonstate actors in 71 TCG schemes. To create the data set, we used as a baseline the aggregate data on 75 TCG initiatives constructed by Hale and Roger (2014), which in turn builds on previous data collection efforts by Hoffmann (2011) and Bulkeley et al. (2014). The 75 TCG initiatives included in the baseline data set had to meet a range of criteria (Hale and Roger 2014). First, to count as an instance of TCG, an initiative had to be transnational in nature. This meant, in practice, that an initiative had to involve nonstate or substate actors from at least two different states as participants in a TCG scheme. Thus, if all of the participants in a particular scheme came from a single state, then it was excluded from the database; if at least one actor came from a different state, it was included. This meant that an initiative like Refrigerants, Naturally!, which has multinational corporations from both the United Kingdom/Netherlands (Unilever) and United States (Coca-Cola) as participants, was included, but schemes like the Regional Greenhouse Gas Initiative that only involve participants from several American states were excluded.

Second, an initiative had to address climate change. Given that climate change is a multidimensional issue that involves nearly all aspects of economic and social activity, TCG schemes focus on many different aspects of the problem. A scheme could therefore be concerned with a range of different substantive activities, but provided that these were framed by the initiative itself as an attempt to address climate change, it would count as an instance of TCG. This meant that a scheme could also combine a focus on climate change with other nonclimate issues, so long as climate change was regarded as one of the central and overarching goals. For example, the Climate Alliance of European Cities and Indigenous Peoples, which combines concerns about climate change and indigenous rights, is included in the database, whereas a transnational certification scheme like the Forest Stewardship Council—which may have implications for the climate but does not explicitly state that addressing climate change is an overarching objective—is excluded.

Finally, in order to enter the database, an initiative had to count as an instance of governance. In many ways, this is the most difficult aspect of TCG to define precisely since the term *governance* itself is an essentially contested concept. However, we argue, along with other work in the field, that the core ideas behind the concept of governance are the notions of "steering" and "publicness" (Andonova, Bestill, and Bulkeley 2009; Bulkeley et al. 2014). An initiative counts as an instance of governance if it somehow seeks to "steer" those who participate toward some common, "public" goal. Here, "steering" means that an initiative aims to somehow change or coordinate the actions of those who participate through the setting or rules, standards, or other kinds of guidelines that aim to regulate the behavior of individuals or corporate bodies or the characteristics of goods or services they produce. More subtly, governance can also be said to arise when an initiative aims at facilitating adherence to such rules through capacity-building programs, technical assistance, climate finance, or efforts to alleviate information asymmetries. However, even if an initiative aims to steer behavior, for it to count as an instance of governance it must steer participants toward an explicitly "public" goal. Thus, the data set excluded any actors or activities aimed solely at achieving "private" goals, such as individual corporations or industry associations, since these each focused primarily on profit-making or lobbying and not attaining broader public objectives or providing some kind of public good.

Constructed in this way, the original database allows us to make descriptive inferences about the world of TCG and thereby provide some broader contextual detail on the changing patterns that the individual articles in the special issue are concerned with. It reveals, for instance, that TCG has grown tremendously over the past 25 years. The earliest initiatives recorded in the database appear in the early 1990s around the time of the 1992 Rio "Earth Summit," which set the agenda for international cooperation on climate change. These included schemes like Energy Cities, an initiative created in 1990 to facilitate locally led energy transitions, and the E8 (later renamed the Global Sustainable Electricity Partnership), which coordinates the activities of some of the world's leading electricity companies. The number of schemes rose slowly throughout the 1990s, as the United Nations climate negotiations began and the global regime started to take shape. At that point, it seems, nonstate and substate actors were willing to leave the governance of climate change up to states. But then, shortly after states signed the Kyoto Protocol in 1997, TCG took off and grew exponentially throughout the 2000s. This pattern of growth can be seen in Figure 1, which shows the cumulative total number of TCG initiatives that have appeared over a period from 1990 to 2010.

However, the world of TCG has not only grown in size; it has become more diverse as well. The database disaggregates TCG into several different kinds of activities, which allows us to track how the composition of initiatives has changed over time. These include *information and networking* schemes, which are designed to share knowledge and experiences and alleviate information asymmetries; *standards and commitment* schemes, which set and enforce specific rules; *operational* schemes, which provide certain collective goods and help to build the infrastructure that allows many other TCG schemes work; and *finance schemes*, which aim to facilitate, shape, and

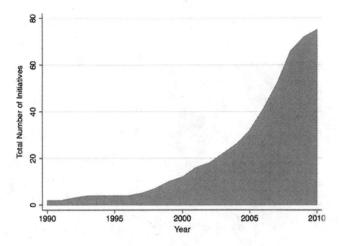

Figure 1. The rise of transnational climate governance, 1990–2010.

sometimes provide flows of capital[3]. Initially, as Figure 2 shows, the world of TCG was largely limited to information and networking schemes, with a small role for those focused on standards and commitments.[4] This persisted until the start of the 2000s, when the world of TCG started to change and diversify. The number of finance and operational schemes started to expand and standards and commitments schemes would rapidly grow to become the largest category of TCG. At present, standards and commitment schemes comprise 44% of all TCG initiatives, while information and networking schemes comprise 31%, operational schemes 14%, and finance schemes 11%.

The kinds of actors involved in TCG have changed over time as well. The data set disaggregates initiatives into three classes composed of different actor types. First, there are those that are comprised entirely of public actors, such as cities and regional governments. These are referred to as "public" or "transgovernmental" schemes. Second, there are those that mainly involve private or nonstate actors, such as individuals, nongovernmental organizations, and firms. These are referred to as "private" or "entrepreneurial" schemes, following the terminology of Green (2013). Finally, there are those that involve varying mixes of private and public actors. These are referred to as "hybrid" schemes. Again, the database reveals a fascinating pattern. Initially, as Figure 3 demonstrates, public actors dominated the world of TCG. Until 1997, the composition of schemes was strongly skewed toward transgovernmental and hybrid schemes. Entrepreneurial schemes typically accounted for less than one-third of the total, and in the early years they were altogether absent. Thus, it seems, private actors were largely willing to leave the governance of climate change entirely up to public authorities. However, this has

---

[3]The typology presented here is derived from Abbott (2012).

[4]Initiatives were coded according to their primary governance activity. Initiatives that perform more than one function equally were coded as performing both functions but then weighted proportionally. For further details, see the Data Appendix for Hale and Roger (2014).

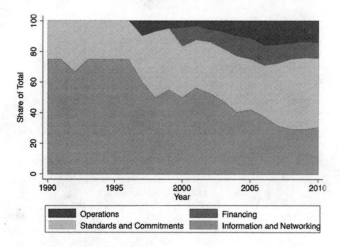

Figure 2. Governance activities, 1990–2010.

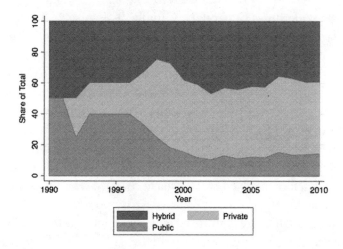

Figure 3. Actor composition, 1990–2010,

changed dramatically. After 1998, the share of entrepreneurial schemes grew significantly; they now constitute the single largest variety of TCG—roughly 46% of all TCG initiatives. Hybrid schemes constitute the second-largest group (40%). Meanwhile, transgovernmental schemes are the smallest, comprising only 14% of the total. Thus, at present, 86% of all TCG schemes involve participation by at least one nonstate actor.

Until now, it has been difficult to say much more about the actors involved. While earlier databases were able to determine the regions in which various initiatives were active, the data were insufficiently fine-grained to determine the actual geographical distribution of the actors participating (see, for example, Bulkeley et al. 2014). It was impossible to say whether, for instance, China had more participants than Vietnam, or whether Mexico had more than Canada, and so on. This barrier also meant that we were unable to make causal inferences about the effect of national-level variables, such as the quality of institutions or the kinds of policies implemented, on levels of participation. In order to address these two constraints, we undertook a major data collection effort that attempted to estimate levels of participation across nation-states. Using the database elaborated by Hale and Roger (2014) as a baseline, we collected participant lists that recorded the actors that took part in each of the 75 initiatives. A large number of these records, which were derived from membership lists and public registries, were accessible through the Web sites of initiatives. Others were obtained through targeted data requests or were inferred from other sources. In this way it was possible to attain participant lists for 71 of the 75 initiatives in the database. Each actor on these lists was then matched with a particular political jurisdiction, typically by relying on self-reporting found on the Web sites of different initiatives. If this proved to be difficult, an actor's geographical base was determined through other publicly available information on their Web sites or promotional materials.

In total, the database indicates that there were at least 14,000 instances of participation in transnational climate governance by substate and non-state actors across 192 states by the year 2012 (the most recent year for which cross-national data is available). It therefore reveals, for the first time, not simply the number of the schemes and the different kinds of extant initiatives but the vast scale of participation in TCG as well. Just 71 initiatives are able to engage thousands of actors from around the world in efforts to address the problem of climate change. However, the data also reveal the extent to which participation in TCG varies across nation-states. Map 1 in Figure 4, for instance, combines all of the different kinds of TCG initiatives together to give us the total number of participants in each country. When aggregated in this way, there are, on average, 76 instances of participation across all of the states. But, given that there is a standard deviation of 282 around this figure, there is clearly significant geographical variation across nation-states. Just as importantly, when we disaggregate the data into different types of initiatives, as is done in Maps 2, 3, and 4, we see altogether different patterns of participation, with countries participating more in some kinds of TCG initiatives and less in others. The database therefore reveals a number of interesting geographic patterns that are not easily explained by existing frameworks. This variation forms the heart of our inquiry into the comparative politics of transnational governance.

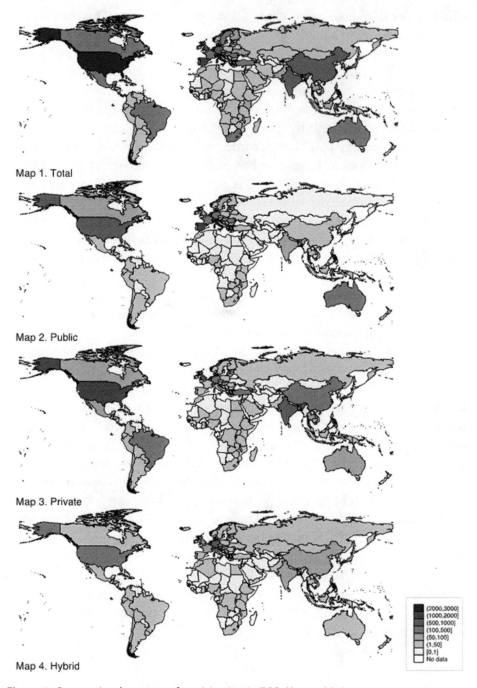

Figure 4. Cross-national patterns of participation in TCG, Year = 2012.

Theoretical approach: The comparative politics of transnational governance

Explanations of transnational governance have emphasized, not surprisingly, the incentives actors have to engage in cross-border networks to advance governance objectives.[5] The motivations behind the creation of transnational initiatives often have international dimensions, such as promoting a set of norms or facilitating international markets. For example, multinational companies and investors have typically supported transnational governance schemes as a means to level the playing field across jurisdictions, to increase the predictability of regulations and/ or to preempt potentially more costly rules. Advocacy groups have, in turn, promoted transnational governance to codify a set of norms in the construction of new governance mechanisms. Most scholars of transnational governance (in the climate realm and beyond) have also emphasized international factors to explain its diffusion across jurisdictions, looking at actors' levels of cultural, political, or economic "connectedness" to the rest of the international system. It is through channels such as international trade, foreign direct investment, and supply chains (Garcia-Johnson 2000; Perkins and Neumayer 2010; Prakash and Potoski 2006), networks of NGOs (Betsill and Bulkeley 2004; Portney and Berry 2014), and the actions of intergovernmental organizations (Andonova 2010; Hale and Roger 2014) that the material and social pressures to adopt transnational rules are transmitted.

These micro-incentives and transnational linkages clearly matter. But at the same time, several studies show that transnational actors are not simply transported outside of their domestic political contexts when they choose to adhere to and implement transnational rules. Bartley (2010), for example, has shown how the adoption of corporate certification schemes for forestry and apparel in Indonesia are affected by local conditions. Scholars have looked at Asia more broadly and found, for example, that the weakness of civil society under China's authoritarian system limits participation in ISO 14001 and other transnational initiatives (Drezner and Lu 2009; Hale and Roger 2012). Policies and public institutions seem to matter, too. Espach (2006) shows that variation in FSC certification and adoption of the Responsible Care standard has been influenced by industrial policies, and Hale and Roger (2015) find that the Chinese government's policies have promoted or obstructed participation in certain TCG schemes. Prakash and Potoski (2014) also find that the stringency of laws and their enforcement characteristics matter for adoption of the ISO 14001 standard. Büthe and Mattli (2011) and Andonova (2014) emphasize the relevance of domestic institutional structures for influencing, respectively, power over private regulations and participation in global public-private partnerships. Finally, Andonova et al. (Forthcoming) find that, contra much of the literature on transnational governance, stronger national policies are associated with greater participation in TCG and that domestic political institutions condition the effect of both transnational linkages and national policies on patterns of engagement.

---

[5]Note that this has been less true in the study of transnational advocacy networks, which scholars often explain precisely as a reaction to adverse domestic political contexts (see Keck and Sikkink 1998).

In sum, a growing number of studies posit that domestic politics clearly "matter" for shaping how actors partake in transnational governance initiatives.

The previous lack of emphasis on domestic politics in most of the literature on transnational governance (with the exceptions noted previously) is particularly surprising given the long tradition in the study of international political economy and environmental politics that focuses on the interplay between domestic and international politics in shaping patterns of international cooperation (Schattschneider 1935). Indeed, one of the chief developments in IR theory in the 1990s was the articulation of more theoretically precise accounts of how domestic politics shaped international cooperation and in turn reflected political realignments in response to international commitments or pressures (Andonova 2003; Dai 2007; DeSombre 2000; Evans, Jacobson, and Putnam 1993; Milner 1997; Milner and Keohane 1996; Moravcsik 1997, among others). In much of this work, openness or "connectedness" to the international system was in fact itself endogenous to domestic politics (Milner and Keohane 1996). National political structures were also found to be important for explaining patterns of transnational activism and norm diffusion (Risse-Kappen 1995).

This special issue breaks new ground by deepening our understanding of exactly how and under what conditions domestic politics "matter" for different varieties of transnational governance. The theoretical approach that informs the collection of articles seeks to examine the missing links between domestic structures and transnational forces as they shape engagement in TCG. Specifically, we consider how country-level factors systematically condition sub- and nonstate actors' participation in transnational governance. Drawing on the international political economy literature, we consider three key dynamics: (1) domestic sources of preferences or strategies regarding transnational action; (2) the impact of domestic institutions for facilitating or hindering the agency of sub- and nonstate actors; and (3) the interplay between public policies and transnational initiatives. Each is explored in more detail in the following sections.

The collection of articles in this special issue strives to provide greater depth and rigor on these questions by analyzing specific elements of this political interface. Each contribution theorizes how different political, economic, and institutional variables are important for understanding the decisions of actors to engage in TCG and demonstrates their causal effects. Some of the articles are able to reverse the causal arrow as well, considering how aspects of transnational governance instead affect features of domestic policy and outcomes. Empirically, the articles draw on the common database, described in the previous section, which captures participation in TCG across jurisdiction by a variety of sub- and nonstate actors. This shared approach allows the articles to disaggregate the phenomenon of TCG in order to increase analytic leverage. Some articles focus on a particular subset of initiatives (Dolšak and Prakash [2017] on the Covenant of Mayors; Hsueh [2017] on some of the larger private sector initiatives, Green [2017] on voluntary carbon standards, Cao and Ward [2017] on private climate governance initiatives), while Michaelowa and Michaelowa [2017] expand the set of initiatives under analysis. Some articles also disaggregate actor types to focus on the particular dynamics surrounding private sector corporations (Hsueh 2017) or cities (Dolšak and Prakash 2017). Grounded in the international political economy tradition and a common methodology, the collection of articles allows us to extract generalizable findings from the dense institutional landscape of the climate regime.

What shapes the preference and strategies of subnational and nonstate actors?

Once transnational entrepreneurs establish a climate initiative, its uptake across jurisdictions depends critically on the willingness of domestic constituencies to endorse it and implement or conform to its norms, standards, or requirements. While actors can be motivated to join a set of initiatives by market-based or normative incentives associated with international interactions, they could also be seeking to address or circumvent problems on the domestic political plane. For instance, the literature on advocacy NGOs has documented how local organizations often link to transnational networks as a strategy to gain resources or information or to cope with domestic institutional barriers (Andonova and Tuta 2014; Keck and Sikkink 1998; True and Mintrom 2001). In the climate realm, actors advocating for strong climate policies may be likely to pursue transnational governance directly to compensate for limited influence at home or in order to influence indirectly the climate engagement of public entities. Our theoretical approach therefore anticipates an interaction between the domestic and international motivations of actors, rather than taking transnational forces for granted as the dominant factor driving transnational engagement. We emphasize the need to better elaborate the theoretical assumptions about the domestic sources of different motivations to participate in transnational governance.

One advantage of working with disaggregated data on participation of sub- and nonstate actors in different types of TCG initiatives is that we can systematically examine theoretical propositions about the motivations and strategies of different kinds of actors, exploiting this rich variation for causal leverage. For example, the linkage between domestic motivations and international norms and incentives is likely to be particularly salient for transgovernmental networks that coordinate collaboration between subunits of governments, municipalities, or their leaders. When such actors engage in TCG, they often target a specific aspect of the larger climate issue—greening energy systems, reducing the footprint of large cities, supporting their resilience, and so on. Public official and organizations, especially at the subnational level, are frequently driven more by pressures from local constituencies or advocacy groups for transnational engagement and less by global networks and supply chains, in which they are less directly embedded. These dynamics are highlighted in the article by Dolšak and Prakash in this special issue, which shows how the strength of local civil society is a key driver of Eastern European cities' engagement in TCG. Cities participating in TCG do so around the nexus between climate change and the local cobenefits of energy efficiency, cleaner transportation systems, city greening, and clean air. Transnational initiatives support and reinforce these local political incentives, which, as Dolšak and Prakash show, depend strongly on civil society groups, with access to resources and broader recognition and political legitimation.

By contrast, much of the literature on private regulation leads us to expect that businesses will be strongly motivated by international normative pressures and market-based incentives in their decisions to join transnational initiatives (Andonova 2009; Falkner 2003; Green 2013; Newell and Paterson 2010; Potoski and Prakash 2009; Prakash and Potoski 2006). As Hsueh's article highlights, however, such assumptions may require some further probing, to account for persistent cross-jurisdictional variation in the willingness of businesses to subscribe to different types of transnational initiatives, even when they are entangled to a similar extent in international markets and supply chains. Her analysis shows that market incentives matter, but not as much as corporate culture and sensitivity to domestic regulations. Internal champions of sustainable business practices are the most important determinant of corporate participation in TCG, she finds, with domestic policy contexts in second place (explaining about 30%–35% of the total variation). These results mirror studies that examine the different corporate social responsibility strategies of oil companies, for example, and point to the relevance of jurisdictional effects as well as the impact of firm-level factors (Kolk and Levy 2001).

More pessimistically, large corporate actors in some political contexts may be more strongly motivated to participate in transnational initiatives intended to divert attention from stricter regulatory efforts either at home or internationally. Indeed, Michaelowa and Michealowa's (2017) article finds that TCG initiatives led by private corporations have fewer concrete mitigation targets than other TCG initiatives, although this is less the case when corporate TCG initiatives are orchestrated by public actors. This result suggests that public regulation is critical for climate mitigation and that some businesses may see TCG as a way to circumvent or preempt more stringent public regulation. One example of this may be the use of transnational governance as a vehicle to export a domestic comparative advantage in cleaner technologies. Companies may adopt voluntary transnational standards under pressure from transnational advocacy or markets, but also to alleviate problems of domestic legitimacy and political risks (Garcia-Johnson 2000). All these considerations suggest that domestic institutional and policy contexts are likely to be an important determinant of participation in TCG. Such an effect may be produced either directly by constricting or enabling agency from below, as we shall elaborate in the next section, or indirectly by conditioning the domestic incentives for transnational action.

A crucial general insight from the articles in the special issue is that sub- and nonstate actors' preferences are shaped by both the domestic and transnational contexts simultaneously. This point comes across strongly in the analysis by Cao and Ward (2017), which models how nonstate actors attempt to allocate their resources between influencing domestic regulations and engaging in transnational private governance. The authors argue that this choice is a function of the domestic opportunities, barriers, and costs that transnational actors face. They argue that, given resource constraints, transnational actors will invest their time in whichever activity is likely to yield a higher mitigation dividends. This contribution reveals how similar actors can pursue different strategies with respect to climate change, either by targeting public authorities or via direct participation in transnational initiatives.

How do institutions mediate participation by subnational and nonstate actors in TCG?

This special issue posits that the influence of transnational factors, such as markets, global actors, or governance networks, is processed through domestic institutions. This conjecture comports with a variety of findings across world politics. The international political economy literature, for instance, has elaborated how the risks of interconnectedness related to trade, foreign investment, resources, or external shocks are mitigated to different degrees by the welfare state and other institutional arrangements. Transnational advocacy networks are, likewise, thought to be most influential in contexts with sufficient institutional permeability to establish a set of cross-cutting insider-outsider coalitions. The regulatory approaches of leading states have also influenced the features of international environmental regimes, and the nature of domestic regulatory institutions has had an imprint on the position of actors in shaping the design or uptake of private regulations (Andonova 2014; Andonova et al. Forthcoming; Büthe and Mattli 2011; Sikkinik 2005).

The formal institutional structures of countries therefore influence the propensity of sub- and nonstate actors to participate in TCG. While the adherence of such actors to transnational rules is not necessarily directly dependent on the state, their activities do not take place in an institutional vacuum. To begin with, national systems that guarantee greater freedom are likely more conducive to leadership and direct engagement by societal and substate actors in transnational networks. Variable degrees of civil and political liberties may have a particularly strong imprint on participation in private transnational schemes, which depends on the agency of nonstate actors. Hybrid initiatives may similarly benefit from institutional contexts that grant stronger voice and initiative to nonstate actors;

they could also reflect the historical evolution of state-society relations in a particular domestic context (Farrell and Newmann 2010; Sending and Neumann 2006). The analyses by Cao and Ward (2017) on nonstate transnational governance, by Dolšak and Prakash (2017) on city networks for climate governance, and by Hsueh (2017) on firm participation in voluntary governance instruments provide new empirical evidence on the influence of political institutions on participation in TCG.

Other institutional features, such as the degree of domestic decentralization both in regulatory and fiscal matters, are likely to be particularly important for the propensity of substate actors such as regions, communities, or municipalities to act on issues related to climate change. In addition to epistemic capacity, subnational public actors need to have sufficient decision-making authority in order to engage in transnational governance. In federal systems and administrative structures that vest greater policy authority at regional and local levels, transnational association is more likely. Subnational authorities that enjoy greater formal authority and fiscal autonomy have benefited more readily from multilevel structures of governance, as research on European integration has illuminated. Greater decentralization in the management of subnational public budgets may, in turn, increase the incentive to seek additional capacity, cobenefits, or efficiency in tackling global and local problems through transnational cooperation. It is not a coincidence that regional networks for climate governance like the Asian Cities Clean Air Initiative have emerged around policy initiatives and common concerns of regional governments.

Beyond these general dynamics, several articles in the special issue stress a crucial causal mechanism connecting domestic institutions with TCG: the presence of NGOs and the capacity of civil society groups. This issue is brought into analytical focus in the article by Dolšak and Prakash (2017). In their study, societal capacity, measured by social capital variables, explains the patterns of engagement of cities in transnational climate initiatives. Institutional control variables such as federalism and democracy matter as well. But, critically, the article finds that domestic civil society is more important than the presence of international NGOs. Cities act because they are responsive to their local communities, not because they have been linked by transnational civil society groups, the article suggest. The findings show how transnational initiatives that involve public authorities cannot be well understood outside of domestic structures. Transgovernmental initiatives often respond to specific local pressures from civil society, experts, and leaders, as well as to transnational opportunities. They have to be enabled by some degree of domestic capacity and political willingness to establish the link between local benefits, global change, and transnational networks. Both Cao and Ward (2017) and Green (2017) also find the presence of NGOs to be a critical driver of participation in TCG, although they find a more international dimension to the work of society groups. For Cao and Ward, NGOs are the vehicle through which TCG emerges, as they arbitrage between domestic regulatory changes and TCG. Strong domestic interests opposing ambitious climate regulations will therefore increase the incentive for NGOs to pursue TCG by making domestic regulation too difficult for green NGOs to obtain. For Green, NGOs are the ones that convince national governments to recognize private regulation of carbon markets. Taken together, these results show how the openness of domestic political structures is a crucial facilitator of the kinds of multilevel state-society interactions from which TCG emerges.

How does TCG interact with formal regulations and policy?

The important questions related to how participation in TCG interacts with public policy similarly require more careful examination. When TCG initiatives started proliferating in the 1990s, and especially after the withdrawal of the United States from the Kyoto Protocol in 2001, they were often discussed in reference to state failure to adopt meaningful policies. Over time, however, it has become clear that the relationship between public policies and transnational governance of climate change is more complex than pure "substitution" or "diversion" hypothesis would imply. On average, national policies and TCG are more often complementary in nature (Andonova et al. Forthcoming). Moreover, important developments in climate governance, such as the development of the voluntary carbon market, the creation of climate finance institutions, and the rise of clean energy initiatives, has depended on public support by states with progressive climate policies, by intergovernmental organizations, as well as nonstate initiatives (Andonova 2010; Bulkeley et al. 2014). According to one estimate, nearly a third of TCG initiatives have been "orchestrated"—that is, initiated, supported, or otherwise steered—by states and intergovernmental organizations (Hale and Roger 2014).

Building on these findings, the articles in the special issue suggest that a more synergistic relationship between transnational governance and public policy is indeed more likely than traditionally assumed. Hsueh (2017), for example, finds a strong correlation between participation by the largest 500 corporations in TCG and the strength of climate policies in the countries in which they are headquartered. Several causal mechanisms may be at work here. Proactive public policies can enable the interest and capacity of actors to seek transnational alliances and partnerships. Such governance networks could be a means to export domestic comparative advantage or leadership in developing and deploying climate-friendly technologies. Transnational actors could also seek some degree of levelling of the regulatory playing field or limiting of the risks from future ratcheting-up of regulations. Finally, public standards could become reference points for certain features of private regulation or other transnational initiatives. As noted, Cao and Ward's (2017) article suggests a specific causal mechanism along these lines: Transnational actors invest their resources to achieve mitigation either in domestic lobbying or in creating TCG initiatives that reach across borders. To the extent that they already have good climate policies at home, they will have more incentive to spend their advocacy "budget" on creating TCG.

Michaelowa and Michaelowa (2017) add an important dimension to this discussion as well by assessing whether TCG initiatives are likely to achieve mitigation of greenhouse gases on their own or to merely complement national regulations. Looking at an expanded set of TCG initiatives, they find that only 13% have at least three of the four institutional design features necessary to achieve mitigation outcomes on their own. While many TCG initiatives have other objectives (like capacity building or knowledge exchange), the findings strongly suggest that TCG initiatives alone are unlikely to fill the "emissions gap"; they are more likely therefore to matter alongside state regulations.

Reversing the causal arrow, several articles show how transnational governance itself can support the development of public policies for climate change in several ways. Transnational networks tend to lend additional legitimacy and resources to domestic proponents of climate action, as discussed already, and even help to create new supportive constituencies by reframing debates or deploying resources domestically. The transnational experience with partnerships for forestry management and with forestry-based carbon offsets has helped to support new ideas and practices at the nexus between forestry management and climate change. The politics of a new policy paradigm framed as "payments for ecosystems services" under the UN REDD+ instrument cannot be separated from or well understood without taking into consideration the influence of prior initiatives. The proliferation of transnational initiatives for clean energy governance, in turn, are closely connected to the expansion of domestic policies on climate and energy. And yet, there has been relatively limited theorizing and systematic empirical data on the connection between transnational processes and the evolution of public policies and standards. The special issue seeks to make a concerted contribution in this direction by examining how transnational activities may impact domestic policies or standards, and to what extent domestic climate policy (or lack thereof) might affect the strategies of actors with respect to transnational governance. For example, Green (2017) finds consistent patterns of interaction between national carbon trading standards and transnational governance. Coding the substantive technical provisions of new national carbon trading systems—the rules governing how carbon is measured—she finds that national governments often incorporate transnational standards into national law. The results show how the fragmentation of the carbon market into a number of national and subnational systems in fact masks a substantive coherence. However, as with Michaelowa and Michaelowa (2017) in this issue, the analysis by Green suggests that private offset standards are rarely used for compliance purposes and are instead used for voluntary offsetting. They therefore tend to be complementary to public regulations.

More generally, Cao and Ward (2017) also postulate that TCG creates linkages not just between specific sub- and nonstate actors but between the larger national contexts in which they are embedded. As mapped out in their network analysis, TCG links between countries can become important vehicles for the transmission of knowledge, policies, norms, resources, or other factors that can affect the domestic politics of climate change within a country. In other words, the growing web of linkages that TCG creates between countries is likely to affect the development of national policies, they surmise.

Implications for the study of world politics

The previous theoretical questions touch on actor motivations and strategies, the domestic institutional environment, and the relationship between public policies and TCG. By applying a common set of theoretical questions to different types of TCG, and then comparing them, the special issue is able to shed new theoretical insight and empirical detail on how different forms of transnational governance are shaped by domestic politics. From these findings, several conclusions emerge that we believe can be generalized to other areas of world politics.

First, the special issue demonstrates the value of employing a diversity of methodologies to study transnational governance and the benefit of combining different forms of analysis. While the bulk of research on transnational governance generally, including in the climate realm, remains qualitative, case focused, and largely inductive, the growing maturity of the literature allows researchers to go further. For example, Hsueh (2017) introduces multilevel modeling to the study of TCG in order to differentiate the causal impact of national factors from firm-level variables. Both Green (2017) and Cao and Ward (2017) employ network analyses to identify patterns within TCG, and in the latter case, to introduce latent space models that control for network effects. Dolšak and Prakash (2017) introduce a conceptualization of civil society as a stock variable, which allows them to measure more accurately the political weight of NGOs at the local level. Michaelowa and Michalowa (2017), in turn, look at the institutional design of TCG initiatives to evaluate their ability to achieve mitigation outcomes. The special issue also shows how combining formal theory (Cao and Ward 2017) with qualitative or quantitative analyses can help pin down causal mechanisms of interest. These innovative methodologies demonstrate the utility of combining theoretical work with detailed empirical studies of transnational governance and complex issue domains. Comparative data and creative empirical approaches are essential for disentangling the multiple drivers of new governance constellations and how they interact with more traditional formal institutions.

Second, the special issue goes beyond the intuitive view that domestic institutions and policies "matter" for transnational governance to show *how* they matter. As we argued previously, institutions help determine the context within which sub- and nonstate actors act, with more liberal and decentralized institutions promoting, on average, higher levels of engagement in TCG. We hypothesize that this result will generalize to other spheres of transnational governance. We also note the correspondence between this finding and the propensity of more democratic governments to participate in more intergovernmental regimes than their authoritarian counterparts. Though the causal mechanisms differ, the idea that regime type affects both intergovernmental and transnational engagement suggests a potentially deeper and richer enmeshment of the international and domestic realms.

Third, we find that actor-level characteristics shape the variable participation in TCG in important ways. Again, this finding corresponds with our theoretical expectations, but the articles in the special issue go further by demonstrating how and where such factors matter. Dolšak and Prakash (2017) show how the strength of local civil society enables cities to engage in transnational governance, suggesting that cities in such contexts develop not only the motivation to engage transnationally but also the skills and competencies to do so. Hsueh's (2017) article on companies, in turn, notes the importance of organizational champions and focal points for driving TCG participation from within. The significance of agency and capacities at the micro level carries important implications for further research on the likely scope but also possible limitations of transnational governance to reach relevant populations, particularly in complex and locally-grounded issues such as health, clean energy, or humanitarian responses.

Finally, we note that public policy interacts with transnational governance in interesting and often unexpected ways. As Cao and Ward (2017), Hsueh (2017), and Green (2017) demonstrate, pro-climate policies tend to correlate with participation in TCG, suggesting that the two realms are not substitutes but complements. Cao and Ward suggest a novel causal mechanism for this symbiotic relationship, arguing that better policies at home give transnational actors more opportunity to invest their resources in transnational actions. This finding seems to stand at odds with other studies that see transnational governance as compensating for lackluster national regulations related to sustainability, labor standards, or other issues. Explaining this cross-issue area variation strikes us a promising path for future research.

Implications for the evolving climate regime

The findings in the special issue carry important implications for the evolving climate regime as well. As the UNFCCC becomes increasingly focused on catalyzing and ratcheting up pledges and actions from both nation-states and sub- and nonstate actors, the relationship between those two key spheres of action becomes central. While various articles put forward specific insights for certain domains, here we collect and highlight the key implications of the special issue's findings for climate policy.

First, it is important to note that not all TCG initiatives are created equal. As Michaelowa and Michaelowa (2017) find, very few TCG initiatives are designed to achieve mitigation outcomes on their own. The idea that such initiatives will therefore fill the current "emissions gap" is in many ways a misunderstanding of their role in climate politics. While a number of initiatives do aim for significant direct reductions, the TCG phenomenon serves a far wider range of purposes and, as this special issue demonstrates, is intimately linked to other spheres of climate policy. We should therefore be cautious of claims that TCG will compensate for lackluster national policies and instead focus on how it interacts with other forms of governance.

Second, several of the articles point to the importance of cities' and firms' capacities to participate in TCG initiatives. Having internal policy champions and technical personnel to devise and implement climate governance is crucial. The implication is that governments, donors, and civil society groups seeking to support TCG may find it useful to invest in core capacity-building as opposed to just program-oriented work. Additionally, as several authors, and especially Dolšak and Prakash (2017) show, a strong local civil society can facilitate effective participation in TCG. These results highlight the continued importance of advocacy groups even as political contestation of climate governance shifts to the transnational realm.

Third, the studies show that national governments play a crucial role in determining the opportunity structures that sub- and nonstate actors face. While certain governments may not be willing or able to broadly expand civil liberties or devolve power to subnational governments, all governments can make more targeted interventions to empower their sub- and nonstate actors to tackle climate change through TCG. Such interventions can include rhetorical support to sub- and nonstate climate action, using the government's convening power to activate sub- and nonstate actors on climate change and link them to international networks, and specific policies that fund or otherwise empower sub- and nonstate actors to take climate actions, such as a challenge fund for local transportation initiatives.

Following the 2015 Paris agreement, countries must now find ways to individually and collectively "ratchet up" their national contributions over the next 10–15 years if the world is to have a reasonable probability of limiting temperature change to 2 degrees Celsius, or even 1.5 degrees, this century. Knowing that the actions of cities, companies, regions, and other sub- and nonstate actors are reinforced by domestic policies suggests that the post-Paris regime may benefit from an upward spiral of climate actions in which domestic and transnational governance of climate change mutually reinforce one another. Building productive linkages across these spheres is, therefore, of central importance if the emerging climate regime is to deliver the much-needed public goods to which it aspires.

Acknowledgments

We are grateful to Xun Cao, Nives Dolšak, Jessica Green, Lily Hsueh, Robert Keohane, Miles Kahler, Taedong Lee, Katja Michaelowa, Axel Michaelowa, Aseem Prakash, and Hugh Ward for comments on earlier versions of this article and overarching theoretical framework of the project, as well as to the editorial team of *International Interactions* for critical feedback and support. Finally, for their help creating the cross-national database of participation in transnational climate governance, we would also like to thank Justin Alger, Jen Iris Allan, Andrea Stucchi, and Kieran Meehan.

Funding

We acknowledge with gratitude the financial support of the Liu Institute for Global Issues at the University of British Columbia, Blavatnik School of Government at Oxford University and the Center for International Environmental Studies at the Graduate Institute, Geneva, for this special issue project.

References

Abbott, Kenneth W. (2012) The Transnational Regime Complex for Climate Change. *Environment and Planning C: Government and Policy* 30(4):571–590.

Andonova, Liliana B. (2003) *Transnational Politics of the Environment: The European Union and Environmental Policy in Central and Eastern Europe*. Cambridge, MA: MIT Press.

Andonova, Liliana B. (2009) Networks, Club Goods, and Partnerships for Sustainability: The Green Power Market Development Group. In *Enhancing the Effectiveness of Sustainability Partnerships*, edited by Derek Vollmer. Washington, DC: The National Academies Press.

Andonova, Liliana B. (2010) Public-Private Partnerships for the Earth: Politics and Patterns of Hybrid Authority in the Multilateral System. *Global Environmental Politics* 10(2):25–53.

Andonova, Liliana B. (2014) Boomerangs to Partnerships? Explaining State Participation in Transnational Partnerships for Sustainability. *Comparative Political Studies* 47(3):481–515.

Andonova, Liliana, Michele Betsill and Harriet Bulkeley. (2009) Transnational Climate Governance. *Global Environmental Politics* 9(2):52–73.

Andonova, Liliana, Thomas N. Hale, and Charles Roger. (Forthcoming). National Policies and Transnational Governance of Climate Change: Substitutes or Complements? *International Studies Quarterly*.

Andonova, Liliana B., and Ioana A Tuta. (2014) Transnational Networks and Paths to EU Environmental Compliance: Evidence from New Member States. *Journal of Common Market Studies* 52(4):775–793.

Avant, Deborah D., Martha Finnemore, and Susan K. Sell. (2010) *Who Governs the Globe?* Cambridge: Cambridge University Press.

Avant, Deborah and Oliver Westerwinter, eds. (2016) *The New Power Politics. Networks and Transnational Security Governance*. Oxford: Oxford University Press.

Bartley, Tim. (2010) Transnational Private Regulation in Practice: The Limits of Forest and Labor Standards Certification in Indonesia. *Business and Politics* 12(3):1–36.

Bartley, Tim. (2011) Transnational Governance as the Layering of Rules : Intersections of Public and Private Standards. *Theoretical Inquiries in Law* 12(2):517–542.

Betsill, Michele M., and Harriet Bulkeley. (2004) Transnational Networks and Global Environmental Governance: The Cities for Climate Protection Program. *International Studies Quarterly* 48(2):471–493.

Bulkeley, Harriet, Liliana B. Andonova, Michele M. Betsill, D Compagnon, Thomas Hale, Matthew J. Hoffmann, Peter Newell, Matthew Paterson, Charles Roger, and Stacy VanDeveer. (2014) *Transnational Climate Change Governance*. Cambridge: Cambridge University Press.

Büthe, Tim, and Walter Mattli. (2011) *The New Global Rulers: The Privatization of Regulation in the World Economy*. Princeton, NJ: Princeton University Press.

Cao, Xun, and Hugh Ward. (2017) Transnational Climate Governance Networks and Domestic Regulatory Action. *International Interactions* 43(1):76–102. doi:10.1080/03050629.2016.1220162

Chan, Mary-Jean, Priyanka De Souza, Thomas Hale, Alice Lang, Dakota McCoy, Sarah St John, and Natalie Weigum. (2014) UNFCCC Parties and Observers' Views on Sub/Non-State Actions and Cooperative Initiatives. Paper presented at workshop on Designing a Global Platform for Climate Actions, Oxford, July 24–25.

Dai, Xinyuan. (2007) *International Institutions and National Policies*. Cambridge: Cambridge University Press.

DeSombre, Elizabeth. (2000) *Domestic Sources of International Environmental Policy: Industry, Environmentalists, and U.S. Power*. Cambridge, MA: MIT Press.

Dolšak, Nives, and Aseem Prakash. (2017) Join the Club: How the Domestic NGO Sector Induces Participation in the Covenant of Mayors Program. *International Interactions* 43 (1):26–47. doi:10.1080/03050629.2017.1226668

Drezner, Daniel, and Mimi Lu. (2009) How Universal Are Club Standards? Emerging Markets and Volunteerism. In *Voluntary Programs: A Club Theory Perspective*, edited by Aseem Prakash and Matthew Potoski. Cambridge, MA: MIT Press.

Espach, Ralph H. (2006) When Is Sustainable Forestry Sustainable? The Forest Stewardship Council in Argentina and Brazil. *Global Environmental Politics* 6(2):55–84.

Evans, Peter, Harold K. Jacobson, and Robert D. Putnam, eds. (1993) *Double-Edged Diplomacy: International Bargaining and Domestic Politics*. Berkeley: University of California Press.

Falkner, Robert. (2003) Private Environmental Governance and International Relations: Exploring the Links and International Relations: *Global Environmental Politics* 3(2):72–87.

Falkner, Robert, Hannes Stephan, and John Vogler. (2010) International Climate Policy after Copenhagen: Towards a "Building Blocks" Approach. *Global Policy* 1(3):252–262.

Farrell, Henry, and Abraham L. Newman. (2010) Making Global Markets: Historical Institutionalism in International Political Economy. *Review of International Political Economy* 17(4): 37–41.

Garcia-Johnson, Ronie. (2000) *Exporting Environmentalism: US Multinational Chemical Corporations in Brazil and Mexico*. Cambridge, MA: MIT Press.

Green, Jessica. (2017) Blurred Lines: Why Do States Recognize Private Carbon Standards? *International Interactions* 43(1):103–128. doi:10.1080/03050629.2016.1210943

Green, Jessica Fischer. (2013) *Rethinking Private Authority: Agents and Entrepreneurs in Global Environmental Governance*. Princeton, NJ: Princeton University Press.

Hale, Thomas. (2016) "All Hands on Deck": The Paris Agreement and Nonstate Climate Action. *Global Environmental Politics* 16(3):12–22.

Hale, Thomas N., and David Held. (2011) *Handbook of Transnational Governance: Institutions and Innovations*. Cambridge: Polity Press.

Hale, Thomas, and Charles Roger. (2012) Chinese Participation in Transnational Climate Governance. In *From Rule Takers to Rule Makers: The Growing Role of Chinese in Global Governance*, edited by Scott Kennedy and Shuaihua Cheng. Research Center for Chinese Politics and Business (RCCPB) and International Centre for Trade and Sustainable Development (ICTSD). Available at http://www.ictsd.org/sites/default/files/research/2012/10/the-growing-role-of-chinese-in-global-governance.pdf.

Hale, Thomas, and Charles Roger. (2014) Orchestration and Transnational Climate Governance. *The Review of International Organizations* 9(1):59–82.

Hale, Thomas, and Charles Roger. (2015) Domestic Politics and Chinese Participation in Transnational Climate Governance. In *China and Global Governance: The Dragon's Learning Curve*, edited by Scott Kennedy. London: Routledge.

Hall, Rodney Bruce, and Thomas J. Biersteker. (2002) *The Emergence of Private Authority in Global Governance*. Cambridge: Cambridge University Press.

Haufler, Virginia. (2005) *A Public Role for the Private Sector: Industry Self-Regulation in the Global Economy*. Washington, DC: Brookings Institution Press.

Held, David, Charles Roger and Eva-Maria Nag. (2013) *Climate Governance in the Developing World*. Cambridge, UK: Polity Press.

Hoffmann, M. (2011) *Climate Governance at the Crossroads: Experimenting with a Global Response after Kyoto*. Oxford: Oxford University Press.

Hsueh, Lily. (2017) Transnational Climate Governance and the Global 500: Examining Private Actor Participation by Firm-Level Factors and Dynamics. *International Interactions* 43(1):48–75. doi:10.1080/03050629.2016.1223929

Keck, Margaret E., and Kathryn Sikkink. (1998) *Activists beyond Borders: Advocacy Networks in International Politics*. Ithaca, NY: Cornell University Press.

Keohane, Robert O., and David G. Victor. (2011) The Regime Complex for Climate Change. *Perspectives on Politics* 9(1):7–23.

Kolk, Ans, and David Levy. (2001) Winds of Change: Corporate Strategy, Climate Change and Oil Multinationals. *European Management Journal* 19(5):501–509.

Michaelowa, Katharina, and Axel Michaelowa. (2017) Transnational Climate Governance Initiatives: Designed for Effective Climate Change Mitigation? *International Interactions* 43(1):129–155.

Milner, Helen V. (1997) *Interests, Institutions and Information: Domestic Politics and International Relations*. Princeton, NJ: Princeton University Press.

Milner, Helen V., and Robert O. Keohane. (1996) *Internationalization and Domestic Politics*. Cambridge: Cambridge University Press.

Moravcsik, Andrew. (1997) Taking Preferences Seriously: A Liberal Theory of International Politics. *International Organization* 51(4):513–553.

Newell, Peter, and Matthew Paterson. (2010) *Climate Capitalism: Global Warming and the Transformation of the Global Economy*. Cambridge: Cambridge University Press.

Ostrom, Elinor. (2009) A Polycentric Approach for Coping with Climate Change. World Bank Policy Research Working Paper, WPS 5095. Washington, DC: World Bank. Available at: http://elibrary.worldbank.org/doi/pdf/10.1596/1813-9450-5095

Perkins, Richard, and Eric Neumayer. (2010) Geographic Variations in the Early Diffusion of Corporate Voluntary Standards: Comparing ISO 14001 and the Global Compact. *Environment and Planning A* 42(2):347–365.

Portney, Kent E., and Jeffrey Berry. (2014) Civil Society and Sustainable Cities. *Comparative Political Studies* 47(3):395–419.

Potoski, Matthew, and Aseem Prakash. (2009) *Voluntary Programs: A Club Theory Perspective*. Cambridge, MA: MIT Press.

Prakash, Aseem, and Matthew Potoski. (2006) *The Voluntary Environmentalists: Green Clubs, ISO 14001, and Voluntary Environmental Regulations*. Cambridge: Cambridge University Press.

Prakash, Aseem, and Matthew Potoski. (2014) Global Private Regimes, Domestic Public Law: ISO 14001 and Pollution Reduction. *Comparative Political Studies* 47(3):369–394.

Risse-Kappen, Thomas. (1995) *Bringing Transnational Relations Back In*. Cambridge: Cambridge University Press.

Roger, Charles, and Peter Dauvergne. (Forthcoming) The Rise of Transnational Governance as a Field of Study. *International Studies Review*.

Schattschneider, E. E. (1935) *Politics, Pressures and the Tariff*. New York: Prentice-Hall.

Sending, Ole J. and Iver B. Neumann. (2006) Governance to Governmentality: Analyzing NGOs, States and Power. *International Studies Quarterly* 50(2):651–672.

Sikkink, Kathryn. (2005) Patterns of Dynamic Multilevel Governance and the Insider-Outsider Coalition. In *Transnational Protest and Global Activism*, edited by Donatella della Porta and Sidney G. Tarrow. Lanham, MD: Rowman & Littlefield, pp. 151–173.

True, Jacqui, and Michael Mintrom. (2001) Transnational Networks and Policy Diffusion: The Case of Gender Mainstreaming. *International Studies Quarterly* 45(1):27–57.

Victor, David G. (2011) *Global Warming Gridlock: Creating More Effective Strategies for Protecting the Planet*. Cambridge: Cambridge University Press.

Widerberg, Oscar, and Johannes Stripple. (2016) The Expanding Field of Cooperative Initiatives for Decarbonization: A Review of Five Databases. *Wiley Interdisciplinary Reviews: Climate Change* 7(4):486–500.

Join the Club: How the Domestic NGO Sector Induces Participation in the Covenant of Mayors Program

Nives Dolšak and Aseem Prakash

ABSTRACT
How does strength of domestic NGOs influence participation in the Covenants of Mayors program? Launched by the European Commission in 2008, this program invites local and regional authorities to voluntarily commit to implementing EU climate change and energy policies. We focus on the transitional countries of Eastern Europe and Eurasia to examine whether the strength of their domestic NGOs correlates with cities' decisions to participate in this transnational program. To operationalize NGO strength, we suggest thinking of it as a stock variable that cumulates over time, instead of a single-year, flow variable. With country year as the unit of analysis, we examine the percentage of urban population covered by the Covenant across a panel of 26 transitional economies for the period 2008–2014. We find that the key variable of interest, cumulative NGO strength, is a statistically significant predictor of program participation, even after controlling for domestic and international factors, including the salience of international NGOs and the years since the country began the formal process to join the European Union.

NGOs are important nonstate policy actors and influence public policy at the international, domestic, and subnational levels. Scholars debate the extent to which the NGOs can influence public policy in the context of the transitional economies of the Eastern and Central Europe and Eurasia with a communist legacy that discouraged civil society. We examine the role of the NGOs in encouraging cities to voluntarily participate in the European Commission's Covenant of Mayors[1] (COM) in the context of 26 transitional countries: Albania, Armenia, Azerbaijan, Belarus, Bosnia and Herzegovina, Bulgaria, Croatia, Czech Republic, Estonia, Georgia, Hungary, Kazakhstan, Kyrgyzstan, Latvia, Lithuania, Macedonia, Moldova, Montenegro, Poland, Romania, Russia, Serbia, Slovakia, Slovenia, Tajikistan, and Ukraine.

---

[1] The Program has recently been renamed as Covenant of Mayors for Climate & Energy. However, given the period of study, we use the original name, Covenant of Mayors.

The COM program was launched by the European Commission in 2008. It seeks to involve "local and regional authorities, voluntarily committing to increasing energy efficiency and use of renewable energy sources on their territories" (Covenant of Mayors n.d.a.). The objective is to reduce carbon dioxide (CO_2) emissions by 20% (with 1992 as the benchmark) by 2020. For the period 2008–2014, the participation levels in the COM program are impressive: 6,275 jurisdictions covering over 190 million inhabitants have joined. However, the participation levels are uneven across the studied 26 countries, ranging from a low of 1% of urban population in Tajikistan or Azerbaijan to a high of 100% in Bosnia and Hercegovina in 2014 (Covenant of Mayors n.d.b.). How do variations in participation levels correlate with the strength of domestic civil society?

This special issue is rooted in the premise that domestic politics plays a crucial role in the success, especially the adoption, of transnational initiatives:

> Prevailing explanations largely focus on global processes of diffusion through economic and social networks, as well as the micro-incentives facing individual sub- and non-state actors. While such theories offer important insights, they assume, often implicitly, that participation can be explained as if it occurred outside the domestic contexts in which actors operate. But this assumption stands at odds both with well-established research on the role of domestic interest groups, policies and institutions in shaping international cooperation, and recent case studies that demonstrate how domestic factors condition transnational forces. (Roger, Hale, and Andonova 2017)

We build on this core idea to show that even in the context of transitional economies of Eastern Europe and Eurasia with communist legacies, civil society can play an important role in shaping the city-level response to a transnational climate governance initiative.

Why participate in a voluntary program? Scholars studying cities' participation in voluntary climate change initiatives note that cities' participation may not seem rational because their voluntary actions create a nonexcludable global public good, while their own costs might significantly exceed their private benefits (Zahran, Brody, Vedlitz, Grover, and Miller 2008). We examine this puzzle through the lens of club theory (Prakash and Potoski 2006). The costs of joining and implementing COM are not trivial. Participating cities are required to create a baseline inventory of their emissions and to implement an energy plan to meet the emissions reduction targets. To accomplish these goals, they have to establish an administrative infrastructure, including a monitoring process. Finally, the participating cities have to submit their plan to the European Union, along with regular implementation reports.

To examine the role of domestic politics in this transnational governance initiative, we focus on domestic NGOs as drivers of COM adoption. Few would disagree that NGOs are important actors in domestic and global politics. Scholars have invested considerable effort in studying the role of transnational NGOs networks in global politics (Keck and Sikkink 1998). They have paid less attention to the role of domestic NGOs in transnational governance. Why might this be so? For one, domestic NGOs tend to be weak in developing countries. To get their voices heard, these NGOs need support from transnational NGOs via the so-called "boomerang effect" (Keck and Sikkink 1998). Hence, it seems that the real "action" is at the global level, not at the domestic level. This is particularly true in the context of environmental issues—hence the focus on transnational instead of domestic actors.

The emphasis on transnational NGOs and the neglect of domestic NGOs is puzzling because the initial justification for focusing on NGOs as policy actors was their embeddedness in domestic politics, their grassroots character, and their ability to generate social capital that could be deployed to political and economic issues (Putnam 1995). Hence, NGOs represented politics from below and were the true agents for aggregating and then transmitting citizens' preferences on key policy issues. While international NGOs certainly have an important role to play in global and domestic politics, a neglect of domestic NGOs undermines our understanding of how NGOs influence transnational governance and domestic politics.

Theoretically, the transitional economies of Eastern and Central Europe and Eurasia present a "hard case" to test the influence of domestic NGOs, which have been nascent in these countries due to their communist legacies. While international NGOs have been active in several of these countries, scholars debate the extent to which domestic NGOs have been able to exercise policy influence. How might then we theoretically think about the strength and policy influence of domestic NGOs in transitional economies? We suggest that the study of the role of civil society in transitional economies should focus on the civil society's cumulative strength, instead of the measures of their annual strength. This is because building trust in NGOs and recognizing their legitimacy as political actors takes place gradually. Furthermore, the social capital that NGOs' activities accumulate and the capital that is then deployed in economic and political sphere is also not a one-shot process. To study the leverage NGOs exercise on governmental policies, scholars need to focus on the strength they have accumulated over a longer time period. To operationalize this key and novel way of thinking about NGO strength, we examine NGO strength as a stock variable that has cumulated over time, instead of an annual, flow variable. We believe this new way of thinking about NGO power in domestic politics should be extended to other issue areas and other developing countries.

Furthermore, transitional economies also show considerable variation in their wealth levels and in the health of their economies. Hence, it is difficult to claim that postmaterialist values are likely to uniformly encourage participation in the COM program. In addition, most transitional economies have joined the European Union at different points in time (and some might yet join). Because the EU exercises significant influence on the domestic policies of its members and potential members, the levels of socialization and policy harmonization induced by the European Union are likely to vary. This allows some additional room for domestic actors to exercise policy leverage.

Efforts to mitigate global climate change have witnessed remarkable participation levels by subnational actors (Lee 2014; Rabe 2004). The emphasis on local governments, specifically cities, is crucial because "80% of energy consumption and CO_2 emissions is associated with urban activity" (European Commission 2015). In the United States, the absence of federal regulation on climate change has created policy space for subnational actors to step in (Dolšak and Houston 2014; Hsueh and Prakash 2012; Zahran et al. 2008). These scholars find state and local governments to be responding to demand-side factors (such as local air pollution, climate-change risks, and public opinion and concern) and the supply/capacity-side factors (such as socioeconomic-capacity dimensions and institutional characteristics). Even beyond climate change, the role of cities in providing the venues for political struggle is recognized to be important across issue areas (Sassen 2001), the Arab spring being a prominent example. At the peril of exaggeration, one might even suggest that there is an urban bias (Bradshaw 1987; Lipton 1977) in politics, with urban actors playing an important role in shaping policy processes. Superior access to media, both traditional and social, gives urban actors policy visibility and influence. The COM program offers an excellent opportunity to study the extent to which domestic environmental NGOs (which tend to be urban-based in transitional economies) have been able to influence city-level participation in a voluntary environmental program.

Empirically, with a country year as our unit of analysis, we examine the percentage of urban populations covered by COM across a panel of 26 transitional economies in Eastern and Central Europe and Eurasia over the 2008–2014 period. Our key variable of interest is the strength of domestic NGOs. Our model controls for a range of variables, domestic and international, that might influence cities' participation in COM. These include: the number of international NGOs in the country (which allows us to differentiate between the policy influence of domestic and international NGOs), economic growth, nitrogen oxides (NOx) pollution levels, fiscal decentralization, and exports as share of GDP. In addition, we control for the number of years since a country signed an EU accession agreement. To check the robustness of our results, we use several measures of NGO strength (employing the USAID NGO Sustainability Index, as we discuss subsequently) as our key independent variable. Our results with regard to the significant effect of the strength of domestic NGOs as a predictor of the COM participation levels are robust across all these specifications. Finally, we extend our analysis to explore whether NGO strength might also influence some measures of program efficacy. Focusing on procedural efficacy, we find that NGO strength correlates with participating cities formally submitting their Sustainable Energy Action Plans to the European Commission.

The Covenant of Mayors program

Nobel Laureate Elinor Ostrom, noted in her presidential address at the 1997 annual meeting of the American Political Science Association that "the theory of collective action is *the* central subject of political science" (Ostrom 1998:1; emphasis in the original). Governance pertains to the organization of sustained collective action by creating rules. Challenges to collective action are particularly salient in the context of transnational endeavors. Furthermore, these challenges pose interesting theoretical issues when collective action is sought to be organized at the level of subnational actors and in the realm of voluntary or nonmandatory actions.

This article examines a unique case of transnational collective action aimed at subnational actors, the Covenant of Mayors (COM) program. COM should be understood in the context of the 1997 Kyoto Protocol that established targets for reductions in greenhouse gas (GHG) emissions. There are 192 parties to this regime: 191 states and the European Union. The European Union sought to implement its Kyoto commitment in a phased manner. The EU-15 committed to reducing their collective emissions to 8% below 1990 levels during phase 2, 2008–2012. The member States that joined the EU since 2004 also committed to reduction targets in the range of 6%–8% (5% in Croatia's case). Overall, the European Union committed that by 2020 it will cut its GHG emissions by 20% below 1990 levels. To do so, the European Union had used both mandatory and voluntary tools. It established the European Union Emissions Trading Scheme (EU-ETS), a "cap and trade" scheme that established mandatory national emission quotas for power plants and some industrial facilities and allowed them to buy and sell emission allowances. The European Union began implementing the EU-ETS in 2005. Alongside this, it launched the COM program in 2008.

Governmental agencies as well as intergovernmental organizations such as the United Nations have been in the forefront of establishing voluntary programs. The United States Environmental Protection Agency has been a pioneer in launching a range of programs, over 60 by some counts, including some programs focusing on climate change mitigation.[2] The UN launched the United Nations Global Compact in 2001. Thus, the European Commission's launch of COM should be viewed as part of the broader

---

[2] http://www3.epa.gov/climatechange/EPAactivities/voluntaryprograms.html

trend, whereby governmental and quasi-governmental actors have deployed both mandatory and voluntary tools toward specific policy objectives.

Although it is a transnational governance tool, the COM supports the efforts of subnational actors on climate change mitigation, especially via adoption of sustainable energy policies. COM is a voluntary, or a nonmandatory, program. It can be conceptualized as a "green club" (Prakash and Potoski 2006) that induces voluntary contribution to public good provision (global climate change mitigation) by promising excludable reputational and goodwill benefits that have the characteristics of club goods. The promise of appropriating these benefits constitutes the incentive for actors to voluntarily incur the costs of participating in the program.

In terms of branding benefits, the European Union has sought to portray COM as an important communication tool with which cities communicate about their efforts to be pro-environment, and more specifically, proactive on the issue of climate change mitigation. The COM Web site notes that "The European Commission has committed to supporting local authorities involved in the Covenant of Mayors and providing public visibility for them" (Covenant of Mayors n.d.c.). Further, the Web site lists several reasons for joining COM. It notes:

> Covenant Signatories find multiple reasons to join the movement, such as: Make a public statement of extra commitment to CO_2 reduction; Create or reinforce the dynamic on CO_2 reduction in your territory; Benefit from encouragement and examples of other pioneers; Share the expertise developed in your own territory with others; Make your territory known as a pioneer; Publicise your achievements visible to the Covenant community and beyond via the Covenant website. (Covenant of Mayors n.d.c.)

Thus, consistent with the literature on voluntary clubs (van't Veld and Kotchen 2011), COM offers important branding benefits, which hold the promise of reputational payoffs to participants.

Reputational benefits often have significant material payoffs. Firms routinely invest in building their brand reputations, which allows them to charge premiums for their products, strengthen the loyalty of their consumers, and reduce what is called "postpurchase dissonance," especially for premium products. There is a well-established literature on how membership in voluntary environmental programs might affect market capitalization of firms. At the country level, reputations are important as well. Countries that have reputations for corruption tend to attract less foreign direct investment, for example. Firms operating in corrupt countries may fear that their products are tarnished by the country's reputation and may join voluntary programs to offset this reputational damage. Consequently, there is some evidence that joining voluntary programs such as ISO 9001 may allow developing countries that have poor reputations for quality to enhance trade (Potoski and Prakash, 2009). Hence, we do not see reputational benefits of joining a program to be mainly ideational; they have concrete material payoffs.

Which actors will bestow these benefits? We suggest that cities might be more willing to recognize such benefits if there are actors who have the ability and incentives to lobby and persuade them in this regard or create a structural context in which such voluntary initiatives are appreciated and recognized. Participation in COM may also strengthen environmental credentials of city politicians with these vocal constituencies. As we discuss in the next section, scholars note the role of NGOs in creating such reputational benefits for environmental issues.

Why study participation in voluntary programs, especially if there is little evidence that they reduce pollution? This subject has been extensively examined in the voluntary program literature because of a lack of apparent motivation for participation. Actors incur nontrivial costs to join these programs, while the benefits from such participation are not always clear, concentrated on the actors incurring the costs, nor excludable. Even if programs are eventually deemed to be ineffective, it is still important to understand the conditions under which actors are willing to join them and why public policy seeks to promote them. Viewed this way, our article also contributes to the literature on voluntary programs that focuses specifically on the subject of participation in such endeavors.

Voluntary programs typically tend to outline two types of commitments: a focus on internal processes/management systems or outcomes. For example, a program could obligate its participants to adopt specific types of policies, without stipulating the targets these participants need to achieve. The rationale is that if appropriate internal systems are in place, the desired outcomes will follow. Prominent examples include the ISO 14001 program sponsored by the International Organization for Standardization, or the Responsible Care program that is sponsored by trade associations representing the Chemical industry. These programs obligate the participating members to adopt management systems with specific features. However, they do not stipulate specific environmental outcomes program members have to achieve (Prakash and Potoski 2011).

Other voluntary programs stipulate specific environmental outcomes that the participants need to meet as part of their membership obligations. COM imposes both process and outcome obligations. In terms of process requirements, it requires its participants to create a baseline emission inventory (BEI) and implement Sustainable Energy Action Plans (SEAP). BEI requires that the participating city document CO_2 emissions caused by fossil fuel consumption of its large emitters. Sustainable Energy Action Plans outline specific actions cities are committing to implement. This is an important first step (which we have termed as procedural effectiveness subsequently) because entities—be it governmental or nongovernmental—are often oblivious of the pollution they emit (Prakash 2000). The creation of baseline inventories forces them to recognize their carbon footprint, which can create internal pressures for policy action. Cities are expected to update these inventories on a regular basis, which allows them to monitor the progress of specific entities in their jurisdictions in reducing CO_2 emissions.

Most voluntary programs recognize the possibility that some participating actors may not fulfill their obligations—the so-called shirking problem (Prakash and Potoski 2006). How might shirking be curbed? Scholars note that the shirking problem is typically addressed in three ways. Scholars subscribing to club theory see shirking mainly as a problem of institutional design. For them, shirking can be curbed if the program incorporates mechanisms to monitor and sanction. While third-party auditors are the gold standard for monitoring, the actor sponsoring the program does not itself sanction the violators, nor does it make information provided by the auditors available to the public for naming and shaming these firms, making monitoring less effective. Some programs ask participants to report on their achievements and then make this information available to the public. This approach is followed by COM: Cities have to submit implementation plans and performance information to the program secretariat, which makes them publicly available. Then interested stakeholders, particularly the NGOs, can use this information to reward and punish participating actors.

Another perspective suggests that shirking can be curbed through peer and community pressure; after all, obeying rules is the norm of appropriate behavior (March and Olsen 1989). Hence, the community of cities participating in COM will exert normative pressure and socialize each other toward honoring program obligations. The third perspective suggests that actors shirk because they do not have the capabilities to meet their obligations. This might hold for small cities with budgetary pressures or insufficient expertise to draw up climate mitigation plans. To address these challenges, national governments as well as the European Union provide financial and technical support.

Joining green clubs typically imposes nontrivial costs (although the literature notes the presence of "greenwashes" that do not impose any serious obligations on their participants, as noted by Laufer [2003]). The creation of BEI and SEAP requires substantial investment in administrative infrastructure. Given that the launch of COM coincided with the European, if not global, economic crisis and budgetary deficits, we expect city governments to think carefully about the political and economic benefits and costs of participating in the COM club. The role of domestic NGOs is crucial in this regard because they can arguably create political and economic benefits for participation. Indeed, voluntary program literature has noted the important role NGOs can play in persuading actors to join specific clubs (Baron 2009; Lenox and Eesley 2009). To what extent NGOs can be successful in their persuasive efforts is an empirical issue we subsequently examine.

Finally, there is a question about the factors governments consider in making policy choices. Scholars debate whether governments think carefully of costs and benefits of policies prior to making policy choices, an issue that is rooted in the broader debate in the literature on rational choice. This article suggests that politicians think of, among other factors, benefits and costs of joining COM prior to joining it. We are not asserting that they think only in terms of benefits and costs; indeed, as we discuss subsequently, our empirical model takes into account the contributions of "nonrational" mechanisms as well. For example, we control for years since the country signed the European Union accession documents. This variable captures the normative and administrative links with the European Union, which can create a common normative community committed to climate change mitigation. In other words, the EU accession process does not directly alter the benefit and cost calculation a mayor of a specific city faces.

NGOs in transitional economies

Scholars debate the extent to which NGOs exercised policy influence in the communist era (Rose, Mishler, and Haerpfer 1997). In the postcommunist era, the influence of domestic NGOs on environmental politics varied across transitional economies (Badescu and Sum 2004; Mondak and Gearing 1998). Consider the following: The Czech Republic faced historically high emissions of SO_2 and NOx even though Czechoslovakia was a signatory of the long-range transboundary air pollution convention agreements. However, it enacted the Clean Air Act in 1991 with NGOs playing an important role in the policy process (Andonova 2005). Poland also faced high domestic air pollution. Its environmental NGOs, however, could not persuade the government to enact something akin to the Clean Air Act (Dolšak 2013). Thus, the ability of domestic NGOs to influence policymaking varies across transitional countries of Eastern Europe and Eurasia. As the U.S. Agency for International Development (2014:1) notes:

> While Poland has more than 100,000 registered associations and foundations, the [civil society organizations] sector in Turkmenistan consists of a mere 106 registered organizations. While it is nearly impossible for the government in Latvia to do anything without meaningfully engaging CSOs [Civil Society Organizations], the situation is quite different in Azerbaijan where CSOs cannot organize any event or activity without the knowledge and permission of the executive powers.

Some countries have adopted laws that restrict the ability of NGOs to secure overseas funding, Russia being a prominent case. Even when NGOs are able to freely obtain international funding, they are not always equipped to effectively deploy it to influence public policies. NGOs in these countries frequently lack the capacity to manage resources with the levels of accountability and transparency required by donors. This leads to credibility problems with domestic audiences and international donors. Furthermore, when the domestic economic situation deteriorates and when the culture of philanthropy is not encouraged, the financial viability of NGOs faces considerable challenge.

NGOs' ability to advocate for policy change is also influenced by their low ability to formulate message in the media, lack of knowledge required for coalition formation, and weakness for demanding policy change and monitoring of enacted policies. When NGOs have a poor public image, they face challenges in recruiting volunteers, encouraging domestic donations, and persuading government to work with them.

Given that NGOs are expected to represent public interest, citizen support and trust becomes an important component of their ability to influence the policy process. Of course, developing trust takes time, particularly because most NGOs served under the umbrella of the communist parties in the pre-1990s. The transition from party-controlled organizations to truly grassroots organization was also challenging because many NGOs, aided with the infusion of Western funds, tended to acquire the semblance of professional organizations that were less interested and capable of grassroots action. Yet, although unevenly so, some NGOs have successfully begun to acquire public trust while maintaining the professional image that is sometimes quite appealing to Western donors. In sum, the acquisition of public trust and policy influence is gradual and cumulative. Both the shadow of the future and experiences of the past drive levels of trustworthiness.

Based on this discussion, we suggest that NGO strength in policy process should be conceptualized as a stock variable instead of a flow variable. We are inspired by Gerring, Bond, Barndt, and Moreno (2005), who suggested that the influence of democracy on development should be studied by thinking of democracy as a stock variable. This is because democracy as a method of governance develops over time, building on the resources accumulated in the past. We explore how this idea applies in the context of NGOs; after all, civil society is a pillar of democracy.

There are important theoretical rationales for our approach. One might argue that the stock of NGOs approximates the concept of social capital, which is an institutional feature that shapes the ability of actors to demand policies and accountability from public authorities and to organize for collective action (Ostrom 1990; Putnam, 1995). Social capital is a stock variable because it is accumulated by repeated interactions over a period of time. While Gerring et al. (2005) construct the democracy stock variable by summing up democracy scores over several decades, following Dolšak (2013) we adopt the same theoretical approach for NGOs but for a much shorter duration (since 1997 when the USAID data became available). We find that this cumulative effect of NGO strength can be observed even after a relatively short period of time. This suggests that there might be "shortcuts" in creating valuable political and social resources such as NGOs and civil society.

Variable operationalization

Our dependent variable is the share of the urban population covered by COM. The COM database lists the cities that have joined the program along with their population. Why focus on population share and not on the number of cities that have participated? With population varying dramatically across cities (from a few hundred to millions), counting the number of cities in each country does not capture the political or policy dynamics. Furthermore, NGOs can be expected to lobby several cities to join this program. While several NGOs tend to be located in the capital city, they are able to influence cities in other parts of the country. Viewed this way, unless one has city-level data on NGOs (which are not available, and this is also problematic because NGOs lobby in several cities) and can map how NGOs target specific cities but not others, it will be theoretically difficult to defend an individual city as the unit of analysis. At a more practical level, while the data on urban population are provided by World Development Indicators, we do not have data on the total number of cities in a given country. Consequently, while we can compute the share of urban population covered by COM, we cannot compute the percentage of cities joining this program. Thus, on both conceptual and practical grounds, our dependent variable is the cumulative share of urban population covered by COM.

Key independent variable

We measure the strength of domestic NGOs using a novel index of NGO sustainability developed by the USAID (2014). While this measure reflects the strength of domestic civil society as a whole, we believe it is an appropriate measure to assess the strength exercised by environmental NGOs as well. Furthermore, it is our sense that domestic environmental NGO strength will strongly correlate with overall strength of civil society given that environmental issues are among the key public concerns in this region of the world. In addition, environmental NGOs were among the first to evolve in these countries in the 1980s and 1990s because they were not viewed as articulating a political challenge to the regime.

The index of NGO sustainability reflects several dimensions of NGO strength that should impact their abilities to influence the policy process. It examines the institutional environment—specifically, the ways in which the legal environment allows them to secure resources. Given that NGOs need to function as organizations, it looks at their internal capacities and skills. It also takes into account their financial viability along with local capacities to support NGOs via philanthropy or fund raising. Because NGOs need to work together to influence the policy process, it also incorporates their abilities to form coalitions. Finally, because media coverage is the oxygen for NGO survival, it looks at how the media cover activities of NGOs. The USAID undertakes expert surveys for each country to assess these dimensions. It seeks opinions from local NGOs, academics, think tanks, government officials, media, and business, as well as international donors (USAID 2014:241). We have reversed the original indicators provided by the USAID so that value 1 indicates the lowest level of NGO sustainability and value 7 indicates the highest. While the majority of our models (1–3 and 8–10) use the combined measure, we report specification checks for subcategories of the measure as well (Models 4–7). The data were downloaded from the USAID 2013 report on the NGO Sustainability Index for Central and Eastern Europe and Eurasia.

International controls

Scholars have noted the impact of the EU accession process on domestic policies in EU candidate countries (Gray 2009). We control for European Union influence on these countries. This process begins with the signing of the EU accession agreement. With this, countries begin to harmonize their environmental regulations, standards, and policies. The length of the accession period is important for two reasons. First, it allows the EU's normative influence longer time to infuse the policy processes in the candidate countries. At the same time, this period also allows these countries to build up local capacities. We measure this in terms of years since the signature of the Europe Agreement (for countries of Central and Eastern Europe) and Stabilization and Association Agreement (for countries of the Western Balkans).

An important factor influencing COM adoption is the engagement of domestic actors with the international economy via trade networks. There is a continuing debate on how engagement with the global economy influences domestic environmental policies. Some scholars find that trade engagement leads to stronger environmental policies (Cao and Prakash 2010), while others find the opposite effect (Andonova, Mansfield, and Milner 2007). Therefore, we control for export salience (exports/GDP) by using data from the World Development Indicators database.

While we focus on the role of the domestic NGOs in the participation in COM, we recognize that international NGOs continue to play an important role in the environmental politics of this region. Hence, we control for the count of International NGOs (INGOs) working in these countries by using data from the Yearbook of International Organizations.

Domestic controls

While the EU-ETS requires member countries to contribute to the provision of a global public good, countries might be motivated to voluntarily undertake climate change mitigation policies if they can reduce domestic air pollution (Dolšak 2009). The ability to corner domestic benefits allows political actors to justify the costs of voluntarily adopting mitigation policies. The political benefits of reducing local pollution might extend well beyond the environmental arena. Indeed, politicians can gather support from NGOs working in areas such as public health as well (Dimas 2008). Our model therefore controls for NOx, which is an important source of local air pollution. NOx emissions are measured in kilograms per capita. Data were accessed at the EU Centre for Emission Inventories and Projections.

The prioritization of environmental concerns on policy agendas may be influenced by business cycles. During periods of lackluster economic growth, environmental concerns might take a back seat (Fagan 1994; Slocock 1996). To control for the impact of the economic cycles on cities' incentives to join COM, we control for the annual GDP growth rate. The data are from the World Bank's World Development Indicators database.

COM is aimed at local and regional governments. Arguably, these governments may have the inclinations and abilities to join such programs only if they have the resources and authority to do so. This, in part, may be influenced by the distribution of power between the national and subnational levels of government. The literature highlights several dimensions of decentralization, including political, administrative, and fiscal (Thiessen 2003). COM might require local governments to make changes in the taxation as well as expenditure policies. We employ a measure of fiscal decentralization because local and regional governments' responses to COM are likely to be influenced by their abilities to impose taxes and decide about expenditures. Our model controls for fiscal decentralization (Iimi 2005; Schneider 2003; Thiessen 2003) operationalized as the percent of total government expenditures attributable to local governments (Dziobek, Alves, El Rayess, Gutiérrez Mangas, and Kufta 2001). The data are from the International Monetary Fund's Government Finance Statistics Yearbook. Descriptive statistics and correlations between variables included in the model are available in the Web appendix.

Model, findings, and extensions

We investigate the theoretical claims using an unbalanced panel of 26 countries for the period 2008–2014. We lag our independent variables by one year to address the issue of reverse causality. To address the issue of heteroscedasticity, we use Hubert White robust standard errors clustered by country (Greene 2012). Our model is specified as:

$$\text{\%Urban Population under COM}_t = \alpha_t + \beta_1 \text{NGO}_{t-1} + \beta_2 X_{t-1} + \varepsilon_t$$

where NGO represents the cumulative score for *NGO strength*, X represents the vector of control variables, and ϵ is the error term.

Table 1 presents the results of our analyses. The first model includes the key independent variable of our interest, cumulative *NGO strength*. Models 2 and 3 control for domestic and international factors respectively. Our analysis suggests that *NGO strength*, the key variable of interest, is statistically significant even after controlling for the salience of international NGOs. In Model 1, an increase of cumulative *NGO strength* (which shows considerable variation, from about 27 in Belarus in the beginning of the studied period to over 99 in Estonia or Poland in the last year of the studied period) by 1 point is associated with a 1.2-percentage point increase in the share of urban population covered by COM ($p < .001$). That is, with an average annual increase of *NGO strength* of about 4.3 points on the NGO sustainability index, we should expect (on average) about a 5-percentage point increase in the share of urban population covered by COM.

Importantly, the effect of the *NGO strength* variable is significant, although we have controlled for INGO presence and for years since the country began the formal process to join the EU. Hence, our analysis provides support for

Table 1. Share of Urban Population Covered by the Covenant of Mayors.

Variable	Model 1	Model 2	Model 3
NGO strength (cumulative)	1.19*** (0.25)	1.28*** (0.33)	1.18*** (0.35)
Years since EU agreement	−0.50	−1.03	−1.29
	(0.86)	(1.07)	(1.25)
Domestic			
NOx emissions per capita		0.87	0.86
		(0.54)	(0.56)
GDP growth		0.07	−0.01
		(0.13)	(0.11)
Fiscal Decentralization		−0.12	−0.17
		(0.39)	(0.45)
International			
INGOs			0.00
			(0.01)
Exports (share of GDP)			0.25
			(0.20)
Constant	−41.89*** (9.09)	−56.78***	−60.31***
		(20.88)	(20.15)
N	156	117	117

Note. Regression for panel data set, random effects.
Robust, cluster corrected standard errors reported in parentheses;
*.05 < p ≤ 0.1; **.01 < p ≤ .05; ***p ≤ .01 (two-tail test).

the claim that domestic NGOs have influenced COM adoption, beyond what they might exercise via their links with INGOs and via the EU accession process. The EU accession process itself does not have a statistically significant effect on COM coverage. This is an important finding because prior research reports the substantial influence of the accession process on domestic policies of EU candidate countries (Gray 2009). Arguably, countries seek to satisfy the EU's requirements regarding formal laws and regulations at the national level only. This sort of EU environmental normative pressure might be less salient at the subnational level and in the context of a voluntary program. For the EU to exercise direct influence on cities in this regard, it should perhaps offer tangible incentives (especially monetary ones that fiscally strapped cities are likely to appreciate) beyond the reputational and informational goodies, to incur private costs of implementing climate change mitigation policies.

We do not find support for the hypothesized impact of the increased fiscal decentralization. The reason may be in that when cities consider joining COM, they count on external financial support. As a matter of fact, cities have received financial assistance to comply with their COM requirements, something beyond the excludable benefits they were expected to gain. Slovenian cities, for example, received support from the Slovenian Ministry of the Environment and Spatial Planning and regional energy agencies for preparation of their sustainable energy action plans. Similarly, Croatian cities received support from German research agencies to prepare their sustainable energy action plans.

Among domestic controls, neither local air pollution (NOx) nor business cycles influence the coverage of urban population under COM. Importantly, neither the presence of international NGOs (INGO) nor the salience of exports influences COM coverage. Some consider INGOs to be important policy actors in transitional economies because domestic NGOs are weak. Arguably, the crackdown on foreign NGOs and on the operations of foreign NGOs in this region might partially explain our finding.

Robustness checks and extensions

We conducted several robustness checks. First, we examined subcomponents of the NGO Index that pertain to NGO advocacy, fiscal viability, public image, and legal environment (Table 2, Models 4–7). As these models indicate, our results are robust to all operationalizations of *NGO strength*.

Second, we undertook additional checks. Some scholars suggest that FDI is an important carrier of environmental norms and wealth correlates with environmental preferences. Hence, we controlled for FDI/GDP, per capita GDP, and per capita GDP squared. While FDI/GDP is not significant and per capita GDP is, their exclusion does not influence our substantive results.

Table 2. Share of Urban Population Covered by the Covenant of Mayors; NGO Capacity Measure Specification Checks.

Variable	Model 4	Model 5	Model 6	Model 7
NGO strength (cumulative)				
NGO advocacy (cumulative)	1.04*** (0.29)			
NGO financial viability (cumulative)		1.17*** (0.43)		
NGO public image (cumulative)			1.20*** (0.35)	
NGO legal environment (cumulative)				1.22*** (0.32)
Years since EU agreement	−1.24	−1.41	−1.43	−1.57
	(1.23)	(1.48)	(1.21)	(1.18)
Domestic				
NOx emissions per capita	0.76	0.5171	0.84	0.98*
	(0.53)	(0.5535)	(0.55)	(0.57)
GDP growth	−0.01	−0.0299	−0.00	−0.02
	(0.10)	(0.1045)	(0.11)	(0.10)
Fiscal Decentralization	−0.22	−0.3027	−0.11	0.13
	(0.43)	(0.4648)	(0.44)	(0.49)
International				
INGOs	0.00	0.00	0.00	−0.00
	(0.01)	(0.01)	(0.01)	(0.01)
Exports (share of GDP)	0.28	0.34	0.25	0.23
	(0.18)	(0.21)	(0.20)	(0.18)
Constant	−57.09***	−46.88**	−62.50***	−67.10***
	(18.74)	(19.53)	(20.67)	(21.53)
N	117	117	117	117

Note. Regression for panel data set, random effects.
Robust, cluster corrected standard errors reported in parentheses;
*.05 < p ≤ 0.1; **.01 < p ≤ .05; ***p ≤ .01 (two-tail test).

Furthermore, Ward and Cao (Forthcoming) in this *International Interactions*' special issue suggest the important role of fossil fuel interest groups in opposing COM participation. Building on this insight, we included a variable measuring the importance of coal in a country's total primary energy supply. We drew on data from the International Energy Agency in this regard and found that even though this variable was significant, its exclusion did not change our key results.

Environmental aid is another factor that might influence incentives and capacities of local governments to join COM. We reestimated our model with environmental aid data provided by Tierney, Nielson, Hawkins, Roberts, Findley, Powers, Parks, Wilson, and Hicks (2011). These data are available for the first 3 years of the 6 years we study and for 17 out of 26 countries included in the analysis. We found that although environmental aid is significant, the inclusion of green aid does not influence the significance of the variable of interest-NGO strength.

NGOs and governments are more likely to support COM adoption when there is a clear public concern regarding environmental issues. Furthermore, not all environmental issues might solicit similar levels of concerns.

Arguably, citizens might be more concerned about local environmental issues than global issues. In particular, citizens might want their governments to provide local environmental public goods as opposed to global public goods such as reductions in carbon emissions. We estimated the models by including various measures of environmental concern. We operationalized commitment to environmental protection as percent of respondents who agreed with the statement that protection of the environment should be given a priority even if it causes slowdown in economic growth. The data were accessed from the World Values Survey (n.d.). To control for concerns about global warming, we used two variables. The first one measures respondents' awareness of global climate change and the second respondents' view that climate change is caused by human activities. Comparable cross-national data on environmental concern and global climate change awareness are collected mostly at one point in time (Gallup poll or World Values Survey) for a subset of countries (Pelham 2009). As a result, we were only able to analyze their impact for a small subset of our sample (52 observations). In this smaller subset, results were consistent with our earlier models.

Might levels of democracy influence assessment of NGO strength? To address this issue, we first included a measure of democracy (Polity IV, scale from −10 to +10, negative numbers indicate authoritarian regimes), and our results hold. Second, we estimated the model without countries with authoritarian regimes (with Polity IV scores below 0). The dropped countries were: Azerbaijan, Belarus, Kazakhstan, and Tajikistan. Again, our results hold.[3]

Finally, we extended our analysis to examine the impact of the NGO strength on the "procedural effectiveness" of the COM. Scholars note the challenges in operationalizing the efficacy of voluntary programs (for that matter, intergovernmental regimes as well) because it is difficult to measure the effects in the short run, and it poses important issues of endogeneity between participation and effectiveness (Borck and Coglianese 2009; Lyon and Maxwell 2007; Prakash and Potoski 2011). One way to think of effectiveness is by focusing on procedural efficacy (as opposed to substantive efficacy that focuses on program outputs). Procedural efficacy can be assessed by examining whether the participating locality has undertaken steps to fulfill its program obligations. The COM was launched in 2008. Prior to 2015, there are no systematic data to assess how participation in COM has influenced city-level emissions of greenhouse gases (substantive efficacy). However, there is a possibility to explore how participating cities are fulfilling their obligations (procedural efficacy) under this program and to what extent this is driven by NGO strength, the key variable of our interest. Participating cities are obliged to formally submit their Sustainable Energy Action Plans.

---

[3]Variables for the above specification checks are included in the replication data set.

Table 3. Share of Urban Population in Cities with Submitted Action Plans.

Variable	Model 8	Model 9	Model 10
NGO strength (cumulative)	0.73***	0.85***	0.73**
	(0.59)	(0.33)	(0.34)
Years since EU agreement	0.68	0.00	−0.10
	(0.94)	(1.13)	(1.21)
Domestic			
NOx emissions per capita		0.75	0.73
		(0.56)	(0.59)
GDP growth		0.15	0.06
		(0.11)	(0.10)
Fiscal Decentralization		0.00	−0.02
		(0.38)	(0.46)
International			
INGOs			−0.00
			(0.01)
Exports (share of GDP)			0.26
			(0.19)
Constant	−25.95***	−43.23**	−44.53**
	(8.23)	(22.32)	(22.25)
N	156	117	117

Note. Regression for panel data set, random effects.
Robust, cluster corrected standard errors reported in parentheses;
*.05 < p ≤ 0.1; **.01 < p ≤.05; ***p ≤ .01 (two-tail test).

While 473 cities in the studied countries have joined COM, only 327 have submitted plans during the studied period. As the Table 3 shows, NGO strength continues to have a statistically significant effect on this dimension of procedural efficacy.

Conclusions

The introductory article by Roger et al. (2017) notes the important role of transnational climate governance initiatives in the abatement of greenhouse gas emissions. Challenging the state-centric view, they suggest that the success of such initiatives will depend on mobilization of subnational and nonstate actors. Because there are variations in the extent to which actors are involved in such initiatives, Roger et al. pose the following question: "How do domestic politics and other country-level variables affect sub- and nonstate actors' participation in transnational climate governance?"

This article responds to this question by focusing on a voluntary program (COM) sponsored by a supranational organization (European Union) and aimed at subnational units (cities). We examine the participation in this program across transitional economies of Central and Eastern Europe and Eurasia by focusing on the role of an important nonstate actor: domestic NGOs. We find that even in the case of these transitional countries with communist legacies where NGOs are of relative nascent origin and NGOs are considered to be less politically powerful, NGO strength correlates with the percentage of urban population covered under this voluntary program. While our model focuses on the cumulative strength of domestic NGOs and controls for the salience of international NGOs, we recognize that the latter often influence domestics politics through the instrumentalities of the former (Andonova and Tuta 2014).

We believe that thinking of NGO strength as a stock variable has a considerable theoretical promise. While Gerring et al. (2005) examined the accumulated democracy stock over several decades, our article adopts the same theoretical approach for NGOs, but for a much shorter duration (since 1997 when the USAID data become available). We find that this cumulative effect of NGO strength can be observed even after a relatively short period of time. This suggests that there might be "shortcuts" in creating valuable political and social resources such as social capital and civil society.

We conceptualize COM as a voluntary club that offers reputational benefits to its participants as an inducement to incur the nontrivial costs of joining COM. Domestic NGOs play a crucial role in the creation of such reputational payoffs via direct advocacy as well as indirectly by structuring the institutional environment in which participation actors function. By their environmental advocacy and lobbying, they seek to persuade city governments to "join the club." The extent to which this club will contribute to climate change mitigation over and above what the cities would have done in any case remains to be seen —an issue future research should closely examine. However, the recruitment into this club, especially during the time of economic crisis, is an important first step. Furthermore, as we report in the article, NGO strength correlates with initial procedural steps such as the creation of Sustainable Energy Action Plans that should eventually lead to lower emissions.

Finally, what policies might be put in place to ensure that participation in voluntary clubs leads to pollution reductions? Arguably, participants may have incentives to garner the reputational benefits without investing substantial amounts in pollution reduction. What might persuade cities to look at the Covenant of Mayors program not merely as a branding exercise but as an opportunity to work toward reducing GHG emissions? The role of financial support from external actors might be crucial here. The subject of effectiveness of climate clubs has assumed added importance because the 2015 Paris Agreement has underscored the important role of voluntary emission reductions. Voluntary clubs such as the Covenant of Mayors can provide a useful template to establish new programs, especially in developing countries.

Acknowledgments

Previous versions of this article were presented at the 2014 Oxford conference on Transnational Climate Governance and Domestic Politics and the 2015 International Studies Association Conference. We thank Liliana Andonova, Thomas Hale, Charles Roger, Jennifer Hadden, and anonymous reviewers for comments on previous drafts.

References

Andonova, Liliana B. (2005) The Europeanization of Environmental Policy in Central and Eastern Europe. In *The Europeanization of Central and Eastern Europe*, edited by Frank Schimmelfennig & Ulrich Dedelmeier. Ithaca, NY: Cornell University Press.

Andonova, Liliana, Edward D. Mansfield, and Helen V. Milner. (2007) International Trade and Environmental Policy in the Postcommunist World. *Comparative Political Studies* 40 (7):782–807.

Andonova, Liliana B., and Ioana A. Tuta. (2014) Transnational Networks and Paths to EU Environmental Compliance: Evidence from New Member States. *Journal of Common Market Studies* 52(4):775–793.

Badescu, Gabriel, and Paul Sum. (2004) Civil Society Development and Democratic Values in Romania and Moldova. *East European Politics and Societies* 18(2):316–341.

Baron, David P. (2009) Clubs, Credence Standards and Social Pressure. In *Voluntary Programs: A Club Theory Approach*, edited by M. Potoski and A Prakash. Cambridge, MA: MIT Press.

Borck, Jonathan C., and Cary Coglianese. (2009) Voluntary Environmental Programs: Assessing Their Effectiveness. *Annual Review Environmental Resources* 34:305–324.

Bradshaw, York W. (1987) Urbanization and Underdevelopment: A Global Study of Modernization, Urban Bias, and Economic Dependency. *American Sociological Review* 52 (2):224–239.

Cao, Xun, and Aseem Prakash. (2010) Trade Competition and Domestic Pollution: A Panel Study, 1980–2003. *International Organization* 64(3):481–503.

Covenant of Mayors. (n.d.a.) About. Available at http://www.covenant ofmayors.eu/about/covenant-of-mayors_en.html. (Accessed February 22, 2014)

Covenant of Mayors. (n.d.b.) Signatories. Available at http://www.covenantofmayors.eu/about/signatories_en.html. (Accessed February 23, 2014)

Covenant of Mayors. (n.d.c.) Support. Frequently Asked Questions. Available at http://www.covenantofmayors.eu/support/faq_en.html?id_faq=5. (Accessed August 14, 2016)

Dimas, Stavros. (2008, January 23) Climate Action: Energy for a Changing World. Speech given at European Commission, Brussels. Available at http://europa.eu/rapid/pressReleasesAction.do?reference=SPEECH/08/37&format=HTML&aged=0&language=EN&guiLanguage=en. (Accessed March 18th, 2008)

Dolšak, Nives. (2009) Climate Change Policy Implementation: A Cross-Sectional Analysis. *Review of Policy Research* 26(5):551–570.

Dolšak, Nives. (2013) Climate Change Policies in the Transitional Economies of Europe and Eurasia. *Voluntas* 24(2):382–402.

Dolšak, Nives, and Kristen Houston. (2014) Newspaper Coverage and Climate Change Legislative Activity across US States. *Global Policy* 5(3):286–297.

Dziobek, Claudia, Miquel Alves, Majdeline El Rayess, Carlos Alberto Gutiérrez Mangas, and Phebby Kufta. (2011) The IMF's Government Finance Statistics Yearbook: Maps of Government for 74 Countries. International Monetary Fund, Working Paper, WP/11/27. Available at http://www.imf.org/external/pubs/cat/longres.aspx?sk=24898.0 (Accessed February 12, 2008)

European Commission. (2015) The Covenant of Mayors: In-Depth Analysis of Sustainable Energy Actions Plans. Available at http://www.eumayors.eu/IMG/pdf/2015-11-13_JRC_SEAPAnalysis.pdf. (Accessed July 12, 2016)

Fagan, Adam. (1994) Environment and Transition in the Czech Republic. *Environmental Politics* 3(3):479–494.

Gerring, John, Philip Bond, William T. Barndt, and Carola Moreno. (2005) Democracy and Economic Growth: A Historical Perspective. *World Politics* 57(3):323–364.

Gray, Julia. (2009) International Organization as a Seal of Approval. *American Journal of Political Science* 53(4):931–949.

Greene, William H. (2012) *Econometric Analysis*. Seventh Edition. Boston: Pearson Education.

Hsueh, Lily, and Aseem Prakash. (2012) Incentivizing Self-Regulation: Federal versus State-Level Voluntary Programs in U.S. Climate Change Policies. *Regulation & Governance* 6:445–473.

Iimi, Atsushi. (2005) Decentralization and Economic Growth Revisited: An Empirical Note. *Journal of Urban Economics* 57(3):449–461.

Keck, Margaret E., and Kathryn Sikkink. (1998) *Activists beyond Borders: Advocacy Networks in International Politics*. Ithaca: Cornell University Press.

Laufer, William S. (2003) Social Accountability and Corporate Greenwashing. *Journal of Business Ethics* 43(3):253–261.

Lee, Taedong. (2014) *Global Cities and Climate Change*. London: Routledge.

Lenox, Michael J., and Charles E. Eesley. (2009) Private Environmental Activism and the Selection and Response of Firm Targets. *Journal of Economic and Management Strategy* 18:45–73.

Lipton, Michael. (1977) *Why Poor People Stay Poor: A Study of Urban Bias in Development*. London: Temple Smith.

Lyon, Thomas P., and John W. Maxwell. (2007) Environmental Public Voluntary Programs Reconsidered. *Policy Study Journal* 35(4):723–750.

March, James G., and Johan Olsen. (1989) *Rediscovering Institutions: The Organizational Basis of Politics*. New York: Free Press.

Mondak, Jeffrey J., and Adam F. Gearing. (1998) Civic Engagement in a Post-Communist State. *Political Psychology* 19(3):615–637.

Ostrom, Elinor. (1990) *Governing the Commons*. New York: Cambridge University Press.

Ostrom, Elinor. (1998) A Behavioral Approach to the Rational Choice Theory of Collective Action. *American Political Science Review* 92(1):1–22.

Pelham, Brett W. (2009) Awareness, Opinions about Global Warming Vary Worldwide. Available at http://www.gallup.com/poll/117772/Awareness-Opinions-Global-Warming-Vary-Worldwide.aspx. (Accessed January 17, 2014)

Potoski, Matthew, and Aseem Prakash. (2009) Information Asymmetries as Trade Barriers: ISO 9000 Increases International Commerce. *Journal of Policy Analysis and Management* 28(2):221–238.

Prakash, Aseem. (2000) *Greening the Firm*. Cambridge: Cambridge University Press.

Prakash Aseem, and Matthew Potoski. (2006) *The Voluntary Environmentalists*. Cambridge: Cambridge University Press.

Prakash, Aseem, and Matthew Potoski. (2011) Voluntary Environmental Programs: A Comparative Perspective. *Journal of Policy Analysis and Management* 31(1):23–138.

Putnam, Robert. (1995) Bowling Alone: America's Declining Social Capital. *Journal of Democracy* 6(1):65–78.

Rabe, Barry. (2004) *Statehouse and Greenhouse: The Emerging Politics of American Climate Change Policy*. Washington, DC: Brookings Institution Press.

Roger, Charles, Thomas Hale, and Liliana B. Andonova. (2017) Domestic Politics and Climate Governance. *International Interactions* 43(1):1–25.

Rose, Richard, William Mishler, and Christian Haerpfer. (1997) Social Capital in Civic and Stressful Societies. *Studies in Comparative International Development* 32(3):85–111.

Sassen, Saskia. (2001) *The Global City*. Princeton, NJ: Princeton University Press.

Schneider, Aaron. (2003) Decentralization: Conceptualization and Measurement. *Studies in Comparative International Development* 38(3):32–56.

Slocock, Brian. (1996) The Paradoxes of Environmental Policy in Eastern Europe: The Dynamics of Policymaking in the Czech Republic. *Environmental Politics* 5(3):501–521.

Thiessen, Ulrich. (2003) Fiscal Decentralization and Economic Growth in High-Income OECD Countries. *Fiscal Studies* 24(3):237–274.

Tierney, Michael J., Daniel L. Nielson, Darren G. Hawkins, J. Timmons Roberts, Michael G. Findley, Ryan M. Powers, Bradley Parks, Sven E. Wilson, and Robert L. Hicks. (2011) More Dollars Than Sense: Refining Our Knowledge of Development Finance Using Aid Data. *World Development* 39(11):1891–1906.

United States Agency for International Development (USAID). (2014, June) 2013 CSO Sustainability Index for Central and Eastern Europe and Eurasia. 17th edition. Available at http://www.usaid.gov/sites/default/files/documents/1863/E%26E%202013%20CSOSI%20Final%2010-29-14.pdf. (Accessed June 1, 2014)

van't Veld, Klaas, and Matthew J. Kotchen. (2011) Green Clubs. *Journal of Environmental Economics and Management* 62:309–322.

World Value Survey. (n.d.) Online Data Analysis. Available at http://www.worldvaluessurvey.org/WVSOnline.jsp. (Accessed on January 16, 2014)

Zahran, Sammy, Samuel D. Brody, Arnoldt Vedlitz, Himanshu Grover, and Caitlyn Miller. (2008) Vulnerability and Capacity: Explaining Local Commitment to Climate-Change Policy. *Environment and Planning C: Government and Policy* 26(3):544–562.

Appendix

Appendix 1
Descriptive Statistics

Variable Code	Variable	Mean	Std. Deviation	Minimum	Maximum
PopCOM	Share of urban population in cities covered by COM (cumulative)	26.30	27.14	0.00	100.00
PopAcPl	Share of urban population in cities with submitted Action Plan (cumulative)	24.32	26.77	0.00	100.00
NGOstr	NGO strength (cumulative)	61.12	15.39	27.50	99.50
NGOadv	NGO advocacy (cumulative)	64.89	16.90	25.40	103.80
NGOfin	NGO financial viability (cumulative)	51.14	16.88	21.80	92.80
NGOpubim	NGO public image (cumulative)	60.40	15.69	26.30	100.00
NGOleg	NGO legal environment (cumulative)	63.70	18.17	12.80	108.70
EU	Years since EU agreement	8.58	8.47	0.00	24.00
NOx	NOx emissions (in kg per capita)	15.61	5.95	4.23	27.48
GDPgrth	GDP growth	2.11	5.67	−17.95	37.48
FisDec	Fiscal Decentralization	22.65	9.38	0.30	45.70
INGO	INGOs	1779.75	1273.95	8.00	4747.00
ExpGDP	Exports (share of GDP)	49.37	19.13	15.04	92.98
EnvComm	Commitment to Environmental Protection	47.57	7.94	31.00	59.00
GWawar	Global Warming Awareness	76.17	14.81	43.00	93.00
GWanth	Global Warming Anthropogenic	51.06	11.37	28.00	81.00
Polity	PolityIV	6.01	5.47	−7.00	10.00

Appendix 2
Correlations

	popcom	popacpl	ngostr	ngoadv	ngofin	ngopubim	ngoleg	eu	nox	gdpgrth
popcom	1.0000									
popacpl	0.9059	1.0000								
ngostr	0.5335	0.5287	1.0000							
ngoadv	0.5088	0.4785	0.9817	1.0000						
ngofin	0.4657	0.4990	0.9798	0.9516	1.0000					
ngopubim	0.5769	0.5669	0.9910	0.9764	0.9584	1.0000				
ngoleg	0.5883	0.5888	0.9540	0.9230	0.9052	0.9542	1.0000			
eu	0.2751	0.3416	0.7716	0.6802	0.8121	0.7649	0.7148	1.0000		
nox	0.0586	0.1540	0.3912	0.3694	0.5393	0.3521	0.1897	0.4850	1.0000	
gdpgrth	-0.0831	-0.0933	-0.1773	-0.1704	-0.1998	-0.1524	-0.1577	-0.1734	-0.1388	1.0000
fisdec	-0.0737	-0.0372	0.1576	0.1663	0.2411	0.1091	-0.0345	0.2115	0.5550	-0.1699
ingo	0.0036	0.0810	0.6448	0.5742	0.7276	0.5754	0.5557	0.7663	0.5837	-0.1989
exppercgdp	0.2787	0.3400	0.3237	0.2367	0.3969	0.2950	0.2558	0.4161	0.4289	-0.1001
envcomm	0.1146	0.1112	-0.1437	-0.1187	-0.1445	-0.1552	-0.1305	-0.3077	-0.0075	-0.0531
gwawar	0.0424	0.0994	0.4517	0.3823	0.5183	0.3944	0.3982	0.5535	0.5583	-0.1617
gwanth	-0.0606	0.0472	0.4280	0.3355	0.5237	0.3463	0.3478	0.6892	0.4679	-0.2356
polity	0.4245	0.4284	0.7394	0.7474	0.6840	0.7402	0.8194	0.5610	0.0743	-0.1881

	fisdec	ingo	expper~p	envcomm	gwawar	gwanth	polity
fisdec	1.0000						
ingo	0.3911	1.0000					
exppercgdp	0.2400	0.1533	1.0000				
envcomm	0.5185	-0.2440	0.1522	1.0000			
gwawar	0.5146	0.6673	0.2639	0.1406	1.0000		
gwanth	0.5492	0.8066	0.4057	0.0015	0.5750	1.0000	
polity	0.1669	0.5053	-0.0696	0.0989	0.4729	0.3465	1.0000

Transnational Climate Governance and the Global 500: Examining Private Actor Participation by Firm-Level Factors and Dynamics

Lily Hsueh

ABSTRACT

This article focuses on the Global 500, which are the world's largest companies by revenue, to examine the factors and dynamics internal to companies that motivate some corporations, but not others, to engage in transnational climate governance. Empirical results based on multilevel mixed-effects analyses, which separately identify the relative weight of firm and country-level factors, suggest that the likelihood that a firm participates in transnational climate governance (TCG) is higher when there exists a "policy supporter" who champions sustainability policies and when a company adopts explicit sustainability practices, such as the incorporation of ESG (Environmental, Social and Governance) principles. Voluntary climate action and carbon disclosure are more likely to take place when a company has a large asset base and certifies with the ISO 14001 environmental management standard. Moreover, the level of civil liberties that corporations enjoy in their respective country of origin is associated with participation in TCG. A decomposition of the variance indicates that firm-level factors account for a majority of the variance in TCG participation. This study has implications for climate change governance and policies, which have increasingly focused on concrete climate solutions and innovations by nonstate and substate actors.

Significant global events and trends—such as the end of the Cold War, globalization, deregulation, and new technologies—over the last century have empowered new actors to engage in the governance of problems and change outcomes in issue areas they care about. Among this diverse set of twenty first-century "global governors" (Avant, Finnemore, and Sell 2010), which includes international organizations, intergovernmental organizations, professional associations, advocacy groups, and the like, are the multinational corporations (MNCs) (Cutler, Haufler, and Porter 1999; Strange 1996).

An area that is currently fertile ground in which to work out the theories about power, interests, and behavioral proclivities of the MNCs, among other "global governors," is transnational climate governance. The United Nations

Framework Convention on Climate Change (UNFCCC) has increasingly recognized the role of global businesses in climate mitigation. At the inaugural 2015 Business & Climate Summit, the UN called global companies to lead the shift toward a "low carbon economy ... highlighting the fundamental role of business in shaping the low carbon transition."[1] In parallel with the top-down, intergovernmental climate talks at the UN Climate Change Conference or COP21, in Paris in December 2015, there was a "Climate Solutions Hub," which showcased concrete climate solutions and innovations initiated by businesses, NGOs, and other civil society actors.

This article highlights the role of global businesses in their participation in transnational climate governance (TCG) and focuses on a specific group of the MNCs—the Global 500, which are the world's largest companies with respect to revenue—to examine how these new global governing "agents" contribute to mitigating climate change. While corporations often "back into governance roles and may even drag their feet" (Avant et al. 2010), global businesses sometimes gain authority because others perceive them as capable of achieving results. With a spotlight on the MNCs, I ask two related questions: Which of the Global 500 firms participate in TCG? What factors compel and condition some corporations, but not others, to engage in TCG?

This article's focus is on the Global 500 firms because there has been little scholarly attention paid to the role of global businesses in creating and joining transnational private climate initiatives. Yet, the Global 500 companies' sheer size, economic contribution, and carbon footprint worldwide warrant a need to investigate the factors that motivate their participation in TCG. Moreover, from a methodological perspective, the Global 500 firms provide a coherent universe of participants and nonparticipants in TCG, which precludes the need for restrictive assumptions about businesses that could have participated but do not participate in TCG.[2] In the concluding section, I provide a brief discussion of the conditions under which this article's results generalize to a broader population of firms.

Existing scholarship on why individual actors engage in transnational governance has emphasized transnational "diffusion" processes, such as advocacy pressures and commodity chains, through which social and material pressures are transmitted (Bartley 2010; Dauvergne and Lister 2010; García-Johnson 2000; Perkins and Neumayer 2010; Prakash and Potoski 2006; Vogel 1995, 2005, 2008, 2010). By contrast, recent work shows that certain domestic political and institutional contexts will favor participation in transnational governance and their effectiveness more than others (Andonova, Hale, and Roger 2014; Berliner and Prakash 2014; Büthe and

---

[1] Source: http://www.theclimategroup.org/what-we-do/news-and-blogs/un-backed-online-portal-to-track-business-and-sub-national-climate-commitments/

[2] For example, restricting the scope of the paper to the Global 500 firms means that I do not have to separately control for international trade, which is presumed to be relatively "fixed" across the Global 500 firms.

Mattli 2011; Hale and Roger 2014; Kollman and Prakash 2001; Koppell 2010; Prakash and Potoski 2014; Roger, Hale, and Andonova 2015). In Andonova et al. (2014), the authors find robust evidence to suggest that participation in TCG will be greatest in countries with strong civil liberties, decentralized government, competent bureaucracies, and pro-environment policies.

This article, in turn, focuses on a third and less emphasized set of factors: dynamics *internal* to private actors—in this case, the MNCs—that shape private actors' participation decisions. While factors external to private actors explain cross-country variation in TCG participation, one needs also to examine microlevel pressures and dynamics internal to firms and other organizations to understand a private actor's full set of incentives and constraints for joining specific types of TCG arrangements. In fact, this article's analysis shows that a relatively small fraction of the variance (30%–35%) in TCG participation is explained by country-level factors and dynamics alone.

This study draws on the public policy and business research literatures to theorize and quantify the importance of management structures within the firm, as well a corporation's espoused values, norms, and practices in signaling its commitment to sustainability. More specifically, the analysis shows how the role of "policy supporters" (Prakash 2001) or in-house champions of sustainability policies and initiatives, namely, managerial- or executive-level sustainability officers, play a critical role in helping to align corporate vision and allocate the necessary resources toward sustainability efforts. Moreover, a MNC's commitment to sustainability is reflected in how the corporation is engaged in explicit forms of corporate social responsibility (CSR), such as how a company projects its mission and incorporates specific ESG (Environmental, Social and Governance) criteria into decision-making processes and day-to-day operations. A global business that adopts explicit CSR programs is more likely to engage in transnational climate governance because these firms will work proactively to ensure that they are ahead of emerging issues to protect their brand reputations and corner new markets and, on a pragmatic level, because the marginal cost of participation is relatively low when sustainability is already integrated into a company's modus operandi.

This article's core contributions are to examine and test these internal factors and dynamics while fully accounting for external factors that have been theorized in the literature through (1) multilevel mixed effects models and (2) original coding of firm-level variables. To my knowledge, this is the first study to employ firm-level data from multiple countries to assess the drivers of transnational climate governance by individual actors.

Unlike the majority of existing research that either focuses on firm-level or country-level explanations and relegating one or the other set of dynamics to fixed effects, this article goes one step further and shows how unique aspects and internal dynamics of firms matter, while employing multilevel mixed-effects models to separately identify the relative weight of internal and external factors. The advantage of multilevel mixed effects models is that these models explicitly account for the fact that firms are nested within countries and that TCG participation by firms from the same country could be driven by national-level factors, as shown by Andonova et al. (2014). Moreover, the multilevel approach enables the identification of scope conditions under which TCG by global businesses might substitute for or complement public (regulatory) institutions, given variation in domestic politics, governance structures and institutions, including quality of environmental policies.

Another contribution that this article makes to transnational climate governance research is to test firm-level hypotheses with original data that I have collected and coded on the world's 500 largest corporations ranked by revenue. Original data on the Global 500 firms include information on the existence of "policy supporters," corporate commitment to sustainability, and the extent of complementary resources and capabilities, as well as data on corporate finances.

This article's key findings indicate that a firm is more likely to participate in TCG when the company has an explicit sustainability focus, such as the incorporation of ESG concerns into corporate decision-making processes and day-to-day operations. Moreover, the existence of a "policy supporter" at the managerial or executive level who promotes sustainability practices and policies is associated with voluntary climate action and carbon disclosure.

The article proceeds in the following way. In the next section, I present hypotheses for how factors and dynamics internal to firms influence business participation decisions. The following section describes transnational climate governance and the Global 500, namely, the Global 500 firms' participation in voluntary climate action and carbon disclosure through two well-known TCG arrangements: Non-State Actor Zone for Climate Action (NAZCA) and the Carbon Disclosure Project (CDP) respectively. NAZCA is not a TCG initiative per se but a web-based data aggregator of voluntary climate action by nonstate and substate actors developed by the UN. By contrast, the CDP is a longstanding and well-known private TCG initiative that encourages voluntary disclosure of greenhouse gas emissions. In the next section, I describe the original data on the Global 500 and present multilevel mixed effects models that are employed for testing the proposed hypotheses. Empirical results and a discussion of these results are reported in the following section. The final section concludes by identifying areas for future research and implications for transnational climate governance.

Theory and hypotheses

Research on why individual actors engage in transnational governance has emphasized transnational "diffusion" processes, such as advocacy pressures and commodity chains, through which social and material pressures are transmitted (Bartley 2010; Dauvergne and Lister 2010; García-Johnson 2000; Perkins and Neumayer 2010; Prakash and Potoski 2006; Vogel 1995, 2005, 2008, 2010). More recent research shows that national levels of openness and connectedness to the rest of the international system are dependent on or endogenous to domestic politics (Berliner and Prakash 2014; Büthe and Mattli 2011; Hale and Roger 2014; Keohane and Milner 1996; Kollman and Prakash 2001; Prakash and Potoski 2014; Roger et al. 2015). In other words, certain domestic contexts will favor participation in transnational governance and their effectiveness more than others. Yet, while factors external to individual firms create incentives or impediments for participation, the main thesis of this article is that microlevel pressures, structures, and dynamics internal to firms could propel or further constrain their participation in TCG initiatives.

Understanding what firm-level factors motivate some companies but not others to engage in TCG is important because climate change has been transformed into a "specific and tangible business risk," which demands corporate responses (Pattberg 2012:614). Climate change gives multinational enterprises "the opportunity to develop 'green' firm-specific advantages, but also help reconfigure ... main sources of firms' profitability, growth, and survival" (Kolk and Pinkse 2008:1359). That being said, the extent to which MNCs are also taking the responsibility to become agents of global change that tackle sustainability issues is highly debated in international business research (Christmann 2004; Christmann and Taylor 2001; Kolk and Levy 2003; Pinkse and Kolk 2012).

This article contributes to this debate by shining the limelight on the Global 500: Global businesses are actively contributing to global climate change mitigation, and some MNCs are more inclined than others to do so due to a broader conglomerate of factors specific to individual firms and also to societal and market forces and at different levels, national, regional, and/or international (Kolk and Pinkse 2005; Kolk and Pinkse 2008; Pattberg 2012). My analysis disentangles firm-level microfoundations from the contextual factors and dynamics. In particular, I emphasize the variables involving the agency of corporate management, which I elaborate by drawing on the literature on "policy supporters" and chief executives. Moreover, I argue that corporate values and practices that are related to sustainability and are reflected in a company's corporate social responsibility (CSR) strategy in terms of its transparency and explicitness further shape a corporation's incentives to engage in TCG. When sustainability is integrated in a corporation's modus operandi, the company is more likely to engage in transnational climate governance because the marginal cost of participation in climate change mitigation is relatively low when the firm is already engaged in proactive environmental management and other related activities.

The literatures on voluntary programs and corporate social performance provide guidance on the nature of these microlevel factors. Prakash (2001) posits that in firms that adopt environmental policies that go beyond the law in a given political economy, two kinds of processes are at work: managers who are "policy supporters" as opposed to "policy-neutrals" and "policy-sceptics" either "capture" top management or induce consensus toward these policies. In particular, Lubin and Esty (2010) suggest that a "chief sustainability officer" helps the executive team align vision of "strategic sustainability initiatives" with business strategy and allocate the necessary resources and responsibilities toward these efforts.

In a study of chief executive officers and voluntary environmental performance, Rivera and De Leon (2005) find that a CEO's environmental expertise appears to be significantly associated with higher corporate participation in voluntary programs and also with higher "beyond-compliance" environmental performance ratings. Likewise, Strand (2013) shows that corporations with a chief social responsibility officer are three times more likely to be included in the Down Jones Sustainability Index (DJSI) than corporations with none.

Hypothesis 1 recapitulates these insights for TCG participation by firms.

H1: *The odds that a firm participates in TCG increases if a "policy supporter" who is at the managerial or executive rank exists inside the firm.*

Sustainability executives exercise leadership and creativity, moving beyond structural constraints as generative agents, similar to the way Avant et al. (2010) describe the new twenty-first century "governors" of global governance. Transformational leaders who are the "policy supporters" within a company can create new interests, new strategies, and new modes of action in global climate change and thus motivate and persuade people on the part of company management to promote proactive climate action and carbon disclosure as central to business objectives. Finally, when "policy supporters" are in top management, they exercise direct control over firm decision-making process and thus can drive and direct priorities and resources toward climate action in ways that advocates and champions in lower ranks would not be able to do.[3,4]

Aside from the existence of specific champions of sustainability inside the firm, a MNC's commitment to sustainability—as they are signaled publicly through corporate values, norms, and practices—could also be a key indicator of a corporation's propensity to engage in transnational climate governance. In their comparative study of corporate social responsibility (CSR), Matten and Moon (2008) distinguish between "implicit" and "explicit" CSR. Companies that engage in "explicit" CSR readily join voluntary social initiatives and articulate and communicate widely their responsibility programs and practices to stakeholders and the public as a reflection of company

---

[3] See, for example, the job description for the Chief Sustainability Officer at The Coco-Cola Company: https://www.linkedin.com/in/bea-perez-8225919

[4] Another example is the job description for the Sustainability Director at Carrefour: https://www.linkedin.com/in/bertrand-swiderski-29173722

discretion and initiative (Matten and Moon 2008; Vidaver-Cohen and Brønn 2013). By contrast, "implicit" CSR is not a voluntary and deliberate corporate decision, but rather, a reflection of a corporation's institutional environment (Porter and Kramer 2006).

For global businesses, explicit CSR may take various forms. These companies have brand reputations to protect, and they work proactively to ensure that they are out in front of emerging issues by detailing how they are upholding their vision and values and then integrating that vision and those values into strategies and operating practices (Scherer and Palazzo 2008; Waddock 2008). As such, many sustainability-inclined firms publicly declare "sustainability" as core to their business in their mission statement and/or create a dedicated Web site that contains detailed information about the company's practices, investments, or special projects related to environmental sustainability (Waddock 2008).

Moreover, companies may embed ESG (Environmental, Social and Governance) criteria into their businesses to screen investments for environmental stewardship, equitable and fair business relationships, and accurate and transparent accounting methods and voting procedures (Gillan, Hartzell, Koch, and Starks 2010; Peiró-Signes and Segarra-Oña 2013). For the MNCs, their explicit CSR may have material consequences: According to the UN's Principles of Responsible Investment, "... environmental, social and corporate governance (ESG) issues can affect the performance of investment portfolios."[5] As an indication of the importance of ESG, several third-party data providers rate companies on their ESG "performance" or activities (Gillan et al. 2010).[6]

H2: *A firm that has adopted explicit corporate social responsibility (CSR) programs and practices is more likely to participate in TCG.*

TCG participation should be the domain of firms that adopt explicit CSR programs and practices through two mechanisms. First, explicit CSR contributes to firm participation in TCG because in order for firms to protect their brand reputations and to corner new markets, these firms will work proactively to ensure that they are ahead of emerging issues. Companies that are already engaged in corporate social responsibility will be, by extension, likely to aspire for consumers and the public at large to perceive them as responsible stewards rather than contributors to adversities, such as ocean acidification or melting glaciers associated with global climate change. Toward this regard, TCG participants are likely to be companies that detail publically their vision and values and describe how they are upholding and integrating that vision into strategies and operating practices through ESG principles.

---

[5]See http://www.unpri.org/
[6]One such leading data provider is MSCI: https://www.msci.com/our-story

Moreover, on a pragmatic level, when a corporation is already engaged in explicit CSR activities, the marginal cost of extending these practices to incorporate climate mitigation is likely to be relatively low because of the shared economies of scale and scope between conventional environment management and climate mitigation.

One might worry that the existence of "policy supporters" within a firm and the adoption of explicit CSR programs by a corporation, as posited in the hypotheses, are correlated in practice. For example, the existence of a Corporate Sustainability manager who promotes sustainable practices could be associated with or a driving force behind a firm's commitment to sustainability or vice versa. I argue that the strength of their association is not ensured. A company could be engaged in explicit CSR without appointing a managerial or executive rank officer to oversee these activities. Likewise, a sustainability officer may not always be able to convince the rest of corporate management to adopt ESG principles or create sustainability-focused mission statements. As noted in the data and model section, these conjectures bear out in practice (see Tables A4 and A5 in the appendix for collinearity diagnostics results).

Transnational climate governance and the Global 500

Transnational climate governance has the primary goal of mitigating and adapting to global climate change. By nature and the name, TCG involves interaction of actors across national borders. Roger et al. (2015) have identified and created a database of 75 transnational climate governance arrangements in 191 countries that have been initiated by companies, NGOs, individuals, and subnational actors. The diversity of the TCG schemes are vast, including C40, WWF Climate Savers initiative, Energy Cities, and the Carbon Disclosure Project (CDP), among others. Nonstate and substate actors engage in a wide range of activities related to climate change mitigation and adaption through these regimes.

This article is concerned with voluntary climate action and carbon disclosure by the Global 500 firms. Information about incidences of a corporation's proactive climate action comes from the Non-State Actor Zone for Climate Action (NAZCA), which is, by design, a data aggregator of climate action that has been created to "provide additional momentum and urgency into the process through to COP21."[7] By contrast, the CDP is a TCG initiative named "the most powerful green NGO you've never heard of" by the Harvard Business Review (Winston 2010).

---

[7]Source: http://newsroom.unfccc.int/lima/new-portal-highlights-city-and-private-sector-climate-action/

NAZCA: Voluntary climate action

The Non-State Actor Zone for Climate Action (NAZCA) is not a TCG initiative in the traditional sense but a web portal developed and launched by the government of Peru in conjunction with the UNFCCC in 2014 to "capture and catalyze climate action" by companies, investors, cities, and subnational regions.[8] In other words, NAZCA serves as a data aggregator of climate mitigation and adaption-related actions by nonstate and substate actors, many of which occur via private or private-public cooperative initiatives.

By year-end 2015, over 2,000 companies, including financial organizations, have made voluntary commitments to climate change mitigation, according to NAZCA.[9] Voluntary corporate actions range from setting specific targets for emissions reduction to improving energy efficiency through fuel-use optimization and to pledging commitments to renewable energy use. In addition to individual actions, many corporate commitments are made in partnership with governments, organizations, and international bodies, including the UN.

Of the over 2,000 corporations that participate in voluntary climate action, 267 companies (~13%) are a part of the Global 500. This means that a little over half of the Global 500 firms have committed to taking some form of voluntary action on climate change.

An example of a Global 500 company that has made individual as well as cooperative commitments to climate action is Wal-Mart Stores, Inc. Wal-Mart is the largest corporation in the world by both revenue and employee size; it is headquartered in the United States with 11,000 stores in 28 countries. As a participant of NAZCA-listed initiatives, Wal-Mart has made eight voluntary commitments related to energy efficiency, emission reductions, and renewable energy. For example, Wal-Mart has pledged to

> eliminate 20 million metric tons of GHG emissions from the lifecycle of products sold by 2015, reduce emissions intensity of direct operations by 80 percent per cases shipped per gallon fuel by 2015 through fleet efficiency initiatives, drive production or procurement of 7 billion kWh of renewable energy by 2020 (600 percent increase vs. 2010), and transition to using 100 percent renewables through renewable energy purchases and onsite generation,

among other pledges.[10]

Moreover, the multinational retail corporation has joined other private and subnational actors to sign the "New York Declaration on Forests," which pledges to "halve the loss of national forests globally by 2020, and end forest

---

[8] Source: http://climateaction.unfccc.int/companyindustries.aspx
[9] The numeric information reported in this article reflects data that were retrieved from the NAZCA Web site on December 15, 2015.
[10] Source: http://climateaction.unfccc.int/company/wal-mart-stores,-inc-

loss by 2030."[11] Also, Wal-Mart, along with other Global 500 companies such as Aviva, BT Group, and Johnson & Johnson, have joined forces as part of RE100, a collaborate initiative of businesses, to set long-term targets on powering their operations entirely with renewable energy.

Among the smallest of the Global 500 (by revenue), Sodexo, a France-based food services and facilities management multinational company, is less ambitious: Sodexo aims to "reduce CO_2 emissions across their entire value chain by 34 percent from 2012 to 2020 through increased energy efficiency and promotion of sustainable consumption." Moreover, Sodexo has committed to joining other private and subnational actors in "adopting a science-based GHG emission reduction target"[12] and "removing commodity-driven deforestation from all supply chains by 2020."[13]

According to NAZCA, "The drivers for this [voluntary climate action] vary significantly but economic opportunity is often the primary motivation given the opportunity represented by energy efficiency, renewable energy and other activities to reduce emissions and improve resiliency."[14] Despite this, the voluntary pledges of climate action listed on NAZCA are not governed by an internationally standardized monitoring, reporting, and verification system, albeit data providers manage periodic reporting cycles that enable tracking and monitoring of climate action. Furthermore, NAZCA includes only cooperative initiatives that have made a commitment to reporting implementation and progress. NAZCA states that it "welcome[s] partnerships with others who would like to do research on this data and make assessments of this type."[15]

CDP: Voluntary carbon disclosure

An even larger number of Global 500 firms (323) voluntarily disclose their carbon emissions to the Carbon Disclosure Project (CDP), which is a long-standing and well-known private TCG initiative founded in 2000 to encourage voluntary disclosure of greenhouse gas emissions, water usage, and voluntary strategies for managing climate change, water, and deforestation risks by private entities. While companies can technically disclose their carbon emissions through other initiatives (or publish their disclosures directly on their own Web sites), the CDP "holds the largest dataset of corporate and city responses to the impacts of climate change and the depletion of natural resources, globally."[16]

---

[11]Source: http://climateaction.unfccc.int/company/wal-mart-stores,-inc-
[12]Source: http://climateaction.unfccc.int/company/sodexo
[13]Source: http://climateaction.unfccc.int/company/sodexo
[14]Source: http://climateaction.unfccc.int/about
[15]Source: http://climateaction.unfccc.int/about
[16]Source: https://www.cdp.net/en-US/Results/Pages/academic-data.aspx

The CDP enjoys much external legitimacy worldwide because each year the CDP invites companies, from Global 500 companies to midsize firms in emerging markets across a wide range of industries, to disclose their climate change, water, and forest-risk information "on behalf of 827 institutional investor signatories with a combined U.S. $100 trillion in assets."[17] Any organization wishing to publicly report their GHG gas emissions, climate change strategies, water stewardship approach, and deforestation risk management can do so through the CDP.[18]

Similar to the NAZCA-listed initiatives, participation in the CDP is voluntary, and the primary motivation, according to the CDP, is also economic opportunity: "Companies that measure their environmental risk are better able to manage it strategically ... creating opportunities to innovate and generate revenue from sustainable products and services."[19] While reporting (including detailed guidance on how to do it) and monitoring of carbon disclosures are part and parcel of participation in the CDP, there are no direct penalties for nonadherence. Despite this, the increasing scrutiny of financial investors, particularly institutional investors, on environmental and carbon asset risks suggests that nonadherence to the CDP could lead to financial consequences (Kim and Lyon 2011; Reid and Toffel 2009; Kolk, Levy, and Pinkse 2008).

Data and models

The unique firm-level data, which form the basis of this article's empirical analysis, are based on original data collection, catalogue, and coding of the world's 500 largest corporations ranked by revenue for their respective fiscal years ended on or before March 31, 2014 (Fortune n.d.).

The MNCs in the article's analysis range across diverse sectors. Figure A1 in the appendix shows the shares of businesses in consumer discretionary (13.8%), consumer staples (6.4%), energy (12.8%), financials (23.2%), health care (4.8%), industrials (16.2%), information technology (10.4%), materials (8.2%), and utilities (4.2%).

Figure 2A in the appendix shows that 26% of the Global 500 companies originate from the United States; most other firms have headquarters in China (19%), Japan (11%), France (6%), Germany (6%), United Kingdom (5%), South Korea (3%), Switzerland (2%), Netherlands (2%), Canada (2%), Australia (2%), Italy (2%), India (2%), Russia (2%), and Spain (2%). Altogether, companies originating from the European Union make up a quarter share of the Global 500.

---

[17]Source: https://www.cdp.net/en-US/Programmes/Pages/climate-change-programs.aspx
[18]Source: https://www.cdp.net/Documents/disclosure/2015/Companies-requested-to-respond-CDP-climate-change.pdf
[19]Source: https://www.cdp.net/en-US/Respond/Pages/companies.aspx

Dependent variables

Participation in TCG is measured as a simple dichotomized variable whereby it is coded as 1 for participation and 0 for nonparticipation. For each Global 500 company, I code *Participation_Climate_Action* for a firm's participation in NAZCA-listed initiatives (that is, voluntary climate action), as well as *Participation_Carbon_Disclosure* for a firm's participation in the CDP (that is, voluntary carbon disclosure).[20]

With respect to regional distribution, companies that engage in proactive climate action and/or carbon disclosure largely originate from the EU and North America (United States and Canada). Firms originating from Asia (with a large share of them based in China) are the least proactive with respect to climate action and carbon disclosure. For example, 77% of companies originating from the EU engage in voluntary climate action, while 70% of corporations headquartered in Asia do not participate in TCG. Regression results reflect this regional distribution of proactive versus less proactive corporations.

The dependent variables are based on the membership data on the Global 500 companies from the NAZCA-listed initiatives and the CDP. Participation on the NAZCA-listed initiatives occurred between mid-2014 and December 2015, while participation in carbon disclosure are based on the 2015 information request by the CDP. A company chooses on an annual basis whether or not to participate in voluntary carbon disclosure; in other words, a company may decide to participate in the CDP in one year but not the next year.[21]

For both the NAZCA-listed initiatives and the CDP, a firm's decision to participate in voluntary climate action and carbon disclosure occurred after the installation of sustainability officers, the creation of mission statements, and the implementation of ESG principles that took place in 2014 or earlier.

Firm-level covariates

For each of the Global 500 firms, I have collected and coded information on the following firm-level independent variables: existence of a policy supporter, including whether the policy supporter is an executive level officer (for example, Chief Sustainability Officer) or a management level officer (for example, Vice President); mission statement; ESG status; employee size; revenues; assets; ISO 14001 certification status; environmental R&D; and government ownership, among other variables.

---

[20] For the rest of the article, a company's participation in proactive climate action and carbon disclosure will be referred to interchangeably as a firm's participation in NAZCA-listed initiatives and a firm's participation in the CDP respectively.

[21] For example, there were 10 companies that disclosed their carbon emissions to the CDP in 2014 but not in 2015.

Table A1 in the appendix describes each of the firm-level variables, how they are constructed and coded, and where they come from. Data sources are corporate Web sites and published reports, such as a company's annual Corporate Social Responsibility reports. Table A1 also includes similar information about the country-level control variables.

With respect to the firm-level variables of interests, three separate variables account for the presence of a designated "policy supporter" in the firm; these indicator variables are mutually exclusive. *Policy supporter—Analyst* is coded as 1 and 0 otherwise if a company houses a designated analyst responsible for climate change, sustainability, or corporate social responsibility (CSR) initiatives within the firm. *Policy supporter—Analyst* is also coded 1 if a firm has a sustainability/CSR committee responsible for setting vision and planning for climate risk management that is distinct from the traditional "Health, Safety, and Environment" roles as part of its Board of Directors.

Policy supporter—Vice President is an indicator variable that accounts for the existence of a management-level officer for sustainability (for example, Vice President or Head of Sustainability). Finally, *Policy supporter—Chief Sustainability Officer* is coded as 1 or 0 otherwise if a company has an executive level position dedicated to issues of sustainability, such as a Chief Sustainability Officer.

Three distinct variables measure the extent to which sustainability is integral to a corporation's mission: *Mission statement* is coded as 1 and 0 otherwise if a company's mission, value, or strategy statement includes the concept of "environmental sustainability" or related concepts in its wording.[22] Appendix A1 presents examples of cases where *Mission statement* is coded as 1.

If a company adopts and incorporates ESG (Environmental, Social and Governance) principles into its decision-making processes and day-to-day operations, as explicitly stated and described in detail on its corporate Web site and CSR publications, *ESG* is coded as 1 or 0 otherwise.

The third sustainability variable is *Dedicated Web site*, which is coded as 1 and 0 otherwise if a company has a dedicated, separate Web site where a company publicizes and documents how it incorporates sustainability in different aspects of its business, including its business practice, products, and/or service delivery.

With respect to firm-level controls, three variables measure firm size: the natural log of a firm's annual, fiscal year *Employee size*—that is, the number of employees—and corporate *Revenues* and *Assets* in millions of dollars. Scholars of voluntary environmental programs and policies have found that larger firms are more likely to participate in voluntary environmental programs (Arora and Cason 1996; DeCanio and Watkins 1998; Videras and Alberini 2000; Khanna, Khoss, Jones,

---

[22]If "sustainability" is mentioned in the context of sustainable economic growth rather than a sustainable environment, *Mission statement* is coded 0.

and Ervin 2007). According to Khanna et al. (2007), this is because larger facilities have a greater capacity to bear the fixed cost of participating in voluntary programs, seeking certification, and providing environmental training to personnel. Moreover, external pressures from regulators, competitors, and the public may also be greater; consequently, larger firms have more incentive than small firms to join voluntary programs, including carbon disclosure to mitigate the potential negative impacts of a tarnished imaged (Aerts, Cormier, and Magnan 2008; Guenther, Guenther, Schiemann, and Weber 2016; Luo, Lan, and Tang 2012).

Aside from firm size, businesses that are already part of a culture of "virtuous" (Vogel 2005) activities will be more likely to participate in activities that reinforce similar norms of voluntary action. Darnall, Jolley, and Handfield (2008) and Arimura, Darnall, and Katayama (2011) find that the adoption of ISO 14001 by participants increases the likelihood of facilities to engage in more-advanced voluntary environmental practices, such as the adoption of green supply chain management. In effect, other private and/or transnational governance activities could help establish a baseline for how much firms engage in TCG and reduce the marginal transaction cost for participation in TCG.

To account for these firm-level complementary resources and commitments, *ISO 14001 (firm-level)* indicates whether a company is certified with ISO 14001. *Environmental R&D* is coded as 1 and 0 otherwise if a company has invested in any form of environmental R&D, such as investments in technologies that increase energy efficiency or investments in improving management processes that incorporate principles of environmental sustainability.[23] Appendix A2 documents examples of environmental R&D investments by the Global 500 firms.

Government-owned is an indicator variable that represents whether a corporation is 50% or higher with respect to government ownership. In their study of environmental management system adoption, Darnall and Edwards (2006) find that government-owned facilities have fewer capabilities and accrue higher EMS adoption costs; this suggests that corporations that are owned partially or wholly by the government may not participate as readily in TCG.

Moreover, the empirical analysis includes a set of industry sector dummies. These sector-specific indicator variables account for cross-sector variation—such as variation in consumer orientation or energy intensity in production—that may influence a corporation's decision to engage in proactive climate action or carbon disclosure but does not change systematically over time within a sector.

Findings on industry sector variation and corporate voluntary action have been mixed. Arora and Cason (1996) find that voluntary program participation rates are

---

[23] The approach of coding a company's investment in environmental R&D as a binary variable is one of expediency in the face of data limitation. Future research should remedy this shortcoming by supplementing this less-precise measure with actual measures of R&D activities, such as corporate expenditures on environmental technologies.

higher in industries with greater consumer contact. By contrast, recent studies have shown that firms that operate in sectors that emit substantial amounts of greenhouse gases are more likely to engage in climate change mitigation activities (Haigh and Griffiths 2012; Hsueh and Prakash 2012; Kolk and Pinkse 2008; Kotchen and Moon 2012). This could be because for firms that operate in energy- and capital-intensive industries, by engaging in proactive climate action they are able to preempt future regulatory tightening and/or more readily circumvent the high fixed costs of adjustment. The bottom line: The direction of the association between industry sectors and participation is not clear a priori.

One might be worried that the firm-level variables are highly correlated. For example, a firm's ISO 14001 certification status may be correlated with its adoption of ESG principles. A collinearity diagnostics of this article's firm-level explanatory variables indicates that the firm-level predictors are independent forces and do not suffer from multicollinearity concerns (see Tables A4 and A5 in the appendix for the scores on different measures of collinearity).

Country-level covariates

Country-level variables contextualize the political economy of the country of origin for each the Global 500 firms. These variables are based on Roger et al.'s (2015) finding that participation in TCG will be greatest in countries with strong civil liberties, decentralized government, competent bureaucracies, and pro-environment policies. Country-level variables include civil liberties, political rights, federalism, GDP per capita, CO_2 emissions, air pollution (PM 10), and the core Environmental Performance Index (EPI). The latter two measures serve as proxies for a country's commitment to environmental protection.

According to Andonova et al. (2014), PM 10 is an effective proxy for national commitment to environmental protection because this pollutant is relatively easy and inexpensive to control, and countries with strong commitments to environmental protection will likely to have done so even if they have high emissions (the correlation between PM10 and CO2 emissions is 0.22). The core EPI focuses on a large range of environmental issues and account for the ambitiousness of a country's environmental policymaking. The country-level data come from various sources and are collected by Roger et al. (2015). I thank these authors for sharing them with me for the purpose of this article's analysis.

Finally, in an effort to thwart endogeneity concerns, all independent firm-level variables are from 2012, 2013, or 2014, and the country-level variables are by and large 10-year averages (2000–2010), all of which precede the dependent variables. The collection of the lagged data and the sequencing of the dependent and explanatory variables are intentional, the purpose of which is to mitigate potential concerns about the direction of impact between the dependent and independent variables.

Table 1 provides summary statistics for the entire set of firm- and country-level covariates.

Model specifications

As explained, the main thesis of this article is that microlevel pressures, structures, and dynamics internal to firms and organizations are the driving forces behind a corporation's participation in transnational climate governance. To test the proposed hypotheses of the association between the firm-level "policy supporter" and explicit CSR or commitment to sustainability covariates and the different measures of TCG participation respectively, this study employs multilevel mixed-effects models, whereby the unit of analysis is the firm.

A major advantage of multilevel mixed-effects models is that multilevel models not only account for the existence of data hierarchies or clustered structures—that is, firm are nested within countries, such that firms from the same country could be correlated—these models separately identify the relative weight of internal and external factors (Gelman and Hill 2006; Raudenbush and Bryk 2002). This gives us, for the first time, empirical leverage to adjudicate between firm-level factors, as hypothesized in this article, and national-level factors, as shown by Roger et al. (2015) and others. A grave consequence of failing to recognize hierarchal structures when they exist is that standard errors of regression coefficients will be underestimated, leading to an overstatement of statistical significance.

This study employs a multilevel mixed-effects logistic model for modeling a global business's participation in voluntary climate action or carbon disclosure. The mixed-effects logistic model is a logistic regression containing both fixed effects and random effects; the observations (the individual companies) comprise the first level, and the countries in which the firms originate comprise the second level. Observations in the same cluster (that is, belonging to the same country) are assumed to be correlated because they share common cluster-level random effects.

Empirical results and discussion

In this section, I report and discuss the empirical results. To begin, a majority of the variance in TCG participation is attributable to the firm and not to the country level: The fraction of the total variance that was between countries (in other words, the residual intraclass correlation) is relatively small, approximately 30% to 35% in the estimated models of participation, leaving the rest to be explained by the firm-level variables, as shown in a

Table 1. Descriptive Statistics of Global 500 Firms ($N = 500$).

Variables	Mean	Std. Dev.	Min	Max
Firm-level variables of interest				
Policy supporter				
Analyst	0.15	0.36	0	1
Vice President	0.38	0.49	0	1
Chief Sustainability Officer	0.05	0.23	0	1
Explicit CSR/Commitment to sustainability				
Mission statement	0.16	0.37	0	1
ESG (Environ., Social and Governance)	0.22	0.41	0	1
Dedicated Web site	0.05	0.22	0	1
Firm-level controls				
Employee size (log)	11.23	1.16	5.17	14.60
Revenues (log)	10.82	0.58	10.07	13.07
Assets (log)	11.35	1.35	7.95	15.00
ISO 14001 (firm-level)	0.66	0.47	0	1
Environ. R&D	0.49	0.50	0	1
Government-owned	0.23	0.42	0	1
Industry sector				
Consumer Discretionary	0.14	0.35	0	1
Consumer Staples	0.06	0.24	0	1
Energy	0.13	0.33	0	1
Financials	0.23	0.42	0	1
Health Care	0.05	0.21	0	1
Industrials	0.16	0.37	0	1
Information Technology	0.10	0.31	0	1
Materials	0.08	0.27	0	1
Utilities	0.04	0.20	0	1
Country-level controls				
GDP/capita (log)	9.58	1.33	6.39	11.04
CO_2 emissions (log)	13.99	1.61	5.60	15.51
Civil liberties	4.45	2.04	0.38	6.00
Political rights	3.44	0.79	1	4.41
Polity	6.22	6.67	−10.00	10.00
Federalism	0.46	0.50	0	1
Air pollution (PPM 10)	40.61	27.20	13.12	150.17
Environ. Performance index	54.62	8.84	33.80	76.20
ISO14001 (country-level) (log)	9.07	1.34	4.03	10.92

decomposition of the variance in Table 2. This suggests that while external factors are important, factors, structures, and dynamics internal to the firm are key to understanding a corporation's participation in proactive climate action and carbon disclosure.

Tables 3 and 4 report the estimated coefficients for the multilevel mixed-effects logistic models of participation in NAZCA-listed initiatives and the CDP respectively. In both tables, Model 1 includes firm-level variables only, and Model 2 includes firm-level and country-level variables. Regression coefficients are presented in terms of odds ratio, and a separate column reports percent impact of the odds in Tables 3 and 4. Robust standard errors are reported in parentheses in both tables.

Table 2. Variance Decomposition: Ratio of Between-Country Variance to Total Variance.

Model	Country-Level Share of Total Variance	Std. Err.
Participation in Voluntary Climate Action	0.35	(0.110)
Participation in Voluntary Carbon Disclosure	0.32	(0.113)

In the following discussion of results, the focus is on Model 2, where both firm- and country-level factors are included. Overall, the regression results provide strong support for Hypothesis 1, which refers to the important role of "policy supporters," and for Hypothesis 2 on a corporation's explicit CSR or commitment to sustainability as drivers of TCG participation.

With respect to H1, which postulates a positive relationship between policy supporters at the managerial or executive level and participation, I find policy supporters at both ranks to be strongly and robustly associated with participation. In both Tables 3 and 4, the key result is that a firm that engages in voluntary climate action is five to seven times more likely to house a policy supporter at the managerial (Vice President) level than otherwise; equivalently, the odds of participation in NAZCA-listed initiatives and the CDP for companies with a sustainability manager are 400% to 600% higher than the odds of participation for companies without such a champion. Similarly, the presence of a Chief Sustainability Officer increases the odds of engaging in proactive climate action or disclosing to the CDP by a factor of close to five. These results suggest that a MNC's decision to engage in climate action and/or disclose its carbon footprint requires the support of high-ranking officers in corporate governance, potentially to fend off shareholder disapproval.

Hypothesis 2 asserts that when a firm engages in explicit forms of corporate social responsibility, it is more likely to participate in TCG, and the results in Table 3 confirms this proposition. The corporate participants of NAZCA-listed initiatives are two to four times more likely to incorporate environmental protection and sustainability as part of its mission or vision statement and embed the principles of ESG (Environmental, Social and Governance) into its decision-making process and day-to-day operations respectively. In other words, the likelihood of proactive climate action by firms with a sustainability mission and ESG-embedded operations are 85% and 289% higher respectively than the odds of proactive climate action by firms that do not adopt explicit CSR.

These affirmative results on the proposed hypotheses underscore that corporate management structures and explicit commitments to sustainability are associated with and likely drivers of a corporation's participation in governance activities that are related to climate change mitigation, which may not yield immediate economic benefits compared to corporate action on more local environmental problems and point source pollution.

Table 3. Multilevel Mixed-Effects Logit Model of Drivers of Participation in Voluntary Climate Action.

	Model 1 Firm-Level			Model 2 Firm & Country-Level		
	Coeff.	Robust Std. Err.	Impact[1] (%)	Coeff.	Robust Std. Err.	Impact[1] (%)
Firm-level variables of interest						
Policy supporter						
Analyst	2.67**	(1.193)	167	2.40**	(0.840)	139
Vice President	8.70***	(2.962)	770	7.12***	(2.386)	612
Chief Sustainability Officer	6.44**	(4.371)	545	4.71**	(2.800)	371
Explicit CSR/Commitment to sustainability						
Mission statement	2.06**	(0.680)	106	1.85*	(0.679)	85
ESG (Environ., Social and Governance)	4.67***	(1.652)	367	3.90***	(1.432)	289
Dedicated Web site	1.00	(0.400)		1.00	(0.508)	
Firm-level controls						
Employee size (log)	1.29*	(0.200)	29	1.40**	(0.210)	40
Revenues (log)	0.61	(0.250)		0.59*	(0.178)	−41
Assets (log)	1.80***	(0.342)	80	1.71***	(0.300)	71
ISO 14001 (firm-level)	1.64	(0.630)		1.36	(0.423)	
Environ. R&D	1.40	(0.423)		1.52	(0.428)	
Government-owned	0.46**	(0.147)	−54	1.00	(0.477)	
Industry sector						
Consumer Staples	2.55***	(0.665)	155	2.56	(1.554)	
Energy	1.41	(0.600)		1.55	(1.00)	
Financials	0.21***	(0.856)		0.25**	(0.154)	−75
Health Care	0.82	(0.271)		1.00	(0.585)	
Industrials	0.80	(0.284)		0.81	(0.351)	
Information Technology	2.22**	(0.726)	122	2.84**	(1.484)	183
Materials	0.55	(0.232)		0.84	(0.510)	
Utilities	1.23	(0.865)		1.24	(0.985)	
Country-level controls						
GDP/capita (log)				0.51*	(0.187)	−49
CO_2 emissions (log)				0.80*	(0.115)	−21
Civil liberties				1.90**	(0.400)	89
Federalism				0.75	(0.301)	
Air pollution (PPM 10)				1.00	(0.015)	
Environ. Performance index				1.00	(0.035)	
ISO14001 (country-level) (log)				1.23	(0.250)	
N (N of groups)	500 (38)			500 (38)		
F-statistics (Wald)	658.99			132.42		
Prob > chi²	0.00			0.00		

Note. ***$p \leq .001$; **$p \leq .05$; *$p \leq .10$.
[1]Impact (%) is (Odds Ratio − 1) × 100. For example, (7.12 − 1) × 100 = 612.

Turning to the results on firm-level and country-level controls, none of the estimated coefficients on these covariates yields statistically significant results of the same order of magnitude as the results on the firm-level variables of interest. Results indicate that corporations that employ a large number of workers have higher odds (by 1.5 times) of engaging in voluntary climate action or carbon disclosure than smaller-size firms. More personnel means

Table 4. Multilevel Mixed-Effects Logit Model of Drivers of Participation in Voluntary Carbon Disclosure.

	Model 1 Firm-Level			Model 2 Firm & Country-Level		
	Coeff.	Robust Std. Err.	Impact[1] (%)	Coeff.	Robust Std. Err.	Impact[1] (%)
Firm-level variables of interest						
Policy supporter						
Analyst	2.14*	(1.000)	114	1.84	(0.731)	
Vice President	5.51***	(1.471)	451	4.91***	(1.428)	391
Chief Sustainability Officer	4.44**	(1.424)	344	3.52***	(1.263)	252
Explicit CSR/Commitment to sustainability						
Mission statement	1.20	(0.320)		1.10	(0.300)	
ESG (Environ., Social and Governance)	1.80*	(0.584)	78	1.47	(0.540)	
Dedicated Web site	0.75	(0.384)		0.81	(0.400)	
Firm-level controls						
Employee size (log)	1.40*	(0.270)	40	1.50**	(0.268)	46
Revenues (log)	0.67	(0.344)		0.72	(0.384)	
Assets (log)	1.80***	(0.168)	76	1.71***	(0.180)	71
ISO 14001 (firm-level)	1.61**	(0.281)	61	1.32*	(0.210)	32
Environ. R&D	1.27	(0.322)		1.31	(0.329)	
Government-owned	0.13**	(0.044)	−87	0.18***	(0.067)	−82
Industry sector						
Consumer Staples	2.33**	(0.854)	133	2.24**	(0.853)	124
Energy	1.13	(0.486)		1.28	(0.550)	
Financials	0.28**	(0.163)	−72	0.33*	(0.191)	−67
Health Care	1.05	(0.598)		1.10	(0.623)	
Industrials	0.82	(0.242)		0.86	(0.258)	
Information Technology	1.50	(0.547)		1.58	(0.620)	
Materials	0.50	(0.260)		0.68	(0.384)	
Utilities	0.65	(0.635)		0.60	(0.560)	
Country-level controls						
GDP/capita (log)				1.00	(0.309)	
CO_2 emissions (log)				0.57**	(0.090)	−43
Civil liberties				1.65**	(0.300)	65
Federalism				1.43	(0.600)	
Air pollution (PPM 10)				1.00	(0.015)	
Environ. Performance index				1.00	(0.033)	
ISO14001 (country-level) (log)				1.76**	(0.420)	76
N (N of groups)	500 (38)			500 (38)		
F-statistics (Wald)	533.27			15234.08		
Prob > chi^2	0.00			0.00		

Note. ***$p \leq .001$; **$p \leq .05$; *$p \leq .10$.
[1]Impact (%) is (Odds Ratio − 1) × 100. For example, (4.91 − 1) × 100 = 391.

greater capacity in terms of human capital to carry out the necessary research and development, experimentation, and other tasks related to climate mitigation and adaption.

Similarly, the possession of large asset holdings is associated with voluntary carbon disclosure among the Global 500 firms. This is likely because there is a technological threshold that firms must meet, which entails costly investments, for undertaking carbon accounting and emissions management required by the CDP.

The odds that a firm engages in voluntary carbon disclosure increases 32% when the corporation is certified with the ISO 14001 environmental management standard compared to counterparts that are not certified, according to the results in Table 4. This result corroborates the fact that environmental management systems facilitate accurate carbon accounting by providing the organization structure, planning, and resources necessary for tracking carbon emissions. Moreover, consistent with previous studies, results show that corporations that are partially owned by the government tend not to voluntarily disclose their carbon emissions.

With respect to industry sectors, companies that are operating in consumer-facing sectors appear to be more likely to commit to voluntary climate action and carbon disclosure. Corporations in the Consumer Staples industry sector are two times more likely to disclose their carbon emissions. Likewise, Information Technology companies that make and sell software, electronics, and related services to consumers have statistically significant higher odds (~3 times) of participating in NAZCA-listed initiatives. By committing to voluntary climate action and carbon disclosures, these corporate actors signal to the market and to consumers with whom they interact on a regular basis that they are socially responsible companies, thus preempting public scrutiny.

By contrast, financial firms are relatively less likely to participate in TCG. This could be because these companies are less carbon-intensive in their operations to begin with. As such, there is little incentive to signal their proactive leadership in climate change mitigation.

Finally, with respect to country-level controls, companies that originate from rich countries that emit substantial CO_2 emissions are on balance less inclined to participate in TCG. Importantly, the presence of strong civil liberties in a corporate actor's country of origin is a statistically significant driver of participation across all multilevel specifications in Tables 3 and 4. Robust civil liberties are associated with a 65% to 90% increase in the odds of proactive climate action and carbon disclosure by corporations, which corroborate Roger et al.'s (2015) finding that institutional structures that promote the agency of actors to engage in "policy advocacy and to create programs and organizations with governance aims" (Roger et al. 2015:15) are an important driver of participation in TCG. In other words, countries with institutions that promote and protect civic engagement by citizens and private entities are ideal host countries to MNCs that engage in proactive policies and practices toward a low-carbon economy.

Similar in the order of magnitude of impact is ISO 14001 adoption levels at the country level in explaining a firm's carbon disclosure. This is in line with the emphasis that Büthe and Mattli (2011) and Andonova (2014) place on the relevance of the state and domestic institutional structures for influencing power over private regulation and participation in global public-private partnerships.

Finally, I conduct robustness checks on the firm- and country-level specifications. I replace *Civil liberties* with two other related measures—*Polity score* and *Political rights* (Table A6, Models 1–4 in the appendix). As these models indicate, the results in Tables 3 and 4 are overall robust to different operationalizations of civil liberties respectively. The alternative specifications underscore the key findings, which are that in-house champions of sustainability at the managerial and executive levels and corporate commitments to sustainability in the form of explicit CSR are important drivers of TCG participation.

Conclusion

This article focuses on the Global 500, which are the world's largest companies with respect to revenue, to make the central argument that while factors external to firms create incentives or impediments for participation, factors, structures, and dynamics internal to firms propel or further constrain their participation in transnational climate governance. On the basis of an original database on the Global 500, I employ multilevel mixed-effects models, which separately identify the relative weight of internal and external factors, to model the participation of global businesses in NAZCA-listed initiatives (that is, voluntary climate action) and the CDP (that is, voluntary carbon disclosure).

A distinct portrait emerges from this article's analysis: As hypothesized, global businesses that house a champion of sustainability in the form of a "policy supporter" at the managerial or executive level have a higher propensity to participate in voluntary climate action and carbon disclosure. These in-house champions of sustainability policies and initiatives help align vision and allocate the necessary resources toward sustainability efforts. More often than not, these MNCs demonstrate explicitly their commitment to sustainability through the adoption of ESG (Environmental, Social and Governance) principles, which are embedded into their decision-making processes and day-to-day operations.

Furthermore, wealthy corporations that employ a large number of workers are more likely to disclose their carbon emissions than companies with smaller asset holdings and employee base. Voluntary climate action and carbon disclosure are more likely to take place when a company certifies with the ISO 14001 environmental management standard.

The article also finds that MNCs that engage in TCG are more likely than nonparticipants to operate in sectors that interface with consumers on a regular basis, such as consumer staples and information technology, and originate from countries with relatively strong civil liberties and higher levels of ISO 14001 certification. Countries with institutions that promote and protect civic engagement by citizens and private entities better enable corporations based there to engage in policy advocacy and to create proactive practices toward a low carbon economy.

An important question that is worth asking, albeit outside of the scope of this analysis, is whether and/or under what conditions the results of this study on global businesses generalize to a broader population of firms. Without the benefit of actual data on other firms, my conjecture is that this article's propositions explain voluntary climate action in the private sector more generally and that, in fact, this study's empirical results are likely to be lower bound estimates in an analysis that includes firms of various sizes and scope of business. If global businesses—which by the virtue of its size, ownership status, and scope of production invite more public scrutiny than privately held firms—require the driving force of sustainability champions at the managerial and executive levels within the firm, it would appear probable that businesses smaller in size and scope would also require internal champions, since studies have shown that by and large privately held companies face fewer stakeholder pressures. This same logic should apply regarding the extent of the embeddedness of sustainability values and principles in influencing the proactive climate action of firms of various sizes and scope of business.

That being said, my conjecture is that in the broader population, for firms lacking "policy supporters" and an existing commitment to sustainability, complementary resources, and domestic political conditions are likely to be even more prominent drivers of proactive climate action and carbon disclosure than for global businesses. Existing firm-level resources and contextual factors, such as robust civil liberties and progressive environmental policies, will likely propel corporations of all sizes based in a given country to engage in TCG.

Several implications for future research follow from this article. First, this article's findings highlight the role of global businesses in climate change mitigation, adaption, and related policies. This is particularly timely and significant because for the first time, in parallel and adjacent to the Conference of the Parties, "COP21," which took place in Paris in December 2015, a "Climate Solutions Hub" initiated by businesses and NGOs, among other civil society actors, showcased concrete climate actions and solutions.

In light of this, this article's findings suggest that there needs to be more scholarly attention paid to the role of global businesses—in particular, to their management structures and explicit demonstrations of corporate commitments toward sustainability. It may very well be that transnational climate governance requires more than big sticks; it also requires leadership and creativity (Avant et al. 2010). With the right leadership and vision, corporations will less likely to "drag their feet."

That being said, questions remain about the link between the scope of participation and effectiveness. For example, existing research has raised doubts about whether corporate carbon disclosure provides information that is valuable for investors, NGOs, or policymakers (Kolk et al. 2008). Future research should address questions such as: Does joining voluntary climate action or carbon disclosure initiatives lead to real changes in firm-level and industry-wide behavior? Or do they generate indirect impacts, such as institutional diffusion or experimentation with new technologies or policy processes? Moreover, are there trade-offs between the scope of participation and effectiveness? And how can these trade-offs be overcome to substantially mitigate greenhouse gas emissions?

A related question that is highly relevant to climate change mitigation is: What happens when companies fail to fulfill their commitments? Currently, there is no penalty for nonadherence to NAZCA-listed initiatives or to the CDP. A significant next step for transnational climate governance would be to publish guidelines and best practices for third-party monitoring and verification in order to strengthen the link between pledges for proactive action and ultimate follow-through by corporations. Companies that are leaders in proactive climate action, such as IT companies and other consumer-facing corporations, should be at the forefront of working to establish best practices for adherence to voluntary commitments for mitigating global climate change.

Answers to these questions have practical implications for public policy. Given slowly unraveling gridlocks over intergovernmental climate governance, there is potential for governments to leverage the assistance of corporations and other subnational and nonstate actors to help achieve greenhouse gas emission targets and other compliance-related objectives. At the same time, the integration of "bottom-up" actions involving subnational and nonstate actors into comprehensive climate governance, including the UNFCCC, could face very different challenges in different countries, as participation of sub- and nonstate actors in TCG are concentrated largely in rich countries with liberal political economies and governance.

Acknowledgments

The author would like to thank Liliana Andonova, Thomas Hale, Charles Rogers, and participants at the Blavatnik School of Government, Oxford University, workshop on transnational climate governance and domestic politics, and participants at the 2015 International Studies Association Conference for helpful and insightful comments and discussions. The author also thanks Won No for excellent research assistance. All errors are my own.

References

Aerts, Walter, Denis Cormier, and Michel Magnan. (2008) Corporate Environmental Disclosure, Financial Markets and the Media: An International Perspective. *Ecological Economics* 64(3):643–659. doi:10.1016/j.ecolecon.2007.04.012.

Andonova, Liliana B. (2014) Boomerangs to Partnerships? Explaining State Participation in Transnational Partnerships for Sustainability. *Comparative Political Studies* 47(3):481–515. doi:10.1177/0010414013509579.

Andonova, Liliana B., Thomas Hale, and Charles Roger. (2014) How Do Domestic Politics Condition Participation in Transnational Climate Governance? Paper presented at the *Political Economy of International Organizations Conference*, Princeton, NJ, January 16–18.

Arimura, Toshi H., Nicole Darnall, and Hajime Katayama. (2011) Is ISO 14001 a Gateway to More Advanced Voluntary Action? The Case of Green Supply Chain Management. *Journal of Environmental Economics and Management* 61(2):170–182.

Arora, Seema, and Timothy N. Cason. (1996) Why Do Firms Volunteer to Exceed Environmental Regulations? Understanding Participation in EPA's 33/50 Program. *Land Economics* 72(4):413–432. doi:10.2307/3146906.

Avant, Deborah D., Martha Finnemore, and Susan K. Sell. (2010) *Who Governs the Globe?* Cambridge, UK: Cambridge University Press.

Bartley, Tim. (2010) Transnational Private Regulation in Practice: The Limits of Forest and Labor Standards Certification in Indonesia. *Business & Politics* 12(3):1–34. doi:10.2202/1469-3569.1321.

Berliner, Daniel, and Aseem Prakash. (2014) Public Authority and Private Rules: How Domestic Regulatory Institutions Shape the Adoption of Global Private Regimes. *International Studies Quarterly* 58(4):793–803. doi:10.1111/isqu.12166.

Büthe, Tim, and Walter Mattli. (2011) *New Global Rulers: The Privatization of Regulation in the World Economy*. Princeton, NJ: Princeton University Press.

Christmann, Petra. (2004) Multinational Companies and the Natural Environment: Determinants of Global Environmental Policy. *Academy of Management Journal* 47(5):747–760. doi:10.2307/20159616.

Christmann, Petra, and Glen Taylor. (2001) Globalization and the Environment: Determinants of Firm Self-Regulation in China. *Journal of International Business Studies* 32(3):439–458.

Cutler, A. Claire, Virginia Haufler, and Tony Porter. (1999) *Private Authority and International Affairs*. Albany, NY: SUNY Press.

Darnall, Nicole, and Daniel Edwards. (2006) Predicting the Cost of Environmental Management System Adoption: The Role of Capabilities, Resources and Ownership Structure. *Strategic Management Journal* 27(4):301–320. doi:10.1002/smj.518.

Darnall, Nicole, G. Jason Jolley, and Robert Handfield. (2008) Environmental Management Systems and Green Supply Chain Management: Complements for Sustainability? *Business Strategy and the Environment* 17(1):30–45. doi:10.1002/bse.557.

Dauvergne, Peter, and Jane Lister. (2010) The Power of Big Box Retail in Global Environmental Governance: Bringing Commodity Chains Back into IR. *Millennium—Journal of International Studies* 39(1):145–160. doi:10.1177/0305829810371018.

DeCanio, Stephen J., and William E. Watkins. (1998) Investment in Energy Efficiency: Do the Characteristics of Firms Matter? *Review of Economics and Statistics* 80(1):95–107. doi:10.1162/003465398557366.

Fortune. (n.d.) Global 500 2014. Available at http://fortune.com/global500/2014/.

García-Johnson, Ronie. (2000) *Exporting Environmentalism: U.S. Multinational Chemical Corporations in Brazil and Mexico*. Cambridge, MA: MIT Press.

Gelman, Andrew, and Jennifer Hill. (2006) *Data Analysis Using Regression and Multilevel/Hierarchical Models.* Cambridge, UK: Cambridge University Press.

Gillan, Stuart, Jay C. Hartzell, Andrew Koch, and Laura T. Starks. (2010) Firms' Environmental, Social and Governance (ESG) Choices, Performance and Managerial Motivation. Unpublished Working Paper. http://www.ie.edu/docs/workshopFinance/LAURASTARKS.pdf.

Guenther, Edeltraud, Thomas Guenther, Frank Schiemann, and Gabriel Weber. (2015 2016) Stakeholder Relevance for Reporting Explanatory Factors of Carbon Disclosure. *Business & Society* 55(3):361–397.

Haigh, Nardia, and Andrew Griffiths. (2012) Surprise as a Catalyst for Including Climatic Change in the Strategic Environment. *Business & Society* 51(1):89–120. doi:10.1177/0007650311427425.

Hale, Thomas, and Charles Roger. (2014) Orchestration and Transnational Climate Governance. *The Review of International Organizations* 9(1):59–82. doi:10.1007/s11558-013-9174-0.

Hsueh, Lily, and Aseem Prakash. (2012) Incentivizing Self-Regulation: Federal vs. State-Level Voluntary Programs in US Climate Change Policies. *Regulation & Governance* 6(4):445–473.

Keohane, Robert O., and Helen V. Milner, eds. (1996) *Internationalization and Domestic Politics.* Cambridge, UK: Cambridge University Press.

Khanna, Madhu, Patricia Koss, Cody Jones, and David Ervin. (2007) Motivations for Voluntary Environmental Management. *Policy Studies Journal* 35(4):751–772. doi:10.1111/j.1541-0072.2007.00246.x.

Kim, Eun-Hee, and Thomas Lyon. (2011) When Does Institutional Investor Activism Increase Shareholder Value?: The Carbon Disclosure Project. *The B.E. Journal of Economic Analysis & Policy* 11(1):1–29. doi:10.2202/1935-1682.2676.

Kolk, Ans, and David Levy. (2003) Multinationals and Global Climate Change: Issues for the Automotive and Oil Industries. In *Multinationals, Environment and Global Competition* (Research in Global Strategic Management, vol. 9), edited by Sarianna M. Lundan. Greenwich, CT: JAI Press, 171–193. http://www.emeraldinsight.com/doi/abs/10.1016/S1064-4857(03)09008-9.

Kolk, Ans, David Levy, and Jonatan Pinkse. (2008) Corporate Responses in an Emerging Climate Regime: The Institutionalization and Commensuration of Carbon Disclosure. *European Accounting Review* 17(4):719–745. doi:10.1080/09638180802489121.

Kolk, Ans, and Jonatan Pinkse. (2005) Business Responses to Climate Change: Identifying Emergent Strategies. *California Management Review* 47(3):6–20. doi:10.2307/41166304.

Kolk, Ans, and Jonatan Pinkse. (2008) A Perspective on Multinational Enterprises and Climate Change: Learning from "An Inconvenient Truth"? *Journal of International Business Studies* 39(8):1359–1378. doi:10.1057/jibs.2008.61.

Kollman, Kelly, and Aseem Prakash. (2001) Green by Choice? Cross-National Variations in Firms' Responses to EMS-Based Environmental Regimes. *World Politics* 53(3):399–430. doi:10.1353/wp.2001.0010.

Koppell, Jonathan G. S. (2010) *World Rule: Accountability, Legitimacy, and the Design of Global Governance.* Chicago: University of Chicago Press.

Kotchen, M., and J. J. Moon. (2012) Corporate Social Responsibility for Irresponsibility. *The B.E. Journal of Economic Analysis & Policy* 12(1). Available at http://environment.yale.edu/kotchen/pubs/csrcsi.pdf.

Lubin, David A., and Daniel C. Esty. (2010) The Sustainability Imperative. *Harvard Business Review* 88(5):42–50.

Luo, Le, Yi-Chen Lan, and Qingliang Tang. (2012) Corporate Incentives to Disclose Carbon Information: Evidence from the CDP Global 500 Report. *Journal of International Financial Management & Accounting* 23(2):93–120. doi:10.1111/j.1467-646X.2012.01055.x.

Matten, Dirk, and Jeremy Moon. (2008) "Implicit" and "Explicit" CSR: A Conceptual Framework for a Comparative Understanding of Corporate Social Responsibility. *Academy of Management Review* 33(2):404–424. doi:10.5465/AMR.2008.31193458.

Pattberg, Philipp. (2012) How Climate Change Became a Business Risk: Analyzing Nonstate Agency in Global Climate Politics. *Environment and Planning C: Government and Policy* 30 (4):613–626. doi:10.1068/c1179.

Peiró-Signes, Angel, and María-del-Val Segarra-Oña. (2013) Trends in ESG Practices: Differences and Similarities across Major Developed Markets. In *Sustainability Appraisal: Quantitative Methods and Mathematical Techniques for Environmental Performance Evaluation*, edited by Marina G. Erechtchoukova, Peter A. Khaiter, and Paulina Golinska. Heidelberg: Springer, 125–140. http://link.springer.com/chapter/10.1007/978-3-642-32081-1_6.

Perkins, Richard, and Eric Neumayer. (2010) Geographic Variations in the Early Diffusion of Corporate Voluntary Standards: Comparing ISO 14001 and the Global Compact. *Environment and Planning A* 42(2):347–365.

Pinkse, Jonatan, and Ans Kolk. (2012) Multinational Enterprises and Climate Change: Exploring Institutional Failures and Embeddedness. *Journal of International Business Studies* 43(3):332–341. doi:10.1057/jibs.2011.56.

Porter, Michael E., and Mark R. Kramer. (2006) Strategy and Society: The Link Between Competitive Advantage and Corporate Social Responsibility. *Harvard Business Review* 84 (12). Available at https://hbr.org/2006/12/strategy-and-society-the-link-between-competitive-advantage-and-corporate-social-responsibility.

Prakash, Aseem. (2001) Why Do Firms Adopt "Beyond-Compliance" Environmental Policies? *Business Strategy and the Environment* 10(5):286–299. doi:10.1002/bse.305.

Prakash, Aseem, and Matthew Potoski. (2006) *The Voluntary Environmentalists: Green Clubs, ISO 14001, and Voluntary Regulations*. Cambridge, UK: Cambridge University Press.

Prakash, Aseem, and Matthew Potoski. (2014) Global Private Regimes, Domestic Public Law ISO 14001 and Pollution Reduction. *Comparative Political Studies* 47(3):369–394. doi:10.1177/0010414013509573.

Raudenbush, Stephen W., and Anthony S. Bryk. (2002) *Hierarchical Linear Models: Applications and Data Analysis Methods*. Second Edition. Thousand Oaks, CA: Sage.

Reid, Erin Marie, and Michael W. Toffel. (2009) *Responding to Public and Private Politics: Corporate Disclosure of Climate Change Strategies*. SSRN Scholarly Paper ID 1237982. Rochester, NY: Social Science Research Network. Available at http://papers.ssrn.com/abstract=1237982.

Rivera, Jorge, and Peter De Leon. (2005) Chief Executive Officers and Voluntary Environmental Performance: Costa Rica's Certification for Sustainable Tourism. *Policy Sciences* 38(2–3):107–127. doi:10.1007/s11077-005-6590-x.

Roger, Charles, Thomas Hale, and Liliana B. Andonova. (2015) How Do Domestic Politics Shape Participation in Transnational Climate Governance? Available at http://www.bsg.ox.ac.uk/sites/www.bsg.ox.ac.uk/files/documents/BSG-WP-2015-001.pdf.

Scherer, Andreas Georg, and Guido Palazzo. (2008) *Handbook of Research on Global Corporate Citizenship*. Cheltenham, UK: Edward Elgar.

Strand, Robert. (2013) The Chief Officer of Corporate Social Responsibility: A Study of Its Presence in Top Management Teams. *Journal of Business Ethics* 112(4):721–734. doi:http://dx.doi.org.ezproxy1.lib.asu.edu/10.1007/s10551-012-1568-z.

Strange, Susan. (1996) *The Retreat of the State: The Diffusion of Power in the World Economy*. New York: Cambridge University Press.

Vidaver-Cohen, Deborah, and Peggy Simcic Brønn. (2013) Reputation, Responsibility, and Stakeholder Support in Scandinavian Firms: A Comparative Analysis. *Journal of Business Ethics* 127(1):49–64. doi:10.1007/s10551-013-1673-7.

Videras, J., and A. Alberini. (2000) The Appeal of Voluntary Environmental Programs: Which Firms Participate and Why? *Contemporary Economic Policy* 18(4):449–460. doi:10.1111/j.1465-7287.2000.tb00041.x.

Vogel, David. (1995) *Trading up: Consumer and Environmental Regulation in a Global Economy*. Cambridge, MA: Harvard University Press.

Vogel, David. (2005) *The Market for Virtue: The Potential and Limits of Corporate Social Responsibility*. Washington, DC: Brookings Institution Press.

Vogel, David. (2008) Private Global Business Regulation. *Annual Review of Political Science* 11:261–282.

Vogel, David. (2010) The Private Regulation of Global Corporate Conduct: Achievements and Limitations. *Business and Society* 49(1):68–87.

Waddock, Sandra. (2008) The Development of Corporate Responsibility/Corporate Citizenship. *Organization Management Journal* 5(1):29–39. doi:10.1057/omj.2008.5.

Winston, Andrew. (2010, October 5) The Most Powerful Green NGO You've Never Heard of. *Harvard Business Review*. Available at https://hbr.org/2010/10/the-most-powerful-green-ngo.

Appendix

The following appendix contains additional figures and tables described in the text of the chapter.

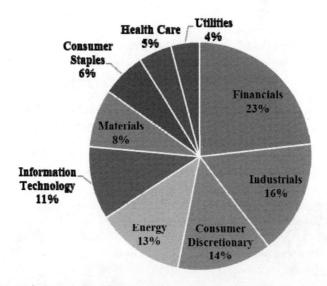

Figure A1. The Global 500 by Industry Sector

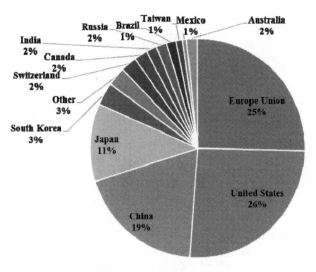

Figure A2. The Global 500 by Country of Origin

Table A1. Variable Description and Construction/Operation

Variable	Brief Description and Operation (Source)
Firm-level variables	
Policy supporter	
Analyst	Coded as 1 and 0 otherwise if the company houses a designated analyst responsible for climate change or sustainability activities or has a sustainability related committee as part of its Board of Directors (Not the traditional "Health, Safety, and Environment" positions or committee) (Corporate websites and sustainability or CSR reports)
Vice President	Coded as 1 and 0 otherwise if the firm or organization has a designated Director or Vice President level officer for sustainability (Corporate websites and sustainability or CSR reports)
Chief Sustainability Officer	Coded as 1 and 0 otherwise if the firm or organization has a designated Chief Sustainability Officer (Corporate websites and sustainability or CSR reports)
Explicit CSR/Commitment to sustainability	
Mission statement	Coded as 1 and 0 otherwise if sustainability is core to the mission of the firm (Corporate websites and sustainability or CSR reports; see Appendix A1 for examples of the author's coding)
Environ., Social and Governance (ESG)	Coded as 1 and 0 otherwise if there is an incorporation of "ESG" (Environmental, Social and Governance) issues into decision-making processes and day-to-day operations (Corporate websites and sustainability or CSR reports)
Dedicated website	Coded as 1 and 0 otherwise if a company has a dedicated, separate website on sustainability
Employee size (log)	Natural log of the number of employees (Fidelity, Bloomberg, or http://fortune.com/global500/2014 with exception for Agricultural Development Bank of China, which is from LinkedIn)
Revenues (log)	Natural log of corporate annual revenues in millions of dollars; revenue figures include consolidated subsidiaries and reported revenues from discontinued operations, but exclude excise taxes. For banks, revenue is the sum of gross interest income and gross noninterest income. For insurance companies, revenue includes premium and annuity income, investment income, realized capital gains or losses, and other income, but excludes deposits. (http://fortune.com/global500/2014)

(Continued)

Table A1. Continued

Variable	Brief Description and Operation (Source)
Assets (log)	Natural log of corporate annual, fiscal year-end assets in millions of dollars (http://fortune.com/global500/2014)
ISO 14001 (firm-level)	Coded as 1 and 0 otherwise if a company is certified with ISO 14001 (corporate websites and sustainability or CSR reports)
Environ. R&D	Coded as 1 and 0 otherwise if a company has invested in environmental R&D (corporate websites and sustainability or CSR reports)
Government-owned	Coded as 1 and 0 otherwise if the company is at least 50% government owned (http://fortune.com/global500/2014)
Industry sector	
Consumer Discretionary	Coded as 1 or 0 otherwise if a company operates in the Consumer Discretionary industry sector (Forbes, CDP, or Fortune if information not available in the former; all companies are classified into 9 sector categories following the Global Industry Classification Standard)
Consumer Staples	Coded as 1 or 0 otherwise if a company operates in the Consumer Staples industry sector
Energy	Coded as 1 or 0 otherwise if a company operates in the Energy industry sector
Financials	Coded as 1 or 0 otherwise if a company operates in the Financials industry sector
Health Care	Coded as 1 or 0 otherwise if a company operates in the Health Care industry sector
Industrials	Coded as 1 or 0 otherwise if a company operates in the Industrials industry sector
Information Technology	Coded as 1 or 0 otherwise if a company operates in the Information Technology or Telecommunication Services industry sector
Materials	Coded as 1 or 0 otherwise if a company operates in the Materials industry sector
Utilities	Coded as 1 or 0 otherwise if a company operates in the Utilities industry sector
Country-level variables	
GDP/capita (log)	Natural log of GDP/capita where GDP is a firm's country of origin's average GDP for 1990–2010 (Andonova et al. 2014; World Bank)
CO2 emissions (log)	Natural log of CO2 emissions where CO2 emissions are a firm's country of origin's average CO2 emissions between 1990 and 2010 (Andonova et al. 2014; World Bank)
Civil liberties	Based on Freedom House's measure of civil liberties, which measures freedom of expression and belief, associational and organizational rights, rule or law, and personal autonomy and individual rights; score transformed by Andonova et al. (2014), such that a higher score means more civil liberties, scale of 0 to 6
Political rights	Based on Freedom House's measure of political rights, which measures a country's electoral process, political pluralism and participation, and functioning of government; score transformed by Andonova et al. (2014), such that a higher score means more political rights, scale of 0 to 6
Polity	A measure of regime type of the country of origin of a firm; follows a scale of –10 to 10 where 10 is a full democracy and –10 is an autocracy (Polity IV Project)
Federal	Coded as 1 or 0 otherwise if a company's country of origin has a federalist system of government (Andonova et al. 2014; Forum of Federations 2012)
Air pollution (PM 10)	A measure of a firm's country of origin's PM 10 concentration in ug/m3; a proxy for a country's commitment to environmental protection since particulate air pollution is relatively easy and inexpensive to control (Andonova et al. 2014; Emerson et al. 2012)

Environ. Performance index	A measure of a firm's country of origin's commitment to environmental protection (Andonova et al. 2014; Emerson et al. 2012)
ISO14001 (country-level) (log)	Natural log of a company's country of origin's total number of ISO 14001 certifications in 2009 (www.iso.org)
European Union	Coded as 1 or 0 otherwise if a company originate from a country that is part of the European Union (United Nations Country Grouping)
North America	Coded as 1 or 0 otherwise if a company originate from a country that is part of North America (United Nations Country Grouping)
Latin America	Coded as 1 or 0 otherwise if a company originate from a country that is part of Latin America (United Nations Country Grouping)
Asia	Coded as 1 or 0 otherwise if a company originate from a country that is part of Asia (United Nations Country Grouping)

A2. Examples of Global 500 companies where *Mission statement* is coded 1

- Chevron

Values – "Protecting People and the Environment"

"We place the highest priority on the health and safety of our workforce and protection of our assets and the environment. We aim to be admired for world-class performance through disciplined application of our Operational Excellence Management System."

Source: http://www.chevron.com/about/chevronway/

- Shandong Energy Group

Enterprise mission – "Green Energy, Humanistic Value"

"Connotation Interpreting: Facing the global energy crisis and the environmental degradation, the sustainable development has become the first choice for the development of energy enterprises. Offering green energy that is safe, high-quality and clean for the economic and social development has been the sacred responsibility of Shandong Energy Group. The Group treads on the heels of the green energy trend by dedicating to the development of a low-carbon economy, laying stress on energy conservation and emission reduction, and developing the new domain in the energy field. Furthermore, the Group actively undertakes the environmental responsibility in order to realize the harmonious development of both the energy and the environment."

Source: http://english.snjt.com/us.jsp?urltype=tree.TreeTempUrl&wbtreeid=1026

- Petrobras

Values – "Sustainable development"

"We pursue business success under a long-term perspective, contributing to economic and social development and to a healthy environment in the communities where we have operations."

Source: http://www.petrobras.com.br/en/about-us/profile/values/

- Petrobras

Values – "Sustainable development"

"We pursue business success under a long-term perspective, contributing to economic and social development and to a healthy environment in the communities where we have operations."

Source: http://www.petrobras.com.br/en/about-us/profile/values/

- Fujitsu

Corporate Values – "Society and Environment"

"In all our actions, we protect the environment and contribute to society. As a good corporate citizen, the Fujitsu Group takes a leading role in sustaining the well-being of society through our business activities."

Source: http://www.fujitsu.com/global/about/philosophy/values/#item1-1

- Dupont

Core Values – "Environmental Stewardship"

"We find science-enabled, sustainable solutions for our customers, always managing our businesses to protect the environment and preserve the earth's natural resources, both for today and for generations into the future."

Source: http://www.dupont.com/corporate-functions/our-company/core-values.html

- Siemens

Strategies: Management model – "Sustainability and citizenship"

"Together with our customers and partners, we want to shape the future by making real what matters and addressing the global issues and trends that are truly crucial. Driven by our passion for engineering excellence, we're committed to the values of our Company's founder. Guiding us for over 165 years, his maxim – "I won't sell the future of my Company for a short-term profit" – demands that we maintain a healthy balance between profit, planet and people."

Source: http://www.siemens.com/annual/14/en/company-report/our-strategy/

- 3M

"Our Values
- Provide our investors an attractive return through sustainable, global growth.
- Respect our social and physical environment around the world."

Source: http://solutions.3m.com/wps/portal/3M/en_US/3M-Company/Information/AboutUs/WhoWeAre/

- ABB

ABB's vision

"As one of the world's leading engineering companies, we help our customers to use electrical power efficiently, to increase industrial productivity and to lower environmental impact in a sustainable way. Power and productivity for a better world."

Source: http://www.abb.com/cawp/czabb014/24410b313424426cc12574a40047093b.aspx

- BASF

"We combine economic success, social responsibility and environmental protection. Through science and innovation, we support our customers in nearly every industry in meeting the current and future needs of society."

Source: https://www.basf.com/us/en/company/about-us/strategy-and-organization.html

A3. Examples of Global 500 companies where *Environmental R&D* is coded 1

- Accenture

"We also help clients develop deep insights on sustainability issues based on our ongoing investments in research, including recent studies on consumer and investor expectations and global executive opinion on corporate sustainability and climate change."

Source: https://www.accenture.com/us-en/service-consulting-sustainability-overview-summary?tab=3

- 3M

"3M's large R&D operations offer both fertile ground for 3P pollution prevention projects and a talented laboratory for developing products and processes aligned with the company's commitment to sustainable development."

Source: http://www.epa.gov/lean/environment/studies/3m.htm

- AT&T

"The AT&T Technology and Environment Awards Program builds on AT&T's legacy of supporting research in fields that focus on the intersection of the economy and the environment."

Source: http://www.att.com/gen/corporate-citizenship?pid=12434

- HSBC Holdings

"Under the HSBC Water Programme, urban freshwater research projects are now up and running in 24 cities, thanks to our partner Earthwatch."

Source: http://www.hsbc.com/citizenship/sustainability

- OMV Group

"Our R&D focus is on fuel cells and therefore on hydrogen. This innovation fits in well with our core business, as our refineries already produce large quantities of hydrogen for industrial use. This element is available in practically unlimited quantities and is as good as emission-free – a major step towards a greener future on the road."

Source: https://www.omv.com/portal/01/com/omv/OMV_Group/sustainability

- Chevron

"Additionally, we operate one of the world's largest geothermal energy portfolios and have significant investments in two of the world's largest CO2 storage projects. We invest in advanced biofuels research and in ways to reduce our equity GHG emissions from flaring and venting. These actions span all phases of technology development, from research to demonstration and deployment, and they significantly inform Chevron's view and involvement in GHG abatement."

Source: http://www.chevron.com/documents/pdf/corporateresponsibility/Chevron_CR_Report_2013.pdf

- Woolsworth

"Areas of research include water use efficiency, nutrient management and reducing carbon footprint."

Source: http://retailsector-woolworths.weebly.com/research-and-development.html

- Cisco

"Since then, Cisco has continued to qualify more halogen free PCB laminate materials and has increased their use in many new products. We will continue to research new laminate materials..."

Source: http://www.cisco.com/assets/csr/pdf/CSR_Report_2014.pdf#page=68

- BAE Systems

"R&D in designing submarines with better waste compacting systems to comply with the Prevention of Pollution From Ships (MARPOL) legislation; Reducing carbon emissions and air pollution from aircraft by running test flights through a simulator, using less fuel…"

Source: http://www.baesystems.com/our-company-rau/corporate-responsibility/working-responsibly/product-stewardship/environmental-impacts;baeSessionId=LUOA1E-gNIkJee3EQjYSrSBpm217ZeDOrR3BDjC6M98XqpTJls8y!-1477725154?_adf.ctrl-state=d484fvrk3_199&_afrLoop=4953238267709000&_afrWindowMode=0&_afrWindowId=null#!%40%40%3F_afrWindowId%3Dnull%26_afrLoop%3D4953238267709000%26_afrWindowMode%3D0%26_adf.ctrl-state%3Dcwzp11wnj_4

- Rolls-Royce

"In 2014 we invested over £1.2 billion in gross Research and Development (R&D). Around two-thirds of this is dedicated to improving environmental performance to lower fuel consumption, emissions and noise."

Source: http://www.rolls-royce.com/sustainability/better-power/products.aspx§rategy-and-governance

Table A4. Correlation Matrix

	Analyst	VP	CSO	Mission statement	ESG	Dedicated website	Employee size (log)	Revenues (log)	Assets (log)	ISO 14001 (firm-level)	Environ. R&D	Government-owned
Analyst	1											
VP	−0.33	1										
CSO	−0.11	−0.19	1									
Mission statement	0.04	−0.01	0.12	1								
ESG	0.02	0.18	0.02	−0.02	1							
Dedicated website	−0.02	0.13	−0.02	−0.03	0.01	1						
Employee size (log)	−0.10	0.14	0.02	−0.04	−0.03	0.07	1					
Revenues (log)	−0.02	0.09	0.01	−0.02	0.11	0.09	0.35	1				
Assets (log)	0.01	0.12	−0.04	−0.11	0.34	−0.03	0.21	0.46	1			
ISO 14001 (firm-level)	0.07	0.13	0.10	0.18	0.14	−0.04	0.06	0.06	−0.04	1		
Environ. R&D	0.09	0.10	0.08	0.15	0.11	−0.01	0.04	0.17	0.07	0.38	1	
Government-owned	−0.02	−0.35	−0.03	−0.01	−0.25	−0.13	0.08	0.03	0.01	−0.15	−0.05	1

Table A5. Collinearity Diagnostics

	VIF	SQRT VIF	Tolerance	R-Squared
Analyst	1.24	1.11	0.81	0.19
VP	1.52	1.23	0.66	0.34
CSO	1.14	1.07	0.88	0.12
Mission statement	1.07	1.03	0.94	0.07
ESG	1.27	1.13	0.79	0.21
Dedicated website	1.05	1.03	0.95	0.05
Employee size	1.20	1.10	0.83	0.17
Revenues	1.45	1.20	0.69	0.31
Assets	1.51	1.23	0.67	0.34
ISO 14001 (firm-level)	1.26	1.12	0.79	0.21
Environ. R&D	1.24	1.11	0.81	0.19
Government-owned	1.28	1.13	0.78	0.22
Mean VIF	1.27			

Table A6. Multilevel Mixed-Effects Logit Model of Drivers of Voluntary Climate Action, Voluntary Carbon Disclosure; Civil Liberties Specification Checks[1]

	Model 1 Voluntary Climate Action	Model 2 Voluntary Climate Action	Model 3 Voluntary Carbon Disclosure	Model 4 Voluntary Carbon Disclosure
Firm-level variables of interest				
Policy supporter				
Analyst	2.50**	2.73***	1.97*	1.97*
	(0.867)	(0.940)	(0.800)	(0.783)
Vice President	6.41**	7.83***	4.85***	5.12***
	(2.194)	(2.602)	(1.544)	(1.356)
Chief Sustainability Officer	5.40**	6.31***	4.40***	3.90***
	(3.200)	(3.800)	(1.500)	(1.371)
Explicit CSR/ Commitment to sustainability				
Mission statement	1.92*	1.91*	1.13	1.10
	(0.714)	(0.700)	(0.322)	(0.310)
Environ., Social and Governance (ESG)	3.89***	4.20***	1.54	1.54
	(1.450)	(1.540)	(0.553)	(0.600)
Dedicated website	1.00	0.93	0.81	0.80
	(0.504)	(0.500)	(0.403)	(0.400)
Firm-level controls				
Employee size (log)	1.32*	1.30*	1.39*	1.42*
	(0.194)	(0.190)	(0.248)	(0.254)
Revenues (log)	0.63	0.61*	0.72	0.73
	(0.200)	(0.180)	(0.400)	(0.400)
Assets (log)	1.71***	1.74***	1.71***	1.71***
	(0.302)	(0.303)	(0.164)	(0.180)
ISO 14001 (firm-level)	1.51	1.50	1.48***	1.34*
	(0.470)	(0.460)	(0.200)	(0.208)
Environ. R&D	1.48	1.45	1.29	1.30
	(0.423)	(0.402)	(0.325)	(0.330)
Government-owned	1.00	0.75	0.18***	0.17***
	(0.434)	(0.346)	(0.063)	(0.062)

Industry sector				
Consumer Staples	2.12	2.42	2.07*	2.17**
	(1.302)	(1.470)	(0.830)	(0.803)
Energy	1.75	1.31	1.31	1.13
	(1.015)	(0.743)	(0.543)	(0.470)
Financials	0.24**	0.22**	0.32**	0.31**
	(0.144)	(0.131)	(0.180)	(0.180)
Health Care	0.80	0.83	1.06	1.05
	(0.522)	(0.535)	(0.604)	(0.610)
Industrials	0.70	0.80	0.78	0.85
	(0.304)	(0.334)	(0.230)	(0.260)
Information Technology	2.66*	2.34*	1.41	1.50
	(1.362)	(1.191)	(0.520)	(0.592)
Materials	0.67	0.70	0.58	0.64
	(0.410)	(0.415)	(0.303)	(0.352)
Utilities	1.10	1.27	0.53	0.61
	(1.000)	(1.000)	(0.532)	(0.592)
Country-level controls				
GDP/capita (log)	0.45**	0.83	1.07	1.21
	(0.183)	(0.250)	(0.400)	(0.370)
CO_2 emissions (log)	0.55***	0.94	0.51***	0.66*
	(0.120)	(0.130)	(0.118)	(0.160)
Civil liberties Political Rights	5.96***		2.11	
	(3.150)		(1.040)	
Polity		1.04		1.10**
		(0.054)		(0.050)
Federalism	1.13	0.77	1.69	1.29
	(0.491)	(0.309)	(0.720)	(0.615)
Air Pollution (PPM 10)	1.00**	1.00	1.00	1.00
	(0.200)	(0.014)	(0.020)	(0.020)
Environ. Performance index	0.93	1.00	0.90	1.00
	(0.041)	(0.034)	(0.042)	(0.042)
ISO14001 (country-level) (log)	1.61*	1.00	1.75**	1.44
	(0.440)	(0.171)	(0.510)	(0.350)
N (N of groups)	500(38)	500(38)	500(38)	500(38)
F-statistics (Wald)	132.84	132.68	22308.13	10903.42
Prob > chi2	0.00	0.00	0.00	0.00

[1] Robust standard errors reported in parentheses
***$P \leq 0.001$; **$P \leq 0.05$; *$P \leq 0.10$

Transnational Climate Governance Networks and Domestic Regulatory Action

Xun Cao and Hugh Ward

ABSTRACT
Transnational climate governance (TCG) creates networks between countries as governments and other organizations enter joint arrangements to further their interests. We argue that actors build TCG, rather than focusing on promoting change at the domestic level, when this is a more efficient way of using their limited resources than lobbying to increase the level of domestic regulation. Based on standard microeconomic theory, we show that actors will respond to higher existing levels of domestic regulation by participating more in TCG because the existence of such domestic legislation frees up resources for them to use in other ways, including activities at the transnational level. We carry out an empirical test based on the strength of the network ties between countries formed by TCG. Results support our main hypothesis on the positive relationship between a country's level of domestic policy output and its participation in TCGs, suggesting that national policies and TCGs are more complements than substitutes as instruments to address global climate change.

Transnational climate governance (TCG) creates networks between countries as governments and other organizations enter joint arrangements to further their interests. Some of these arrangements are sponsored by, or strongly steered by, the actions of states or international organizations. In this article, we focus on other arrangements—specifically those that are led by corporations, NGOs, or subnational units of government such as cities (Bulkeley, Andonova, Betsill, Hale, Hoffmann, Newell, Paterson, Roger, and Vandeveer 2014; Hale and Roger 2014). We call these *transnational climate governance* (TCG) (Andonova, Betsill, and Bulkeley 2007; Green 2014; Hale and Rogers 2014). Why do such actors use their resources to build TCG rather than focusing on promoting change at the domestic level?[1] Our argument is that they do so when this is a more efficient way of using their limited resources

---
Color versions of one or more of the figures in the article can be found online at www.tandfonline.com/gini
[1] Herein for brevity we drop the "sub/nonstate" prefix.

than lobbying for action at the national level to increase domestic regulation. We highlight that the more legislative action there has been at the domestic level, the greater the participation of actors in TCG. This is because if they can bank on the domestic legislative environment being favorable to their interest in climate change governance, organizations are less resource constrained in relation to participating in TCG.

Currently we lack a firm understanding of the domestic conditions that influence participation in transnational ties. Andonova (2014) provides a number of answers to another important question: What factors condition TCG arrangements where states *do play* an important leadership or conditioning role? Her specific focus is on arrangements arising from the Johannesburg Earth Summit, not all of which specifically concern climate change. Hale and Roger (2014) focus on transnational governance of climate change but specifically on arrangements led by states (comprising around 30% of the total). The pioneering study of domestic influences using large-n statistical methods is that of Andonova, Hale, and Roger (2014). They suggest that when governments hold pro-environmental views, this facilitates organizations' involvement in TCG. They find some evidence that pro-environmental policies promote organizations' involvement and quite strong evidence that state capacity does so. We build on this study by providing a strong theoretical rationale for the idea that a favorable domestic regulatory environment encourages participation.

In addition to introducing a new measure for domestic climate change policy capturing the number of relevant domestic legislative instruments, we make three core contributions. First we use a rational agent perspective to develop specific hypotheses about domestic influences on action. This approach has proven extremely useful, alongside others, in constructing descriptive narratives about TCG (Bulkeley et al. 2014; Schäferhoff, Campe, and Kaan 2009). For instance, Green (2014) uses a rational choice supply/demand model to develop hypotheses about why states delegate authority to private actors in some instances while private organizations develop "entrepreneurial authority" in others. Our argument complements Green's. First, we add that domestic legislative action can, in some circumstances, provide similar benefits to international cooperation between states—and to private authority. Second, we stress that organizations face trade-offs in pursuing goals associated with climate governance because they have finite resources.

Our second contribution is to bring a network perspective to bear on the study of TCG. Although TCG has been widely cast in the literature, and even defined, as a network phenomenon (Andonova, Betsill, and Bulkeley 2009), surprisingly little use has been made of concepts from social network analysis and associated methods that are now becoming widely used in political science (Hafner-Burton, Kahler, and Montgomery 2009; Ward, Stovel, and Sacks 2011) and are starting to be used in the global environmental politics literature (Ward 2006; Cao and Prakash 2010 and 2102; Kalbhenn 2011, Spilker 2012; Ward and Cao 2012; Schaffer and Bernauer 2014; Grundig and Ward 2015; Böhmelt and Vollenweider 2015). We add to the small number of studies in the recent literature using formal social network analysis. Lee and van de Meene (2012) study the directed network formed when one city involved in the C40Cities TCG program learns from another affiliated city. Green (2013) uses social network analysis to examine links when one greenhouse gas emissions standard recognizes another, enabling her to analyze which standards are central to this network. Widerberg (2014) moves beyond enumerating organizations involved in the climate regime complex (Keohane and Victor 2011; Abbott 2012) to map links between them, using affiliation to institutions and hyperlinks on organizations' Web sites to other organizations. There is growing recognition in social network theory that it is often inappropriate to treat network ties as givens when they actually emerge from the strategic choices of agents (Jackson 2008:257–319). By considering the domestic factors that influence networks built by rational actors, we start to endogenize the network.

Our third contribution is to recognize that, in testing models of how networks develop, it is important to recognize that observations are not independent and to use appropriate econometric methods to deal with this. Looking at network ties helps us to answer our question about the effects of domestic legislation on organizations' participation in transnational arrangements. However, care needs to be exercised in making statistical inferences. Several organizations in states j and k may be involved in negotiating an arrangement. If negotiations are successful, to use the language of social network theory (Wasserman and Faust 1994), a co-affiliation link is created between j and k. If, as will frequently be true empirically, organizations in some other state, i, are involved, network links are also created between j and i and between k and i. This is a 'friend of your friend is likely to be your friend' effect. Notice that this implies that the probability of a tie between j and k is unlikely to be independent of the occurrence of other links in the network involving j, k, and third states. If such interdependencies are not taken into account, we are liable to get biased estimates of the effects of domestic covariates, as detailed in the section on latent-space models (Hoff, Raftery, and Handcock 2002).

TCG as a network phenomenon

When organizations in countries i and j are involved in a TCG arrangement, they strengthen the network tie between the two countries. Our article is different from others in this special issue in that our empirical focus is on explaining the strength of such network ties, based on our model of the trade-off that individual organizations face. The network is only strengthened if an actor in country *i* and an actor in country *j* are willing to participate in an arrangement. Thus we argue that the overall strength of the network tie (allowing for multiple organizations on each side) increases with the degree of development of legislation in the country that has the lowest level of domestic legislative action. This is a "weakest link" argument (Hirshleifer 1983); it is the incentives of the actors most loath to participate that govern connections.[2] Thus we adopt a rational agent perspective but, in line with a systemic approach to TCG (Bulkeley et. al. 2014), we emphasize that ties between countries are an emergent consequence of rational action of individual actors.

At first sight, to focus on network ties between countries rather than network ties between particular actors may seem a rather odd perspective, albeit that our argument derives from a theory of the domestic influences on organizations. However, transnational ties do more than link the agents explicitly involved in them. They create ties between countries, and second-order links between agents within them, along which information and normative influences flow. Although we do not deal in depth with information and influence flows in this article, their potential importance helps to justify our research question. Even relatively functionally diffuse ties of this sort may play a role in promoting sustainability (Ward 2006). As conduits for information flows between societies, they may also lead to policy diffusion (Simmons, Dobbin, and Garrett 2006) and even to subsequent convergence of environmental policy between societies (Holzinger, Knill, and Sommerer 2008).

In this regard, it is important to note that one characteristic form of TCG involves information exchange. Indeed, Bulkeley et al. (2014) calculate that 90% of the 60 TCG arrangements they look at perform this function, and furthermore, nearly the same proportion function to build capacity.[3] For instance, an important focus for TCG has been networks between cities (Bulkeley 2010; Lee and van de Meene 2012). Between 2008 and 2010, the World Economic Forum's SlimCity program allowed city mayors and businesses to exchange information about using energy efficiently at the city level (World Economic Forum 2009). The mayor of San Francisco and the Governor of Rio de Janeiro were both involved in this initiative. Each may have learned from the other about how to use energy efficiently. But they were also enmeshed in regional and national networks at the domestic level. For instance, San Francisco is also a member of the US Mayor's Climate Protection Agreement. Information mayors learned through SlimCity can be

---

[2] Hirshleifer's (1983) is an argument about public goods provision. Effective transnational climate governance is a public good, but its production often also co-generates private good benefits for participants—for example, profits from participation in markets for carbon offsets. For applications of weakest link arguments to democratic peace and international conflict, see Dixon (1993) and Oneal and Russett (1997).

[3] As shown in the introduction to this special issue's Figure 2, the proportion of arrangements mapped in the data we use providing information and networking services fell from around 75% in 1990 to around 30% in 2010 (Roger, Hale, and Andonova 2017). However, the proportion is still substantial.

passed on through these domestic networks, even though many actors in these domestic networks are not directly involved in Slimcity. Moreover, what mayors know and can transmit directly to other actors involved in SlimCity is partly a function of the information they receive through domestic networks. Also, when cities network internationally, they create opportunities for their mayors and officers to act as policy and norm entrepreneurs (Bulkeley 2010). Cities learn from each other directly by participating in networks (Lee and van de Meene 2012). In addition, cities' involvement in TCG generates second-order links between business communities and citizens' groups in cities, even if they are not directly linked, and it creates second-order links with cities not directly involved in TCG.

Domestic lobbying activity can be costly in terms of time and money spent gathering information, maintaining personal ties, and making contributions to politicians' election funds. Participation in TCG is not cost-free, either. Information exchange requires time and effort to package information for others and to assimilate information the organization receives. Because they can informationally benefit some actors that do not bear the costs of TCG arrangements, the links we emphasize have the public-goods property of nonexcludability. Nevertheless, it may be rational for organizations to use resources in building them because only participants get access to certain benefits, such as direct or enhanced access to information.

According to Bulkeley et al. (2014), some 50% of the TCG arrangements they looked at functioned to set standards. Like information exchange, adhering to a standard also has opportunity costs because standards preclude potentially profitable activities.[4] Standard-setting also creates links between countries.[5] As Potoski and Prakash (2005) argue, corporations adhering to a credible environmental standard enjoy reputational benefits with customers, suppliers, and government regulators that they can only get by joining the "green club." If a corporation in country *i* voluntarily offsets some of its carbon emissions against schemes accredited by, say, *The Gold Standard*, this can have a network externality effect on corporations in country *j*, increasing the value they place on offsetting. There is what Ostrom (2012) calls a *nested externality*: In this case, action on a transgovernmental scale creates an externality linking national markets.

Theory

Focusing on transnational ties enables us to ask whether organizations develop transnational arrangements partly because this is a rational course

---

[4]Additional costs for involvement in transnational networks involve the allocation of administrative staff and resource for participation, meeting commitments, and/or resources toward increasing capacity for action.
[5]In 2010 around 44% of TCG arrangements concerned standard setting and commitments (Roger et al. 2017).

of action for them given the degree of development of national policy in the country where they are based and given the transaction costs associated with forging links with other organizations. It is a commonplace that corporations make rational use of resources so as to achieve desired ends; the same assumption can be argued to be plausible for NGOs and subnational governments. Resource mobilization theories of social movements suggest that NGOs have endemic problems with mobilizing their latent support and must use resources wisely to maintain support and flows of resources from members (Edwards and McCarthy 2004). An important motive for local politicians is to win elections by making rational choices over the policies and taxes they offer (Besley and Case 1995). We assume organizations make rational decisions about forming transnational ties.

The literature suggests that organizations pursue a number of purposes through TCG: information sharing, rule setting, provision of collective goods, financial functions, capacity building, and implementation (Andonova et al. 2007). Governance arrangements "purposively steer constituent members to act" (Andonova et al. 2007:5). Regulation by states through domestic policy can aim to do the same thing, though sometimes through different means. For instance, cities concerned with their carbon emissions could lobby their government to set (binding or nonbinding) targets for cities, or they could act to set up a TCG arrangement like C40Cities (Lee and van de Meene 2012) to encourage action through sharing of information. Similarly, NGOs and corporations concerned about the low quality of some carbon offsets could have lobbied for state regulation of the domestic market rather than initiating a transnational arrangement.[6] We assume that there is usually at least some overlap between what organizations can get through transnational arrangements and what they can get through lobbying to tighten domestic regulation, though we concede that this may not always be the case. This does not commit us to the view that organizations see lobbying and building transnational governance as equally efficient responses. For instance, national regulation of carbon offsets might well be viewed as relatively inefficient by domestic interests because the standard would only apply to one market.[7] We allow for organizations' perceptions of relative efficiency via their utility function over national policy and transnational activity.

On the assumption that TCG and domestic regulation are partial substitutes, organizations face a trade-off between them because they face a resource constraint. Let the utility function of organization o in country j's be

---

[6]Green (2017) shows that some governments' domestic legislation recognizes private offset standards, often alongside national standards. Again this suggests a degree of substitutability.

[7]Although, if the country was economically powerful enough, it might diffuse through the "California Effect" whereby foreign corporations comply to gain better access (Vogel 1995).

$$U(p, t, p_\Sigma)$$

where p is the level of national policy, t is o's level of transnational activity, and p_Σ is the level of policy in the rest of the world outside j. (We simplify notation by dropping subscripts o and j.) Then we assume:

$$\delta U/\delta p > 0; \ \delta U/\delta t > 0; \ \delta^2 U/\delta p^2 < 0; \ \delta^2 U/\delta t^2 < 0; \ \delta^2 U/\delta p_{\Sigma^2} < 0$$

that is, o's utility increases with the level of domestic and international policy and its transnational activity, but marginal utilities are declining.

Because climate change is a global problem that cannot be solved by action at the national level in any one country, it can be assumed that all organizations have some concern about what happens in other national jurisdictions. Nevertheless, we expect their degree of concern to vary. A mayor may want to share information with mayors in other cities, but if her motives primarily center on reelection, she may not be particularly concerned with outcomes in cities overseas—unless her voters are, too. If she could obtain the same information more easily at the domestic level, it might well be rational to do so. On the other hand, the supporters of many environmental NGOs are strongly internationalist in outlook, so their leaders have (or must act as if they have) inherent concern for outcomes overseas. We expect the marginal rate of substitution between domestic policy and transnational action[8] to vary systematically across different types of organization. Figure 1 shows three of o's indifference curves for fixed p_Σ in (p, t) space, labelled I1, I2, and I3. The more o cares about transnational action compared to domestic policy, the flatter the indifference curve through a particular point.

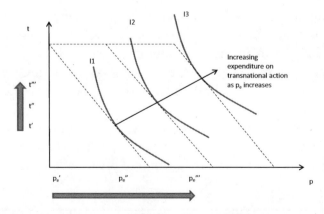

Figure 1. The effect of increasing domestic policy on transnational activity.

---

[8]Equal to $(\delta U/\delta p)/(\delta U/\delta t) > 0$.

Let the level of policy in country *j* if *o* does not lobby be p_e. Suppose that *o* spends l unit of resource on lobbying. Then we assume that the level of policy becomes:

$$p = p_e + l/\pi$$

where $\pi > 0$ represents the costs of lobbying. Pushing policy forward is not costless because *o* faces resistance from a counterlobby that could consist of domestic producers of fossil fuels, heavy industrial users of energy, or government departments primarily concerned with competitiveness or (narrowly defined) economic development. The greater the power of the counter lobby, the larger the value of π. In general, there could be strategic interdependence between *o* and other organizations. We assume that organization *o* does not expect others to react. This may be reasonable where large numbers of others are involved in an arrangement, so that it is difficult for organizations to carry out a strategic analysis. Following the trend toward using game theory in the recent literature on environmental political economy (for example, Bechtel and Urpelainen 2015), in the appendix, a preliminary analysis suggests that our main argument generalizes if there are complementarities, so when o_i puts more effort into TCG, the marginal benefit o_j gets from investing in TCG increases.

We assume that *o* cannot affect policy in the rest of the world directly. If it can do so at all, it does so indirectly through its transnational governance activities—for instance, by helping to "boomerang" back global civil society's views on the government of one of its transnational partners (Keck and Sikkink 1998). This is an idealization because groups can and do affect policy outside their domestic system, even if costs are typically higher. Our central arguments generalize if we relax this assumption, however.

If *o* expends t units of resource on transnational activity, its involvement is t/τ, $\tau > 0$. One factor affecting the efficiency of such activity is transaction costs with organizations in other jurisdictions, τ. As these go up, we expect τ to increase.

Organization *o* faces a resource constraint:

$$l + t \leq r$$

Using dotted lines, Figure 1 shows *o*'s feasibility frontier in (p, t) space for three different levels of current domestic policy: p_e', p_e'', and p_e'''. Organization *o* gets p_e units of public policy even if it expends no resources on lobbying. It can increase the level of public policy up to $p_e + r/\pi$ by expending all its resources on lobbying.[9] On the other hand, if it expends nothing on lobbying, it can afford r/τ units of transnational activity. The

---

[9] As we assume that *o* cannot affect the level of p_Σ, it would be irrational to spend resources on lobbying outside its jurisdiction.

downward sloping portion of the feasibility frontier has slope $-\pi/\tau$. As p_e increases, the frontier expands outward, as shown.

Organization o has a resource income r. However, this is not its only source. In formal terms, p_e is analogous to a portion of consumer income that must be spent and, moreover, must be spent on one particular good. As o's "income" (in this sense) goes up, its optimal mix of domestic lobbying and building transnational governance will change. As in standard consumer theory, optima are points of tangency between the feasibility frontier and indifference curves. We make the further assumption that both transnational action and domestic policy are normal goods, with positive income elasticity of demand. Then as o's "income" from existing domestic policy goes up, it chooses more transnational action, as shown in Figure 1: As domestic policy increases from p_e' through p_e'' to p_e''', o's transnational activity goes up from t' through t" to t'". Because o has fixed *disposable* income r, all of which it spends, domestic lobbying goes down from $(r - t'/\tau)$, through $(r - t''/\tau)$ to $(r - t'''/\tau)$.[10]

Because this is a critical assumption in our model, it is worth pausing to think about why the feasibility frontier could expand outwards with the current level of domestic policy, p_e. First, this would be so if domestic legislation can partially substitute for international governance *and* there is some degree of institutional "stickiness" in policy. If organizations had continually to defend the status-quo level of regulation, they would be unable to "bank" on it when deploying their resources elsewhere. However, we think that it is generally the case that it is harder to change the legislative equilibrium than to defend a status-quo policy once it is in place, as theories of punctuated equilibria in policymaking suggest (Baumgartner and Jones 1993; Jones and Baumgartner 2005). While there are examples of governments rolling back climate change regulation, we do not think this is common so far.

Moreover, domestic legislation may free resources in less obvious ways, too. From the perspective of new institutional economics, the transaction costs of investing in a common language, exchange of information, and trust are crucial to explaining the form taken by institutions. Applying this insight to transnational advocacy coalitions, Prakash and Gugerty (2010) argue that they will emerge in areas where there is considerable uncertainty and high costs to learning, so that up-front investment costs are high. Although domestic legislation may not *directly* substitute for transnational governance, it may reduce transaction costs for organizations under its jurisdiction—for instance, by providing a common perceptual frame and a degree of trust *at the domestic level* between organizations from the country concerned that helps when they get involved in a *transnational* initiative.

---

[10] Note that o still enjoys a higher level of domestic policy the greater its "income" (consistent with policy being a normal good), even though it lobbies less.

Figure 2 illustrates the effect of changing the marginal rate of substitution, other things equal. As transnational governance becomes more important to the organization, indifference curves become flatter (I2 instead of I1), and the organization chooses more transnational activity (t" instead of t') and less lobbying. For instance, an international NGO might have the flatter curve I2 compared with a local politician more concerned with domestic politics.

Figure 3 illustrates the effect of increasing the price of domestic lobbying, π, other things equal. The maximum domestic policy that can be attained falls, and the sloping portion of the budget constraint becomes steeper. The price of domestic lobbying might go up if, for example, the size of the domestic carbon lobby was large, as is the case in the United States and Russia. As policy is a normal good, the organization carries out less lobbying, resulting in a lower level of domestic policy. The effect on transnational action is indeterminate: The relative price of lobbying increases, encouraging more transnational activity (the substitution effect), but the increased price of

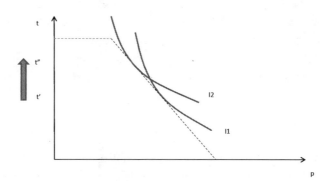

Figure 2. The effect of increasing emphasis on transnational issues in the utility function.

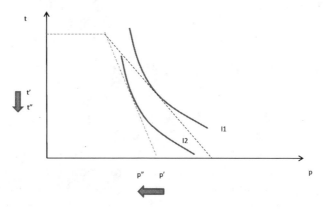

Figure 3. The effect of increasing the price of domestic lobbying.

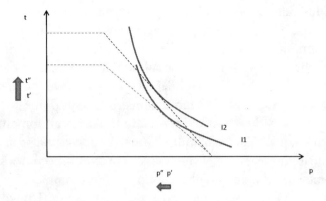

Figure 4. The effect of decreasing the price of transnational action.

lobbying reduces o's income, which tends to reduce transnational activity (the income effect); the sum of these effects could be positive or negative.[11]

Figure 4 illustrates the effect of *decreasing* the price of transnational action, τ, other things equal. For instance, such action may be less costly for an NGO already heavily involved at the international level than for a city that has largely operated at the domestic level to date. This time more transnational action is chosen in equilibrium, but the effect on domestic lobbying is also indeterminate.

In summary, our key theoretical expectations at the organizational level of analysis can be summarized as follows:

1. The greater the level of current national policy output, the more effort o will put into creating transnational ties, other things equal;
2. The greater the priority o puts on transnational payoffs, the more effort it will put into creating transnational ties, other things equal;
3. The lower the transaction costs for dealing outside its national base, the more effort o will put into creating transnational ties, other things equal.

We return to these points in our development of hypotheses.

From the individual organization to the state-dyadic level: Weakest links

Now we move from the microlevel of the incentives facing individual transnational agents to the national and dyadic levels at which ties between countries exist. The tie between countries i and j is strengthened when an organization from i and an organization from j both join an arrangement. Thus we focus on the organization with the smaller incentive to join. Note

---

[11] In Figure 3 the income effect predominates, and transnational action decreases.

that the patterns of domestic incentives we focus on are common to all organizations in a particular country.

Our dependent variable is the number of transnational links between countries i and j in the transnational governance network, that is, the number of arrangements that have at least one organization in i and at least one organization in j as a member. To use terminology from network theory, we model the value of the edge between i and j in a nondirected graph representing co-affiliation (Wasserman and Faust 1994). In modelling this, we use a weakest-link argument.

An arrangement links i and j only if it includes at least one organization from each country. First, a link could be forged when organizations from i and j agree with others to initiate an arrangement. No link is created between i and j if either organization prefers not to go ahead.[12] The probability of a potential co-affiliation tie *increases* as the incentives of the organization most loath to go ahead in i and j *increase*. Second, an organization o from j, say, may or may not decide to join an existing organization. Again, what governs whether a link is forged between i and j is how loath o is to join. In developing testable implications, we focus on national-level factors governing this, rather than the idiosyncratic ones characterizing particular organizations, which are difficult to capture empirically. Thus:

H1: *The value of the transnational link between* i *and* j *will increase with the level of development of national policy in the member of the dyad with the least-developed national policy to combat climate change (in line with point 1 in the summary of the previous section).*

A strong domestic environmental constituency correlates positively and significantly with national participation in public-private partnerships for sustainability (Andonova 2014). We assume that environmental NGOs have a strong support constituency for international action; hence they place considerable emphasis on transnational payoffs. In addition, pressure from environmental NGOs may increase the incentives of other organizations like cities to become involved in transnational arrangement (Dolšak and Prakash 2017). Then:

H2: *The value of the transnational link between* i *and* j *should increase with the number of environmental NGOs in the member of the dyad with the lowest number of environmental NGOs (in line with previous point 2).*

---

[12] Negotiations in relation to the same arrangement could continue between other dyads, but even if they succeed, no link is created between o_i and o_j.

Although, consistent with the emphasis of this special issue, our main focus is on domestic politics, international factors enter via transaction costs. These should go up with the geographical distance between i and j. We also assume that transaction costs for negotiating transnational arrangements are lowered by trade ties between i and j. In line with classic liberal arguments, Dorussen and Ward (2010) find that conflict between countries falls with both direct and indirect ties in the trade network, the importance of indirect ties, especially, suggesting that this partly relates to information flows. If organizations know more about each other's societies and values, it should be easier to reach agreement. So (in line with previous point 3):

H3: *The value of the transnational link between* i *and* j *should decrease with the distance between them, and*

H4: *The value of the transnational link between* i *and* j *should increase with dyadic trade between* i *and* j.

Data

Shared TCGs

Our dependent variable is the shared number of TCGs between two countries during the 1990 and 2013 period. We use data discussed in Roger et al. (2017). We exclude "orchestrated" transnational climate governance arrangements where a state or IGO has played an important role. The data give starting dates and ending dates for arrangements, from 1990 onwards. Most came into operation after 2000. All but about 10% were still extant in 2013. However, the data set does not provide the time a country joined and/or left a TCG but only whether it was part of TCG during the period 1990 onwards. As it is impossible for us to create yearly cross-sections, we treat the data as a single cross-section. We then use the country-level data to calculate a co-affiliation network where the value of the edge between country i and country j is the number of arrangements that came into operation between 1990 and 2013 having one or more member organizations in both i and j.

Figure 5 is a visual representation of the network. The closer countries are in the figure, the more ties there are between them, and the larger the font size used for a county's acronym, the more arrangements it has entered in total.[13] The figure brings out the fact that ties are predominantly between rich developed countries themselves and between rich developed countries and newly emerging economies like China, India,

---

[13]For clarity, we do not draw edges for values ≤ 5. Many countries are not involved in global TCG networks.

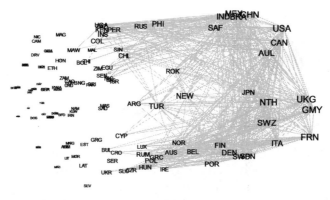

Figure 5. The transnational governance network between countries.

and Brazil. Moreover, there is clustering such as a large European bloc in the lower right; a Scandinavian bloc to the right of them; a United States, Canada, and Australia bloc; and a China, India, Brazil, Mexico, and South Africa bloc. Note that there are 135 countries in this figure, but only 70 of them are included in the latent space model analysis because of missing data on the right-hand side variables.[14] Table A5 of the appendix lists the countries, their acronyms, and whether they are included in the empirical analysis.

Key explanatory variables

Four salient factors affect the chances of a link existing between two countries via TCG: (1–3) the shared number of TCGs between two countries should increase with the level of development of national policy, the number of domestic environmental NGOs, and the density of trade between the two countries; (4) it should decrease with the distance between the two countries. Following the previous discussion, we use the weakest link approach to create the dyadic version of these variables.

Our measure of national policy is drawn from the IEA/IRENA global renewable energy policies and measures database.[15] This gives information on national policies under the following broad headings: economic instruments, information and education, policy support, regulatory instruments, research and development, and voluntary approaches. The date each policy came into force and ended is given. Our base measure of national policy, *domestic legislation*, is the number of listed policies and measures that were in force at some time during the period 1990–2013. For dyad i, j we take the lower of the national values. Other empirical studies of TCG have used a

---

[14]The variable most responsible for this is the domestic legislation variable: Only about 100 countries are included in the data set.
[15]See http://www.iea.org/policiesandmeasures/renewableenergy/.

general Environmental Performance Index (Andonova et al. 2014; Hsueh 2017) or particulate air pollution (Andonova et al. 2014) as proxies for national policy on climate change. Our measure is more closely related to climate change, although it does not directly capture carbon taxes (Ward and Cao 2012) or energy conservation policy.[16]

We measure the number of environmental NGOs (*green NGOs*) by the average number of environmental NGOs registered in a country with the International Union for Conservation of Nature (IUCN) between 1990 and 2006 (Bernauer, Böhmelt, and Koubi 2013). We also take the lower of the national values. To capture general trade network ties between countries, we started with Gleditsch's (2002) trade data, taking the average level of bilateral trade measured in real terms for the period 1990 to 2000. Because of missing values in the bilateral trade data, we then estimated a gravity model of trade, calibrated using Gleditsch's data, and used this to create a proxy for total dyadic trade, *trade proxy*.[17] For the effects of distance in geography, we use Gleditsch and Ward's (2001) minimum distance data (*distance*). This records the shortest distance between points on the outer boundaries for two polities, as long as the shortest distance is less than 950 kilometers.

Control variables[18]

Although our theory predicts that the size of the counterlobby will reduce the amount of domestic lobbying by an organization (previous point 3), it suggests that the effects on transnational involvement are indeterminate. Nevertheless, the theory leads us to expect some effect, so it is important to control for this possibility. A number of factors may be cited that could increase the power of the counterlobby. For instance, it is likely to go up as the number of domestic veto players increase because this increases the chances that one veto will be opposed to further domestic legislation, increasing its price. However, specifically we contend that the domestic fossil fuel production industry is likely to be opposed. Hence our measure of the size of the counterlobby against extending national policy is *fossil fuel production*—a country's oil, gas, and coal production per capita, measured

---

[16] Adopted policies could be numerous but not particularly strong. One reason is that energy-intensive groups might be able to block a strong policy by agreeing to a number of less-significant policies. Ideally, one should code the strength of each domestic policy, but this is hard to operationalize across countries. A country's environmental treaty commitment often strongly correlates with its domestic efforts (Cao and Prakash 2012); green taxes are can be considered a strong policy because they often affect energy-intensive sectors directly. Our domestic policy variable gains some credibility from correlating with the total number of environmental treaties variable at 0.49 and with per capita green taxes variable at 0.24.

[17] A gravity model specifies that dyadic trade increases with the size of each economy and decreases with the distance between them. For an application to international conflict, see Hegre, Oneal, and Russett (2010). Results do not change between using the actual bilateral trade and the imputed trade proxy variable.

[18] Unless we note another source, data are from the World Bank Development Indicators.

in millions of tons of oil equivalent for 1990–2005 (Bättig and Bernauer 2009). For each dyad, we take the lower of the national values.

In order to control for the effect of trade openness, we create *trade share*— the share of total trade in GDP, based on trade proxy variable, for the dyad member with the smallest share. We use two variables to control for a country's environmental conditions: *CCI* is the climate vulnerability index (Guillaumont and Simonet 2011), and *CO2 pc* is CO_2 emissions per capita. Similarly, we follow the weakest link approach to create the dyadic version of the variables.

Because many TCGs surround carbon trading, it is important to control for the size of a country's financial sector, as some financial organizations may have an interest. However, it is quite difficult to find a convincing proxy. Because of wider data availability, ultimately we used *bank deposits per GDP*—bank deposits normalized by GDP for the dyad member with the smallest financial sector.[19] Because the corporate sector's interest in environmental issues may affect a country's TCG involvement, we control for the number of ISO14001 certificates normalized by the size of GDP. As suggested by Andonova et al.'s (2014) study, we include measures of democracy and decentralization: *Polity* is the democracy score of the country with the lower-level democracy within a dyad on the 21-point Polity IV scale (Marshall, Jaggers, and Gurr 2011); *federation* is a federalism dummy variable indicating whether both countries are federal states. *EU* is a dummy variable that takes the value 1 if both countries are EU member states. Finally, we also control for the effects of *real GDP per capita* and *population* size, also following the weakest link approach. Wealth is often associated with environmental values, therefore increasing the level of environmental demand from the citizens, part of which might be translated into transnational actions. A large country, by the sheer size of its economy and connections with other countries, might have a higher chance of forming TCG ties.[20]

Latent space model

Justification

The dependent variable of this study belongs to the relational ("dyadic") data type, which consists of measurements that are made on pairs of objects or under pairs of conditions. Statistical modeling of relational data often poses a challenge to standard statistical models that assume independence among observations. Interdependencies among dyadic observations are prevalent in most relational

---

[19]The bank deposit variable might be problematic because, for instance, not all financial institutions are involved in carbon trading.

[20]We provide a detailed discussion of the effects of control variables in the appendix.

data (Wasserman and Faust 1994; Hoff, Raftery, and Handcock 2002). This concern is relevant for this study because of the possibility of autocorrelation among dyadic observations of the dependent variable: The shared numbers of transnational arrangements are likely to be highly correlated between dyads of countries. For example, if Germany shares many ties with France, and France shares many with Italy, it is very likely that Germany shares a large number of ties with Italy (unless the ties shared between Germany and France and the ties shared between France and Italy do not overlap). This kind of autocorrelation between dyadic observations is often called "third-order dependence" in the statistical literature. Ignoring third-order dependence in dyadic data and treating dyads Germany-France, France-Italy, and Germany-Italy as independent observations can cause bias in parameter estimates (Hoff 2005).

The statistical literature has proposed a series of latent space to control for autocorrelation among dyadic observations (Hoff et al. 2002; Hoff 2005). Countries' unobserved characteristics are captured by latent vectors: for example, we can use two latent vectors, z_i and z_j, to locate countries in i and j in the latent space, capturing third-order dependence (autocorrelation) in the dyadic observations of transnational ties among them. The latent space model has recently been applied in the political science literature, but it has mainly been used to model actual flows such as trade and migration (Ward and Hoff 2007; Breunig, Cao, and Luedtke 2012; Cao and Ward 2014). In this study, we use the following latent space model:

$$y_{i,j} = \beta'_d x_{i,j} + a_i + b_j + \epsilon_{i,j} + z'_i z_j$$

where $y_{i,j}$ is the number of transnational ties between country i and j,[21] $\beta'_d x_{i,j}$ represents covariates (for example, domestic legislation, green NGOs, size of domestic energy sector, and dyadic trade volume), and a_i and b_j the country random effects. $\epsilon_{i,j}$ is a normally distributed random error. Therefore, without the cross-product of latent vectors $(z'_i z_j)$, $y_{i,j} = \beta'_d x_{i,j} + a_i + b_j + \epsilon_{i,j}$ is a typical random effects regression setup with a dyadic dependent variable.

The cross-product of latent vectors of i and j—$z'_i z_j$—is added to control for third-order dependence/autocorrelation in dyadic observations of the dependent variable ($y_{i,j}$'s).[22] Note that we have not exhausted all potentially relevant variables (for example, common culture between two countries). However, the latent space model controls for these by country random effects (a_i and b_j) and the cross-product of countries' latent

---

[21]We use a Poisson link function.

[22]The dimensionality of the latent vectors can be chosen depending on the purpose of the model: If the goal is descriptive, then a choice of k = 1, 2, or 3 would allow for a simple graphical presentation; alternatively, one could examine model fit as a function of k based on the log-likelihood or use a cross-validation criterion if one is primarily concerned with predictive performance (see Hoff 2005). The goal for this article is to control for higher-order dependencies. Log-likelihoods suggest that model fits better when k = 2 or 3; to be consistent, we set k = 3. Results when setting k = 2 are in the second model specification of Table A2 of the appendix.

positions ($z'_i z_j$). The former (a_i and b_j) control for domestic variables, and the latter ($z'_i z_j$) can be considered as taking up the unexplained interactive/dyadic effects.[23]

Empirical results

Table 1 summarizes the posterior distributions of the effects of covariates and the variances of country random effects, random error, and the three latent dimensions. We include density plots to show the 95% confidence intervals (by blue vertical lines) in Figure 6. We are first of all interested in whether the four variables implied by our theories affect chances of TCG ties between countries. We *italicize* these four variables in Table 1: *Trade proxy, Distance, Domestic legislation, and Green NGOs*. Specifically, Table 1 shows the lower and upper bounds of the 95% confidence intervals, the mean, and the standard deviation of the posterior distributions. Here, we find no evidence that the level of bilateral trade affects TCG participation (H4 is not suported). The distance between countries also has no effect on their shared TCGs (H3 is not supported). These two nonresults seem to suggest that transaction costs for organizations to deal with organizations outside their national base hardly affects their TCG efforts.

Table 1. Summary of Posterior Distribution: The Effects of Covariates, Error Structures, and Latent Dimensions.

	2.5%	Mean	97.5%	σ
Constant	−2.0345	−0.4579	0.5937	0.6566
Trade proxy	−0.0009	0.0001	0.0009	0.0005
Distance	−0.0104	−0.0026	0.0052	0.0040
Domestic legislation	0.0014	0.0235	0.0432	0.0104
Energy production	−0.0179	0.0018	0.0195	0.0096
Green NGOs	0.0003	0.0103	0.0205	0.0052
Trade share	0.0147	0.0526	0.0902	0.0191
Real GDP per capita	0.0048	0.0119	0.0185	0.0034
Polity	−0.0184	0.0040	0.0245	0.0109
CCI	−1.0621	−0.1742	0.7523	0.4591
CO_2 pc	−0.0123	0.0097	0.0319	0.0116
EU	−0.0640	0.1333	0.3225	0.0963
Bank deposits per GDP	−0.1698	0.0406	0.2482	0.1078
Federation	−0.0212	0.1235	0.2641	0.0732
Population	−0.0001	0.0002	0.0005	0.0002
ISO14000 per GDP	−0.0127	0.0137	0.0381	0.0134
Variance of Country Random Effects (σ_a^2)	1.5067	4.2789	11.6405	3.0839
Error Variance (σ_γ^2)	0.0059	0.0083	0.0112	0.0013
Variance of Latent Dimensions 1 (σ_{z1}^2)	0.2630	0.3914	0.5882	0.0836
Variance of Latent Dimensions 2 (σ_{z2}^2)	0.0228	0.0630	0.1427	0.0329
Variance of Latent Dimensions 3 (σ_{z3}^2)	0.0188	0.0405	0.0977	0.0195
Log Likelihood (L-L)	−2979.10	−2950.17	−2918.43	15.53

[23]The latent positions and the latent space model are estimated by Bayesian Markov chain Monte Carlo. Empirical Bayes priors are used.

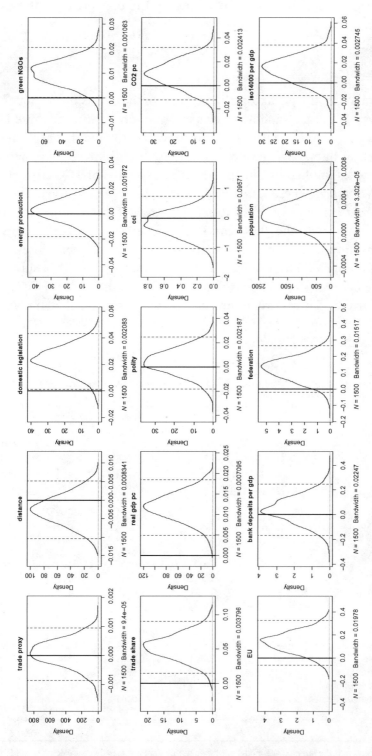

Figure 6. Density plots of posterior distributions of the effects of 15 covariates. Note we indicate the 95% confidence intervals by dashed vertical lines and add solid vertical lines to indicate zeros. One way to evaluate the statistical significance level is whether the 95% confidence intervals bounded blue vertical lines include zero or not.

On the other hand, we find that domestic legislations and domestic green NGOs are both positively associated with shared TCGs between countries (H1 and H2 are supported). This confirms our central theoretical claim that TCG links between two countries increase with the level of development of national policy, and our subsidiary claim that the strength of domestic support constituency for international action matters. In terms of the substantive effects, holding all variables at their mean levels, the mean predicted TCG between any two countries is about 0.75 (mean of a Poisson distribution). If we increase the value of the domestic legislation variable by one standard deviation, that is, from a mean of 2.03 to about 4.29, the mean predicted between-country TCGs increase by about 5.5% (to 0.79). Moreover, a two standard deviation increase in the domestic legislation variable increases the mean predicted between-country TCGs by about 11%. The substantive effect of the domestic green NGOs variable is smaller but still not negligible: Here a one standard deviation increase from the mean increases the mean predicted TCGs by about 3.4% and a two standard deviation increase by about 7%.[24]

In addition to the aforementioned four variables, we include a number of controls. Looking at Table 1 and Figure 6, few of them matter for TCG connections between countries. However, we do find that countries with a higher level of trade to GDP share (*trade openness*) are associated with more links, suggesting that countries that are more open economically also have organizations more proactive in relation to building transnational climate governance. Moreover, we also find that *real GDP per capita* matters as wealthier countries are associated with higher number of links.

The size of the counterlobby is of particular interest because our theory suggests that it should matter, although the direction of the relationship is not predicted. Looking at both Table 1 and Figure 6, we also see no evidence that the size of domestic counterlobby, measured by a country's oil, gas, and coal production per capita, affects the number of TCGs shared by two countries. In order to assess robustness, we also use another indicator: *fossil fuel energy consumption as a percentage of total energy consumption*. The results are presented among robustness checks in Table 2. Table 2 shows the lower and upper bounds of both the 90% and 95% confidence intervals. Here, we also find no association between the importance of fossil fuel energy consumption and TCG network links.

Insitutional constraints at the domestic level may inhibit both domestic and transnational action, so as a robustness check we add Henisz' (2002)

---

[24]Our predicted substantive effects are calculated only using covariates, that is, $\beta'_d x_{i,j}$ in $y_{i,j} = \beta'_d x_{i,j} + a_i + b_j + \epsilon_{i,j} + z'_i z_j$; a careful reading of Table 1 suggests that there is significant amount of variance not explained by the covariates ($\beta'_d x_{i,j}$). Actually, the variance of country Random Effects () is relatively large with the estimated mean around 4.28, suggesting that country random effects ($a_i + b_j$) explain quite a significant amount of variation in the DV.

Table 2. Latent Space Model Estimates for Shared TCGs: Robustness Checks.

	2.5%	5%	Mean	95%	97.5%	σ
Constant	−2.1547	−1.8188	−0.5569	0.4433	0.6298	0.7025
Trade proxy	−0.0009	−0.0007	0.0001	0.0008	0.0010	0.0005
Distance	−0.0107	−0.0094	−0.0028	0.0041	0.0051	0.0041
Domestic legislation	0.0033	0.0064	0.0236	0.0405	0.0432	0.0103
Fossil fuel (% of total energy)	−0.0036	−0.0030	0.0009	0.0049	0.0057	0.0023
Green NGOs	−0.0001	0.0020	0.0101	0.0179	0.0196	0.0050
Trade share	0.0137	0.0194	0.0513	0.0823	0.0886	0.0189
Real GDP per capita	0.0043	0.0054	0.0113	0.0171	0.0179	0.0035
Civil liberty	−0.0846	−0.0697	−0.0009	0.0653	0.0792	0.0414
Veto player	−0.2676	−0.1911	0.2242	0.6015	0.6898	0.2434
CCI	−1.0834	−0.9495	−0.1877	0.5300	0.6873	0.4525
CO2 pc	−0.0137	−0.0099	0.0087	0.0274	0.0302	0.0114
EU	−0.0587	−0.0207	0.1377	0.2894	0.3190	0.0939
Bank deposits per GDP	−0.1872	−0.1383	0.0386	0.2196	0.2424	0.1101
Federation	−0.0165	0.0016	0.1185	0.2324	0.2488	0.0714
Population	−0.0001	−0.0001	0.0002	0.0005	0.0005	0.0002
ISO14000 per GDP	−0.0140	−0.0087	0.0128	0.0349	0.0399	0.0134
Variance of Country Random Effects (σ_a^2)	1.5460	1.6584	4.3811	10.7956	12.2195	3.2100
Error Variance (σ_y^2)	0.0060	0.0062	0.0083	0.0107	0.0113	0.0014
Variance of Latent Dimensions 1 (σ_{z1}^2)	0.2604	0.2771	0.3900	0.5307	0.5663	0.0785
Variance of Latent Dimensions 2 (σ_{z2}^2)	0.0231	0.0256	0.0572	0.1154	0.1317	0.0290
Variance of Latent Dimensions 3 (σ_{z3}^2)	0.0198	0.0220	0.0469	0.1043	0.1227	0.0259
Log Likelihood (L-L)	−2977.67	−2974.14	−2950.89	−2924.94	−2920.96	14.89

widely used measure of domestic *veto players*.[25] We substitute a specific measure of *civil liberties* for our more general measure of democracy (*polity*), as freedom of expression and association may be more crucial for the green lobby than free elections in which green parties have little success.[26] Interestingly, we find neither of these variables affects TCGs links, even at lower levels of significance. In Table 2, H1 is still supported, but we do find that the *green NGO* variable is now only significant at the 90% level, so support for H2 is somewhat weaker.

Conclusions

Our theory suggests that, dependent on characteristics of the weakest link in the dyad, the number of network ties between two countries should increase with domestic legislation (H1), the number of domestic environmental NGOs (H2), and the density of trade between the two countries (H4). It should decrease with the distance between the two countries (H3). We find that H1 and (somewhat more weakly) H2 are supported. Few other domestic covariates are significant, though ties are greater if the

---

[25]We use the country scores averaged over the 1990 and 2004 period.
[26]Civil liberties allow for the freedoms of expression and belief, associational and organizational rights, rule of law, and personal autonomy without interference from the state. Data are provided by the Freedom House. Countries are graded between 1 (*most free*) and 7 (*least free*). We used the country scores averaged over 1990–2008.

weakest link is richer and a more open economy. Neither vulnerability to climate change nor CO_2 production per capita matters, so ties appear not to be driven by the seriousness of climate change as an issue for the weakest link. While ties appear to be promoted by a powerful domestic green lobby (H2), there is no evidence that a bigger financial sector (that might benefit from carbon trading) or more firms adopting voluntary environmental management standards matter. Moreover, there is no evidence that the size of the carbon counterlobby matters. While it is gratifying that we find the anticipated effects of domestic legislation using a more direct indicator, there is clearly considerably more work to do in developing theory.

Our approach could be developed in a number of ways. We highlight that involvement in TCG is linked with the ability to exert pressure, so that domestic lobbying relates to international governance. Because of this, domestic institutional variables found to be important in the comparative political economy literature should relate to TCG: majoritarian versus proportional representation, presidential versus parliamentary, and the nature of the party system (Persson and Tabellini 2005) or corporatism (Scruggs 2003). We argue that transnational ties do more than link the organizations directly involved. They are conduits through which information can flow between countries, linking organizations not directly involved in TCG. As such, they present the possibility of diffusion of policy and learning. In further research, the TCG network discussed in this article could be used to study policy diffusion by employing the spatial lag methods that have recently found application in the international environmental politics literature (Ward and Cao 2012). Another question suggested by our emphasis on the relation between TCG and domestic politics is whether domestic policy outputs are made more effective in terms of their impact on carbon emissions by involvement in TCG networks. For instance, does centrality in the TCG network condition effectiveness?

We find that ties are strongest between rich countries and between rich countries and some NICs (Bulkeley et al. 2014:117–133). In relation to rich countries, ties are denser between countries with developed national climate change legislation and strong environmental movements. If it turns out the network does promote information transfer and diffusion, on the one hand it tends most strongly to link countries most responsible for greenhouse gas emissions. On the other, it may not function so well to link developed countries and poorer ones that are peripheral to the network. In other words, the current network structure of the global TCG network might not help the information flows between the rich and poor countries as much as we would like to see.

While recognizing the role that states can play in forging governance arrangements over climate change, the literature sees governance by nonstate actors as an important complement to international regimes and state-led governance networks. Flexibility mechanisms under the Kyoto Protocol encourage the involvement of a range of nonstate actors, and the weakness of the regime encourages the formation of "coalitions of the willing" from "outside" the regime (Andonova et al. 2007:4). On the other hand, there are serious concerns about weak governance of carbon markets that have emerged under the Kyoto Protocol (Newell and Paterson 2010:141–160) and about the need to develop new accountability mechanisms (Keohane 2006). Different forms of accountability mechanisms (Bäckstrand 2008) and different bases of legitimacy (Bulkeley et al. 2014:134–157) may be appropriate for different sorts of TCG arrangements, and some accountability mechanisms could involve corporations or governments, rather than civil society or citizens as a whole. However, Lidskog and Elander (2010) argue that addressing climate change in a democratic and efficient manner requires greater integration between the climate change regime, built by states, and TCG. We suggest this implies greater grass-roots and citizen involvement. De Búrca, Keohane, and Sabel (2014; see also Stevenson and Dryzek 2012) propose "global experimentalist governance," which implies continual review of both international and transnational governance through a deliberative and inclusive process reaching down to citizens at the grass-roots level, facilitating learning and reflection on the overall process of governance. In such a conception, adequate flows of information are crucial: Otherwise, justification of practices through deliberation cannot function in a satisfactory manner. When a country is peripheral to the network we focus on, its government and citizens will receive relatively little information compared to those from a country central to the network. From this perspective transnational climate change governance is not open enough to deliberative justification—and it is certainly not open enough to justification to poor citizens in poor countries. The emergent network we study tends to exclude poor countries, and because of this, TCG is less shaped by the preferences of their citizens. Therefore TCG may be less responsive to the very people who are most likely to suffer the negative consequences of climate change.

References

Abbott, Kenneth W. (2012) The Transnational Regime Complex for Climate Change. *Environment and Planning C: Government and Policy* 30(4):571–590.

Andonova, Liliana B. (2014) Boomerangs to Partnerships? Explaining State Participation in Transnational Partnerships for Sustainability. *Comparative Political Studies* 47(3):481–515.

Andonova, Liliana B., Michele M. Betsill, and Harriet Bulkeley. (2007) Transnational Climate Change Governance. Paper Presented at the Amsterdam Conference on the Human Dimensions of Global Environmental Change, Amsterdam, May 24–26.

Andonova, Liliana B., Michele M. Betsill, and Harriet Bulkeley. (2009) Transnational Climate Governance. *Global Environmental Politics* 9(2):52–73.

Andonova, Liliana B., Thomas Hale, and Charles Roger. (2014) How Do Domestic Politics Condition Participation in Transnational Climate Governance? Paper Presented at the Political Economy of International Organizations Conference, Princeton, NJ, January 16–18.

Bäckstrand, Karin. (2008) Accountability of Networked Climate Governance: The Rise of Transnational Climate Partnerships. *Global Environmental Politics* 8(3):74–102.

Bättig, Michèle B., and Thomas Bernauer. (2009) National Institutions and Global Public Goods: Are Democracies More Cooperative in Climate Change Policy? *International Organization* 63(2):281–308.

Baumgartner, Frank R., and Bryan D. Jones. (1993) *Agendas and Instability in American Politics*. Chicago: University of Chicago Press.

Bechtel, Michael M., and Johannes Urpelainen. (2015) All Policies Are Glocal: International Environmental Policy Making with Strategic Subnational Governments. *British Journal of Political Science* 45(3):559–582.

Bernauer, Thomas, Tobias Böhmelt, and Vally Koubi. (2013) Is There a Democracy-Civil Society Paradox in Global Environmental Governance? *Global Environmental Politics* 13(1):88–107.

Besley, Tim, and Anne Case. (1995) Incumbent Behavior: Vote Seeking, Tax Setting and Yardstick Competition. *American Economic Review* 85(1):25–45.

Böhmelt, Tobias and Jürg Vollenweider. (2015) Information Flows and Social Capital through Linkages: The Effectiveness of the CLRTAP Network. *International Environmental Agreements* 15(2):105–123.

Breunig, Christian, Xun Cao, and Adam Luedtke. (2012) Global Migration and Political Regime Type: A Democratic Disadvantage. *British Journal of Political Science* 42(4):825–854.

Bulkeley, Harriet. (2010) Cities and the Governing of Climate Change. *Annual Review of Environment and Resources* 35:229–254.

Bulkeley, Harriet, Liliana B. Andonova, Michele M. Betsill, Thomas Hale, Matthew J. Hoffmann, Peter Newell, Matthew Paterson, Charles Roger, and Stacy D. Vandeveer. (2014) *Transnational Climate Governance*. Cambridge: Cambridge University Press.

Cao, Xun, and Aseem Prakash. (2010) Trade Competition and Domestic Pollution: A Panel Study, 1980–2003. *International Organization* 64(3):481–503.

Cao, Xun, and Aseem Prakash. (2012) Trade Competition and Environmental Regulations: Domestic Political Constraints and Issue Visibility. *Journal of Politics* 74(1):66–82.

Cao, Xun, and Michael D. Ward. (2014) Do Democracies Attract Portfolio Investment? *International Interactions* 40(2):216–245.

De Búrca, Gráinne, Robert O. Keohane, and Charles Sabel. (2014) Global Experimentalist Governance. *British Journal of Political Science* 44(3):477–486.

Dixon, William J. (1993) Democracy and the Management of International Conflict. *Journal of Conflict Resolution* 37(1):42–68.

Dolšak, Nives, and Aseem Prakash. (2017) Join the Club: How Domestic NGOs Induce Participation in the Covenant of Mayors Program. *International Interactions* 43(1):26–47.

Dorussen, Han, and Hugh Ward. (2010) Trade Links and the Kantian Peace: A Network-Theoretic Approach to Communication, Inter-Cultural Understanding, and Conflict. *Journal of Peace Research* 47(1):29–42.

Edwards, Bob, and John D. McCarthy. (2004) Resources and Social Movement Mobilization. In *The Blackwell Companion to Social Movements*, edited by David A. Snow, Sarah A. Soule, and Hanspeter Kriesi. Oxford: Blackwell.

Gleditsch, Kristian S. (2002) Expanded Trade and GDP Data. *Journal of Conflict Resolution* 46(5):712–724.

Gleditsch, Kristian S., and Michael D. Ward. (2001) Measuring Space: A Minimum-Distance Database and Applications to International Studies. *Journal of Peace Research* 38(6):739–758.

Green, Jessica. F. (2013) Order out of Chaos: Public and Private Rules for Managing Carbon. *Global Environmental Politics* 13(2):1–25.

Green, Jessica F. (2014) *Rethinking Private Authority: Agents and Entrepreneurs in Global Environmental Governance*. Princeton: Princeton University Press.

Green, Jessica F. (2017) Blurred Lines: Why Do States Recognize Private Carbon Standards? *International Interactions* 43(1):103–128.

Grundig, Frank, and Hugh Ward. (2015) Structural Group Leadership and Regime Effectiveness. *Political Studies* 63(1):221–239.

Guillaumont, Patrick, and Catherine Simonet. (2011) Data from "Building an Index of Physical Vulnerability to Climate Change." Fondation pour les études et recherches sur le développement international. Retrieved from: http://www.ferdi.fr/en/indicator/index-structural-vulnerability-climate-change

Hafner-Burton, Emilie M., Miles Kahler, and Alexander H. Montgomery. (2009) Network Analysis for International Relations. *International Organization* 63(3):559–592.

Hale, Thomas, and Charles Roger. (2014) Orchestration and Transnational Climate Governance. *Review of International Organizations* 9(1):59–82.

Hegre, Håvard, John R. Oneal, and Bruce Russett. (2010) Trade Does Promote Peace: New Simultaneous Estimates of the Reciprocal Effects of Trade and Conflict. *Journal of Peace Research* 47(6):763–774.

Henisz, Witold J. (2002) The Institutional Environment for Infrastructure Investment. *Industrial and Corporate Change* 11(2):355–389.

Hirshleifer, Jack. (1983) From Weakest-Link to Best-Shot: The Voluntary Provision of Public Goods. *Public Choice* 41(3):371–386.

Hoff, Peter D. (2005) Bilinear Mixed Effects Models for Dyadic Data. *Journal of the American Statistical Association* 100(2):286–295.

Hoff, Peter D., Adrian E. Raftery, and Mark S. Handcock. (2002) Latent Space Approaches to Social Network Analysis. *Journal of the American Statistical Association* 97(469):1090–1098.

Holzinger, Katharina, Christoph Knill, and Thomas Sommerer. (2008) Environmental Policy Convergence: The Impact of International Harmonization, Transnational Communication, and Regulatory Competition. *International Organization* 62(4):553–587.

Hsueh, Lily. (2017) Who Sets the Agenda in Global Climate Change? Explaining Private Actor Participation by Internal Firm-Level Factors and Dynamics. *International Interactions* 43(1):48–75.

Jackson, Matthew O. (2008) *Social and Economic Networks*. Princeton, NJ: Princeton University Press.

Jones, Bryan D., and Frank R. Baumgartner. (2005) *The Politics of Attention: How Government Prioritizes Problems*. Chicago: University of Chicago Press.

Kalbhenn, Anna. (2011) Liberal Peace and Shared Resources—A Fair-Weather Phenomenon? *Journal of Peace Research* 48(6):715–735.

Keck, Margaret E., and Kathryn Sikkink. (1998) *Activists beyond Borders: Advocacy Networks in International Politics*. Ithaca, NY: Cornell University Press.

Keohane, Robert O. (2006) Accountability in World Politics. *Scandinavian Political Studies* 29(2):75–87.

Keohane, Robert O., and David G. Victor. (2011) The Regime Complex for Climate Change. *Perspectives on Politics* 9(1):7–23.

Lee, Taedong, and Susan van de Meene. (2012) Who Teaches and Who Learns? Policy Learning through the C40 Cities Climate Network. *Policy Sciences* 45(3):199–220.

Lidskog, Rolf, and Ingemar Elander. (2010) Addressing Climate Change Democratically: Multi-Level Governance, Transnational Networks and Governmental Structures. *Sustainable Development* 18(1):32–41.

Marshall, Monty G., Keith Jaggers, and Ted Robert Gurr. (2011) Polity IV Project: Dataset Users' Manual. Center for Systemic Peace: Polity IV Project. Retrieved from: http://www.systemicpeace.org/polity/polity4.htm

Newell, Peter, and Matthew Paterson. (2010) *Climate Capitalism: Global Warming and the Transformation of the Global Economy*. Cambridge: Cambridge University Press.

Oneal, John R., and Bruce Russett. (1997) The Classical Liberals were Right. *International Studies Quarterly* 41(4):267–293.

Ostrom, Elinor. (2012) Nested Externalities and Polycentric Institutions: Must We Wait For Global Solutions to Climate Change before Taking Actions at Other Scales? *Economic Theory* 49(2):353–369.

Persson, Torsten, and Guido Tabellini. (2005) *The Economic Effects of Constitutions*. Cambridge, MA: The MIT Press.

Potoski, Matthew, and Aseem Prakash. (2005) Green Clubs and Voluntary Governance: ISO 14001 and Firms' Regulatory Compliance. *American Journal of Political Science* 49(2):235–248.

Prakash, Aseem, and Mary Kay Gugerty. (2010) Advocacy Organizations and Collective Action: An Introduction. In *Advocacy Organizations and Collective Action*, edited by Assem Prakash and Mary Kay Gugerty. New York: Cambridge University Press.

Roger, Charles, Thomas Hale, and Liliana B. Andonova. (2017) Domestic Politics and Climate Governance. *International Interactions* 43(1):1–25.

Schäferhoff, Marco, Sabine Campe, and Christopher Kaan. (2009) Transnational Public-Private Partnerships in International Relations: Making Sense of Concepts, Research Frameworks, and Results. *International Studies Review* 11(4):451–474.

Schaffer, Lena M., and Thomas Bernauer. (2014) Explaining the Adoption of Renewable Energy Policies. *Energy Policy* 68:15–27.

Scruggs, Lyle. (2003) *Sustaining Abundance: Environmental Performance in Industrial Democracies*. Cambridge: Cambridge University Press.

Simmons, Beth, Frank Dobbin, and Geoffrey Garrett. (2006) Introduction: The International Diffusion of Liberalism. *International Organization* 60(4):781–810.

Spilker, Gabriele. (2012) Helpful Organizations: Membership in Inter-Governmental Organizations and Environmental Quality in Developing Countries. *British Journal of Political Science* 42(2):345–370.

Stevenson, Hayley, and John S. Dryzek. (2012) The Discursive Democratisation of Global Climate Governance. *Environmental Politics* 21(2):189–210.

Vogel, David. (1995) *Trading up: Consumer and Environmental Regulation in a Global Economy*. Cambridge: Harvard University Press.

Ward, Hugh. (2006) International Linkage and Environmental Sustainability: The Effectiveness of the Regime Network. *Journal of Peace Research* 43(2):149–166.

Ward, Hugh, and Xun Cao. (2012) Domestic and International Influences on Green Taxation. *Comparative Political Studies* 45(4):1075–1103.

Ward, Michael D., and Peter D. Hoff. (2007) Persistent Patterns of International Commerce. *Journal of Peace Research* 44(2):157–175.

Ward, Michael D., Katherine Stovel, and Audrey Sacks. (2011) Network Analysis and Political Science. *Annual Review of Political Science* 14:245–264.

Wasserman, Stanley, and Katherine Faust. (1994) *Social Network Analysis: Methods and Applications*. Cambridge: Cambridge University Press.

Widerberg, Oscar. (2014) Mapping Institutions and Actors in Global Climate Governance: A Network Approach. Working Paper. Institute for Environmental Studies (IVM), VU University Amsterdam.

World Economic Forum. (2009) Slimcity: A Cross-Industry, Public-Private Initiative on Urban Sustainability. Available at http://www.weforum.org/pdf/ip/ec/SlimCity.pdf.

Appendix

1. Generalising the theoretical model to allow for strategic rationality

We developed our argument that an increase in domestic legislation increases the amount of resources an organization will allocate to transnational activity on the assumption of parametric rationality. Specifically, organisations do not take into account possible reactions by other organizations to its choice of transnational activity level. What if organisations take into account the possibility that organizations in other countries react to its choice? We illustrate that the key issue is whether other organizations react by increasing or by decreasing transnational effort. If they react by increasing effort and some modelling assumptions hold, then our argument generalizes.

Because we are interested in dyadic ties, we consider the interaction between two organizations that might be part of a larger arrangement. Consider organizations o_1 and o_2. Generalize utility functions so that each organization cares about the other's level of transnational effort, so they take the form[1]

$$U_1(p_1, t_1, t_2) \text{ and } U_2(p_2, t_1, t_2)$$

This time o_i's chosen level of effort depends on t_j; so it has a reaction function $R_i(p_i, t_j)$. Equilibria occur where reaction functions cross – see figure 1.[2] As drawn, $R_1(p_1, t_2)$ is steeper in the vicinity of the equilibrium than $R_2(p_2, t_1)$. Under this condition the equilibrium is stable: small deviations from equilibrium generate action-reaction sequences leading back to it.[3] We will assume stable equilibria, because they are more plausible. Multiple equilibria can occur, but we will assume that the equilibrium is unique.

---

[1] For notational convenience we ignore the dependence of utility functions on other organisations actions and policy in the rest of the world.
[2] Reaction functions need not be linear.
[3] With the linear reaction functions shown the equilibrium is globally stable.

The critical issue is how o_1 and o_2 react to changes in each other's level of transnational activity. Consider figure A1. Here we assume that reaction functions are increasing in the level of activity of the other organization. In many instances we find this plausible, because other organizations' actions are *strategic complements*. The gains to be made for ENGOs and local or city governments from getting involved in transnational networks go up the more effort others put in: more information is available; in the case of standards, a more widely recognised standard with more effort put into compliance is of greater benefit; etc. If the marginal gains from investing in transnational activity go up due to o_2 putting in more effort, o_1 will rationally invest more.

Now suppose the level of domestic legislation o_1 faces goes up from p_1 to p_1'. For exactly the same reasons suggested in text in the parametric case (illustrated in figure 1), o_1 will wish to allocate more to transnational activity for any given level of t_2, i.e. o_1's reaction function shift to the right to $R_1(p_1', t_2)$. Because we deal with stable equilibria and because there is strategic complementarity, in the new equilibrium both o_1 and o_2 invest more in transnational activity because of the shift from p_1 to p_1'.

Now suppose that there is a minimum level of effort that each organization must expend in equilibrium in order that the co-affiliation link is formed, respectively τ_1 and τ_2. In figure A1 in the initial equilibrium, only o_2 is willing to put enough effort in. In general the weakest link is the organization furthest from meeting the necessary minimum in an equilibrium. Given p_1, o_1 is the weakest link. However with p_1', in the second equilibrium, both o_1 and o_2 are willing to put in enough effort.[4] With unique stable equilibria and positive complementarity, it can never be the case that when domestic policy in one country increases this precludes the possibility of a link: because equilibrium transnational effort increases for both o_1 and o_2, either the change enables the constraint to be met for one or both organizations where this was not previously the case or the constraint is still not met for at least one.

In contrast figure 2 shows the situation where we assume a unique stable equilibrium where organizations react by reducing their transnational effort as that of the other organization increases. Here after an increase from p_1 to p_1', o_2's effort drop below τ_2, though o_1's effort increases so that it meets its constraint. However, we find it difficult to think of reasons why other organizations would react negatively in the assumed manner.

2. Robustness Checks

Using environmental treaties as a proxy for domestic legislations: using our key explanatory variable, domestic legislations, generates a large number of missing values and reduces the number of countries included in the analysis to 70. To increase the number of countries, we use a country's environmental treaty commitment, which often strongly correlates with its domestic efforts (Neumayer 2002; Ehrlich 2009; Cao and Prakash 2012), to replace the domestic legislation variable in robustness checks. Note that our domestic policy variable correlates with the total number environmental treaties variable at 0.49. Using this treaty variable instead of the domestic legislation variable, we are able to inrease the number of countries included from 70 to 103. Table 1 of this memo reports the empirical findings. Here, the results in Table A1 hold regarding environmental treaties (proxy for domestic legislations), green NGOs, and per capita GDP.

---

[4] In which case there is no weakest link in the sense we have defined in this appendix.

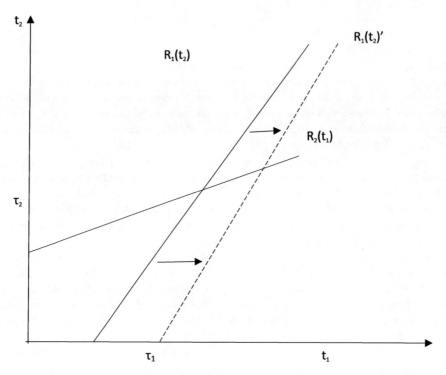

Figure A1: Effect on equilibrium of shift in domestic policy from p_1 to p_1' assuming complementarity.

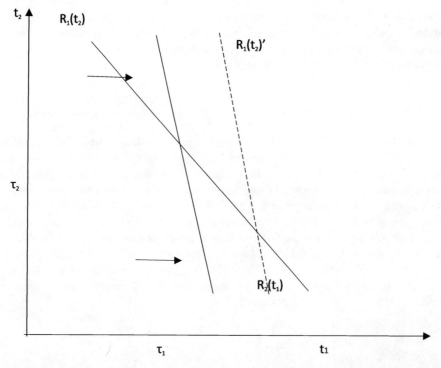

Figure A2: Effect on equilibrium of shift in domestic policy from p_1 to p_1' not assuming complementarity.

Table A1: Latent space model estimates for shared TCGs using environmental treaties as a proxy for domestic legislations.

	2.5%	Mean	97.5%	$\hat{\sigma}$
Constant	−9.5682	−6.6107	−3.8217	1.5200
Trade proxy	−0.0010	−0.0000	0.0009	0.0005
Distance	−0.0101	−0.0033	0.0034	0.0035
Environmental treaties	0.0004	0.0036	0.0062	0.0015
Green NGOs	0.0003	0.0103	0.0211	0.0054
Energy production	−0.0205	−0.0015	0.0168	0.0095
Trade share	−0.0130	0.0147	0.0388	0.0138
Real GDP per capita	0.0028	0.0097	0.0165	0.0035
Polity	−0.0284	−0.0088	0.0094	0.0099
CCI	−0.8122	−0.0866	0.6345	0.3767
CO2 pc	−0.0068	0.0170	0.0384	0.0119
EU	−0.1297	0.0695	0.2494	0.1004
Bank deposits per GDP	−0.1026	0.0889	0.2800	0.0982
Federation	−0.1324	0.0127	0.1380	0.0701
Population	−0.0002	0.0002	0.0004	0.0002
ISO14000 per GDP	−0.0139	0.0043	0.0226	0.0098
Variance of Country Random Effects (σ^2_a)	41.6879	55.2254	74.0745	7.8311
Error Variance (σ^2_y)	0.0060	0.0082	0.0110	0.0012
Variance of Latent Dimensions 1 (σ^2_{z1})	0.4229	0.5708	0.7579	0.0919
Variance of Latent Dimensions 2 (σ^2_{z2})	0.0315	0.0953	0.1601	0.0314
Variance of Latent Dimensions 3 (σ^2_{z3})	0.0191	0.0420	0.1150	0.0232
Log Likelihood (L-L)	−4391.82	−4359.05	−4332.47	15.43

Common language, similarity in regime types, and other robustness checks: Clustering of countries in Figure 5 of the paper seems to suggest that proximity in space does not correlate with transnational links in TCGs. We have experimented with additional variables to capture the costliness of transnational links: common language and dissimilarity in political regime (we define this as the absolute difference between two countries' polity scores). The results are presented in the third model specification of Table A2 in this appendix (M3: additional control variables). Neither of these additional controls is statistically significant. Note that other model specifications of Table A2 also reports results when we drop the bank deposit variable (M1: no bank deposit variable) and we set the number of latent dimensions to 2 instead of 3 (M2: k=2). In both cases, the main results do not change.

Over dispersion and a negative binomial regression: With a mean of 2.65 and standard deviation of 3.26, the count dependent variable is over dispersed to some extent. The latent space model does not provide a negative binomial or over-dispersed Poisson link function. We did experiment with estimating a simple negative binomial regression: results are reported in Table A3 of this appendix. The key difference between the negative binomial estimates and those from latent space model is that the negative binomial regression shows more statistically significant relationships. This is because a negative binomial regression treats all observations as independent from each other while the latent space model does not: in the manuscript, we have provided justification for the usage of latent space model despite the fact that a simple negative binomial model provides better empirical support for our theoretical expectations, for example, the variable *Energy production* is negative and significant in Table A3 of this appendix, therefore supporting our expectation on the effect of domestic counter lobby on TCG; we find no such effect in various latent space models we have run though.

Table A2: Latent space model estimates for shared TCGs, further robustness checks.

	M1: no bank deposit variable			M2: k=2			M3: additional control variables		
	2.5%	Mean	97.5%	2.5%	Mean	97.5%	2.5%	Mean	97.5%
Constant	−2.7615	−1.0936	0.4597	−2.0699	−0.5959	0.5849	−2.7468	−1.0496	0.4437
Trade proxy	−0.0008	0.0001	0.0010	−0.0009	0.0001	0.0010	−0.0009	0.0001	0.0010
Distance	−0.0114	−0.0028	0.0051	−0.0099	−0.0026	0.0049	−0.0106	−0.0025	0.0058
Domestic legislation	0.0011	0.0225	0.0421	0.0045	0.0240	0.0438	0.0064	0.0247	0.0431
Green NGOs	−0.0005	0.0094	0.0212	0.0007	0.0104	0.0200	0.0004	0.0100	0.0195
Fossil fuel (% of total energy)	−0.0031	0.0013	0.0061	−0.0032	0.0010	0.0055	−0.0035	0.0011	0.0057
Trade share	0.0150	0.0523	0.0896	0.0169	0.0537	0.0875	0.0135	0.0533	0.0899
Real GDP per capita	0.0050	0.0117	0.0189	0.0049	0.0114	0.0181	0.0039	0.0111	0.0176
Civil liberty	−0.0797	0.0022	0.0813	−0.0780	−0.0022	0.0898	−0.1237	−0.0209	0.0876
Veto player	−0.3163	0.1723	0.6643	−0.2632	0.2073	0.6554	−0.2600	0.2584	0.7119
CCI	−1.0128	−0.1087	0.7039	−1.1133	−0.1917	0.6892	−1.1751	−0.2589	0.6056
CO2 pc	−0.0155	0.0083	0.0312	−0.0143	0.0079	0.0315	−0.0160	0.0070	0.0300
EU	−0.0800	0.1375	0.3080	−0.0700	0.1213	0.3037	−0.0809	0.1338	0.3216
Bank deposits per GDP				−0.2084	0.0301	0.2673	−0.2020	0.0226	0.2247
Federation	−0.0218	0.1153	0.2588	−0.0205	0.1252	0.2712	−0.0247	0.1193	0.2575
Population	−0.0002	0.0002	0.0005	−0.0001	0.0002	0.0005	−0.0001	0.0002	0.0005
ISO14000 per GDP	−0.0126	0.0139	0.0377	−0.0148	0.0128	0.0422	−0.0137	0.0132	0.0385
Common language							−0.0636	0.0327	0.1319
Polity dissimilarity							−0.0084	0.0066	0.0222
Variance of Country Random Effects (σ_α^2)	3.3877	7.9516	12.8139	1.6020	4.3432	10.1398	5.5933	8.9834	14.1599
Error Variance (σ_ν^2)	0.0059	0.0083	0.0113	0.0064	0.0090	0.0124	0.0059	0.0083	0.0113
Variance of Latent Dimensions 1 (σ_{z1}^2)	0.2677	0.4018	0.5817	0.2731	0.3992	0.5887	0.2600	0.4091	0.5799
Variance of Latent Dimensions 2 (σ_{z2}^2)	0.0225	0.0607	0.1435	0.0242	0.0630	0.1382	0.0222	0.0493	0.1104
Variance of Latent Dimensions 3 (σ_{z3}^2)	0.0191	0.0442	0.1143				0.0194	0.0488	0.1221
Log Likelihood (L-L)	−2972.36	−2944.77	−2915.19	−2977.79	−2950.08	−2919.05	−2975.22	−2947.22	−2918.98

Table A3: A negative binomial estimation for shared TCGs.

	Estimate	Std. Error	z value	Pr(>|z|)
Constant	−0.2384	0.1141	−2.09	0.0367
Trade proxy	−0.0003	0.0008	−0.38	0.7023
Distance	0.0943	0.0235	4.01	0.0001
Domestic legislation	0.0762	0.0075	10.13	0.0000
Green NGOs	0.0527	0.0047	11.25	0.0000
Energy production	−11.4664	4.3490	−2.64	0.0084
Trade share	0.2384	0.0262	9.10	0.0000
Real GDP per capita	0.0125	0.0027	4.64	0.0000
Polity	0.0358	0.0032	11.03	0.0000
CCI	0.1637	0.2288	0.72	0.4745
CO2 pc	0.0074	0.0093	0.80	0.4244
EU	0.3365	0.0697	4.83	0.0000
Bank deposits per GDP	−0.0760	0.0818	−0.93	0.3527
Federation	0.5099	0.0766	6.66	0.0000
Population	0.0056	0.0003	17.66	0.0000
ISO14000 per GDP	70.0392	12.3839	5.66	0.0000
N. observations				2265
Log-likelihood				−3991.208

3. Operationalization of control variables

In the paper, because of word limits, we can't give a justification for weakest link for each control variable. We therefore give justifications in the appendix, along the lines in the table below. For variables following the weakest link approach, we took the minimum value for the dyad. When the table says smallest, it means the smaller of the two values if no missing data, or if data is missing for one country the value for the other (because variables appear to have generated using the Stata minimum collapse).

Table A4: Control variable operationalization and justifications.

Variable	Operationalization	Justification
Distance	dyadic	Not using *weakest link*; distance reduces interactions therefore lowers chances of TCG.
Energy production	Smallest value	Theory is indeterminate because of income effect and substitution effect going opposite ways when the price of lobbying goes up.
Trade share	Smallest value	Trade contacts could relate to background information that could keep transaction costs down, hence to the relative price of TCG and domestic legislation. On the other hand if a country doesn't trade much, its organizations would have less interest in carbon markets and standards (slope of indifference curves steeper in figure 2).

(*Continued*)

Table A4. Continued

Variable	Operationalization	Justification
Real GDP per capita	Smallest value	Poorer country organizations might have less interest in TCG (slope of indifference curves flatter in figure 2), so probably ok in theory terms.
Polity	Smaller	Organizations from less democratic countries could be more constrained from building ties, or less interested in international governance, so probably ok.
CCI	Smaller	Organizations from less vulnerable countries could be less interested in ties, so probably ok.
CO2 pc	Smaller	We could argue that organizations from smaller emitters are less interested in TCG; on the other hand the cost of domestic legislation could be higher with large emissions.
EU	Smaller	Probably ok, because EU action pushed climate politics domestically
Bank deposits per GDP	Smaller	If deposits proxy size of financial sector, smaller financial sector has less interest in building carbon markets through TCG, so probably ok.
Federation	Smaller	Probably ok as federal systems give more encouragement for mayors and local politicians to get into TCG
Population	Smaller	Small country; smaller organizations; harder to participate in TCG. Probably ok
ISO14000 per GDP	Smaller	If ISO1400 proxies business interest, probably ok as smaller registrations implies less business interest in TCG.

Blurred Lines: Public-Private Interactions in Carbon Regulations

Jessica F. Green

ABSTRACT
Carbon markets are flourishing around the globe, created both by governments and by nonstate actors. In this article, I investigate when and why governments choose to interact with and use private rules about carbon offsets in public regulatory arrangements. The analysis demonstrates that there is "blurring" between public and private authority, insofar that there are a multiple interactions between the two spheres. However, a closer look reveals that most of these are of a relatively weak nature, since private standards are used for voluntary rather than compliance purposes. To explain this trend, I use qualitative and quantitative analysis and find that NGOs are the main catalysts for the interaction between public and private rules. States are most likely to interact with private regulations when they have large numbers of NGOs active within their borders. In short, private authority is largely a complement to public regulatory arrangements. While previous work that suggests that private authority arises when there are gaps in public rules, the analysis here demonstrates that at the domestic level, this logic does not hold.

Why Do States Recognize Private Regulations?

In the past 15 years, carbon offsets have emerged as a new and prominent regulatory tool. In the public sphere, the Clean Development Mechanism (CDM) of the Kyoto Protocol has been the main public offset market. In the private sphere, a vibrant voluntary market has emerged, in which offsets are created using standards crafted by nonstate actors and then traded among firms and other nonstate actors. Globally, carbon markets were valued at just under US$50 billion in 2015, and this only covers 12% of global emissions (World Bank and Ecofys 2014).

These reductions in greenhouse gas emissions are used to "neutralize" emissions made elsewhere and have transformed from a distant glint in the eye of a few diplomats to a vast global market, in both the public and the private sectors. Carbon offset markets are now some of the largest and best-developed pollution

---

Color versions of one or more of the figures in the article can be found online at www.tandfonline.com/gini.

markets and will only grow in importance as states increasingly implement carbon pricing policies to address climate change.

Traditionally, these two markets have been largely separate. The CDM was created to help states meet their Kyoto targets. The voluntary market was for do-gooders, usually corporations, to atone for their carbon sins. However, the shape of the climate change regime is rapidly shifting due, in large measure, to the Paris Agreement of December 2015 and the process leading up to it. Among many other attributes, the Paris Agreement emphasizes the role of nonstate and transnational actors to help states collectively reach the goal of keeping global temperatures from rising beyond 1.5 degrees Celsius. The Paris Agreement further solidifies a pattern that has been percolating over the last few years: the blurring between public and private rules.

Both of these empirical trends—the growth in carbon markets and the new role for nonstate actors in the Paris Agreement—indicate the need to understand carbon offset markets and their interactions with national and international policy.

This article examines how the lines between public and private carbon markets are gradually eroding—though not in ways that profoundly alter the distribution of authority. Specifically, it provides the first in-depth analysis of the interaction between public and private markets at the transnational *and* national levels. Using new data and network analysis, I find that the interactions between the Kyoto and voluntary markets are growing. As domestic carbon regulations are put in place around the globe, some countries have chosen to utilize private standards in their public rules in various ways. However, these interactions are not an indication of a deep transfer of authority from states to nonstate actors. My analysis shows that interactions are driven by nonstate actors, specifically by civil society, and are rarely used for compliance with national regulations. The data illustrate that states are willing to accept private offsets in their *voluntary* carbon initiatives but seldom do so for compliance purposes. Of the 41 states[1] with policies that include offsetting provisions, only three—Switzerland, the United States, and Canada—use private rules in some capacity for compliance purposes.

These findings have mixed implications for the role of private regulation in the climate regime and domestic climate policies. Private carbon regulations are by no means replacing public power, and their peripheral role vis-à-vis domestic regulation shows that their value as a complement is also somewhat limited. Yet their relatively widespread use in voluntary public rules suggests that governments view them as a legitimate strategy in an "all of the above" approach to mitigating greenhouse gas emissions.

---

[1] This includes the 28 member states of the European Union (EU). If the EU is counted as one state (since it has a collective commitment as set forth in its Intended Nationally Determined Contribution), then the number of relevant states falls to 14. I discuss this decision further subsequently.

The article makes four important contributions with regard to regulation and transnational actors. First, using network analysis, it provides descriptive analysis of the nature of interactions between public and private authority. Second, because the universe of cases is small, I am able to disaggregate the dependent variable—interactions—into two different types. This allows for better understanding of what interactions *really* mean for climate politics at the domestic level. Third, the analysis moves beyond many of the useful, though largely untested, typologies that describe interactions by systematically analyzing various extant explanations for public-private interactions. The findings demonstrate that private rule makers' regulatory impact on national policy is limited. This suggests that the likelihood of institutionalizing private authority through public policy is low and that private rule makers should seek other avenues for effecting policy change. Finally, by shifting the analysis from the transnational to the domestic level, the findings add important nuance to previous work, which argues that private authority arises when there are gaps in public rules. The analysis here demonstrates that at the domestic level, this logic does not hold.

Public/Private Interactions: Definitions and Theory

Private authority can be understood as situations in which nonstate actors make rules or set standards that other actors in world politics adopt (Green 2014). Entrepreneurial authority can be understood as one form of private authority in which "private actors strike out on their own, serving as de facto rule makers in world politics" (Green 2014:7). For example, entrepreneurial authority occurs when an NGO or group of NGOs decides what practices constitute "sustainable fishing." These actors create rules without the explicit permission of the state and persuade others to adopt them. Since authority is a reciprocal relationship between rule maker and rule adopter, rule makers do not enjoy authority unless someone decides to follow the rules (Lake 2009; Raz 1990). Similar to entrepreneurial authority, Cashore, Auld, and Newsome (2004) have described private standard-setting as "non-state market driven" governance, which uses authority generated by the supply chain to change environmental practices. In the context of climate governance, Hoffmann (2011) refers to climate "experiments" that are engaged in rule making independent from the Kyoto process or national regulatory measures, and occur transnationally.

Figure 1 demonstrates the growth in entrepreneurial authority in the area of carbon offsets.[2] There has been a veritable explosion in private offset standards in the last 15 years. This rapid growth motivates the research question: Are these standards relevant to international and national climate policies, and if so, how?

---

[2] I describe how these data were gathered in the section on Research Design and Data.

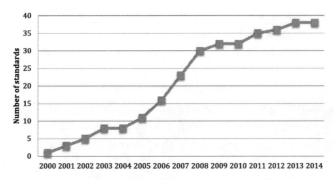

Figure 1. Growth in private regulation on carbon offsets.

An examination of the interactions between public and private offset standards provides some preliminary insights into this question.

There are a variety of explanations for the emergence of private authority. Some argue that private regulations emerge when there is a "gap" in global rules (Cashore et al. 2004) or a lack of state capacity (Borzel and Risse 2005). Others maintain that private regulations are a way for business and industry to protect their interests, through a globalized version of regulatory capture (Buthe and Mattli 2011). Still others maintain that private regulation is a strategy for nonstate actors motivated by their desire to "do good" in a way that is consonant with global norms of neoliberalism (Bernstein 2001).

Though the focus of this article is private rules' interactions rather than their emergence, it is important to note that actors likely have diverse motivations for creating these rules. While some may create regulations to create public goods, others may simply seek regulatory authority; that is, private regulations do not necessarily serve collective interests (Scott, Cafaggi, and Senden 2011). These varying interests are also reflected in the thematic focus of various private carbon standards: For instance, some focus on biodiversity, while others on improving livelihoods or the well-being of women.

Interactions are "the myriad ways in which governance actors and institutions engage with and react to one another" (Eberlein, Abbott, Black, Meidinger, and Wood 2014:12). There are a number of other scholars who view public-private interactions in similar terms. For example, Abbott and Snidal's (2009:48) work on regulatory standard setting demonstrates that "the simple view of the state as centralized, mandatory regulator is inapplicable in the transnational realm." Oberthur and Stokke (2011:4) examine institutional interactions—"situations in which one institution affects the development or performance of another institution." Some work on regime complexity also examines how public and private rules overlap (Abbott 2012; Green 2013).

These interactions can take place at multiple levels: micro, meso, or macro (Eberlein et al. 2014). At the microlevel, they occur between individuals. At the mesolevel, they occur between rule-making organizations. Rule makers may be private or public or both (Eberlein et al. 2014:8). Most broadly, at the macrolevel, interactions occur across different regulatory issue areas, such as between trade and environmental regulations. As will be discussed further, this article examines interactions at the mesolevel—primarily between public and private regulators.

Interactions can take on a number of forms. Eberlein et al. (2014) offer four categories: competition, coordination, cooptation, and chaos. When examining interactions between public and private rules, competition is unlikely, since private regulation is voluntary (Green and Auld 2016). More probable are coordination interactions, where actors emulate each other or undertake conscious coordination or division of labor, or cooptation interactions, where private rules are subsumed into public ones. In another form of cooptation, private pressure on global regulatory processes can give rise to capture (Mattli and Woods 2009). Since private standards always exist within a broader field of laws and regulations, Bartley (2011) characterizes the interaction between public and private rules as "layering." For example, private standards can require compliance with international law, go beyond compliance, or they may be de facto equivalents to public rules (Bartley 2011:525).

Other works are more sanguine, emphasizing the complementary nature of public/private interactions over time. Vogel (2005) suggests that corporate social responsibility can provide incentives for private firms to move "beyond compliance" and exceed regulatory requirements. Similarly, Cashore, Auld, Bernstein, and McDermott (2007) suggest that properly constructed, public policies can help "ratchet up" the effects of private regulations. Mayer and Gereffi (2010:19) argue similarly that private governance must be "supplemented and reinforced by public institutions" in order to be effective. Knill and Lekhmuhl (2002) acknowledge the "synergetic relationships" between public and private authority, which vary with the governance capacity of each actor. Gulbrandsen (2014) argues that state responses vary from mutually reinforcing to state reappropriation of authority, depending on the structure of the policy domain and the evolution of the issue area. Abbott, Green, and Keohane (2016) view the provision of complementary private rules as a strategy to preserve organizational autonomy. Delegation to private actors is yet another positive interaction, where states select private actors to carry out specific governance functions (Buthe 2008; Buthe and Mattli 2011; Green 2014). Others view private regulations as a realm of experimentation, where rules are set up to be regularly reviewed and revised; lessons can then be passed along to public rule makers (Sabel and Victor 2015; Sabel and Zeitlin 2010).

Hypotheses

I offer three explanations for the interactions between public and private authority. These can be roughly sorted into *intrinsic* and *extrinsic* explanations.

The intrinsic explanations posit that recognition of private authority is driven by governmental factors—their preferences and capabilities. The extrinsic explanation suggests that actors *outside* of government, including civil society and firms, are the primary reason that offset programs recognize private authority.

The first hypothesis is that recognition of private authority occurs when the government lacks capacity or the technical expertise necessary to create or enforce rules. This hypothesis is consistent with accounts of private authority that attribute its emergence to instances in which states are unable to govern—a dominant explanation in the literature. Cashore et al. (2004) argue that NGOs created private forestry standards in part to respond to states' failure to craft a multilateral forest agreement in 1992. Büthe and Mattli (2011:5) argue that the privatization of governance with respect to international technical standard setting is driven "in part, by governments' lack of requisite technical expertise, financial resources or flexibility to deal expeditiously with ever more complex ... regulatory tasks." It is also consistent with conceptualizations of limited statehood, in which states may "lack the ability to implement and enforce rules ... with regard to specific policy areas" (Krasner and Risse 2014). Note that this view does not require that the state be a "failed state," only that it is more efficient for actors *other* than the government to carry out the regulatory tasks.

This argument follows theories of delegation: Delegation is premised on specialization and the resulting division of labor. When states have insufficient capacity to create or enforce rules—that is, they do not possess adequate specialization—they delegate to those who are more expert in the area, choosing to "buy" expertise rather than "make" it in-house (Alchian and Demsetz 1972). And, as Tierney et al. note, "gains from specialization are likely to be greatest when the task to be performed is frequent, repetitive and requires specific expertise or knowledge" (Hawkins, Lake, Nielson, and Tierney 2006:14).

H1: *Governments that lack technical expertise are more likely to incorporate private rules into national policy, all else equal.*

If this hypothesis holds, two observable implications should follow. First, developed countries—which presumably have greater regulatory capacity—should be *less* likely to recognize private standards. Second, states should *only* utilize private standards in their climate regulation; that is, we should only observe *strong* forms of interaction—instances in which government programs accept private standards for compliance purposes. (The distinction between strong and weak interactions is described further in the following section.) They should not also have their own government-created standards, since doing so would be an indication of sufficient capacity.

A second possible explanation, also grounded in rationalist theories of institutions, is that recognition of private authority is simply a way for governments to lower the costs of governing. Recognition of multiple private standards can save governments the time and trouble of developing their own standards. Governments choose to "buy" standards not because they lack the capacity to develop them but rather because it is simply more expedient—both politically and economically—to do so (Alchian and Demsetz 1972). Recognition of multiple private standards can increase the availability of low-cost carbon offsets, since presumably a larger market means greater efficiency and liquidity. It can also lower risks for market participants who can potentially participate in multiple markets.

H2: *Governments in carbon-intensive economies are more likely to incorporate private rules into national policy, all else equal.*

Carbon-intensive countries will face higher costs when reducing emissions; this will likely translate to political opposition. As such, governments of carbon-intensive countries will try to lower the costs of reductions as much as possible. There are two observable implications of this hypothesis. First, governments should interact with private standards that dominate the voluntary market. These market leaders are already widely accepted by consumers (often institutional consumers like firms), who would benefit from their incorporation into regulatory regimes. Use of these already-implemented standards is likely to lessen objections from reluctant interests. Governments should also interact with those private standards that are the most "prestigious"—those that are the most recognized by *other* standards. The same logic applies here: The most prestigious standards, as defined by network analysis, have the most interaction with other standards. Therefore, they are the most likely to enhance compatibility across regulatory regimes and thus liquidity. For example, if the Gold Standard is accepted as a legitimate offset standard in markets A and B, it allows firms that purchase Gold Standard offsets to participate in both markets.

Second, countries that interact with private standards as a way to lower transaction costs should be more likely to link their markets to others, as a further way to lower transaction costs. "Linked" markets accept each others' offsets, thereby expanding the total number of credits available, thus lowering the costs of compliance (Green, Sterner, and Wagner 2014).

The third and final explanation is that interactions can be explained by factors *extrinsic* to governments. Specifically, H3 posits that nonstate actors, often private regulators themselves, drive interactions: They create rules and then push for their use by governments. This hypothesis stands in contrast to much of the received wisdom about private authority, which suggests that private regulation arises as a way to fill a gap in public rules (Cashore et al. 2004; Gulbrandsen 2004). Thus, by focusing on interactions, rather than emergence of private regulation, H3 departs from standard accounts in the literature; it posits that the presence of private authority, coupled with its political power, is the main explanation for its recognition. Andonova and Levy (2004) make a similar argument with respect to public-private partnerships, which tend to be initiated by international organizations. Thus, the engine of these new governance initiatives is not an unfulfilled need but rather a savvy entrepreneur.

If H3 is correct, we should expect states with more NGOs and greener firms to be the ones interacting with private offset regulations. These nations are more likely to have private actors organized and prepared to supply regulations.

H3: *Governments with an active civil society and a green private sector are more likely to incorporate private rules into national policy, all else equal.*

Research Design and Data

Research Design

The research design proceeds in three steps. First, I conduct network analysis to understand the relationship among private standards. Before examining interactions between public and private rules, it is important to understand whether some private standards are more influential than others. I describe the compilation of this data in further detail in the following. Second, I use quantitative analysis to uncover whether there are relationships between public-private interactions and the independent variables put forth in the hypotheses. Finally, descriptive inference and qualitative data probe the causal mechanisms. This mixed-method research design proceeds sequentially. The network and quantitative analyses provide the starting point for probing mechanisms that are examined qualitatively, both through descriptive inference and interview research (Tarrow 2004).

The following network data are a useful contribution to the study of transnational climate governance. They provide an in-depth analysis of the *content* of rules, rather than a mere counting of their presence. Understanding interactions through an analysis of shared content is a relatively new approach to studying private regulation (Green 2013; Hafner-Burton, Kahler, and Montgomery 2009) and provides a useful baseline data for future longitudinal studies. In addition, this is one of few studies that examines the content of rules as the basis for network analysis. Other studies focus on shared membership (Hafner-Burton and Montgomery 2009; Hadden 2015; Widerberg 2016) as the basis for analysis. This is a relatively weak tie, as actors may be the members of the same organization without sharing other traits. By contrast, looking at the content of rules provides a robust and internally valid measure of the relationship between rule-making organizations.

The quantitative analysis then presents new data, in which the dependent variable is interactions between the *contents* of the rules—offset standards. There are a number of different types of organizations that generate standards. Offset *standards* are the rules that define the scope of eligible activities and provide detailed instructions on calculating a baseline and the projected reductions. Offset *programs* are the organizations that actually issue the offsets. In some cases, standards are created by the issuing organization.[3] In other cases, an organization has created a standard but does not issue the actual offsets. For example, the International Organization for Standardization has created a suite of carbon-related standards, but it does not carry out offset projects or certify them. For the purposes of this analysis, the institutional form of the rule-making organization is less important that the rules themselves. For this reason, I refer generally to offset standards, though in some instances, this may be coterminous with an offset program, an add-on standard, or refer to a set of rules that have no corresponding program.[4] All different organizational forms share the common feature of having rules that govern offsets.

Data and Methods

According to data that I compiled, in 2014 there were 39 different transnational private regulations governing carbon offsets created by NGOs, firms, and networks comprised of both. Standards are included in this analysis if they meet three criteria. First, they must be private—created and administered by nonstate actors. Second, they must deal primarily with carbon measurement and offsetting. Thus, general sustainability standards are excluded. Third, they must operate transnationally—in two or more countries. To be included, the offset standard must also promulgate at least some independent rules. There are a number of carbon retailers, which simply sell offsets generated by others' rules; these are not included in the data set.

I compiled this information by triangulating among a number of sources (Kollmuss, Zink, and Polycarp 2008; Peters-Stanley and González 2014; World Bank and Ecofys 2014). The data were initially collected in 2009, using the sources previously stated. I updated the data in 2014 by rechecking all of the Web sites and consulting policy reports by the World Bank and Ecosystem Marketplace to see if there were additional standards to add.

Nonstate actors, as characterized previously, created all of the offset standards in the data set. For example, the Climate, Community and Biodiversity (CCBA) standard was created by five international NGOs to ensure that climate mitigation activities also promoted poverty alleviation. By contrast, the Verified Carbon Standard was created by several business

---

[3] This is not universally true. For example, anyone can propose an offset standard (or methodology) to the Clean Development Mechanism. After peer review, it decides whether or not to accept the proposed standard.
[4] I am grateful to an anonymous reviewer for this useful distinction.

NGOs, including the International Emissions Trading Association (an industry group), the World Business Council on Sustainable Development, and the World Economic Forum. Some standards differentiate themselves through the provision of other "co-benefits" in addition to the reduction of carbon emissions, such as improvements in health, economic, and environmental quality.

The network analysis provides a broad overview of how the different private standards relate to each other. It is meant to show the "big picture" of the relative importance of standards, rather than a detailed analysis of individual relationships. Although, as I have suggested, some have slightly different goals, these standards are in the same policy space and compete for resources and for regulatory share (Abbott et al. 2016). In some cases, the relationships are complementary. For example, the CCBA is an "add-on" standard, which provides additional sustainability criteria for existing projects. It is often coupled with the VCS standard. In other cases, the relationships are competitive. For example, both Plan Vivo and the CCBA are add-on standards with the same goal of promoting local sustainability. Finally, in some cases, the relationship is unclear.

To evaluate the relationships among offset standards, I read the contents of each standard. I coded each one for interactions with other standards—to see whether they build upon or use the contents of other private standards. I refer to this process of referencing other rules as an "interaction." Interaction was determined by triangulating among several sources. First, I used the Web site for each organization to see whether they self-identify as linked to any other standards in the data set. Second, I read the documents for each of the standards. Almost all of the standards have a publicly available document that explains how the rules work. This includes what other standards they build on or recognize. The network includes both the original 39 private standards, as well as any other standards they build on or recognize. These may include public standards, or in some cases, carbon accounting standards. Thus, the total number of nodes in the network (60) is greater than the number of carbon standards.

For example, the Verified Carbon Standard (VCS), a leading private offset regulation, states that "[a]ny methodology developed under the United Nations Clean Development Mechanism can be used for projects and programs registering with VCS. The same is true for methodologies developed by the Climate Action Reserve with the exception of their forest protocols."[5] Virtually all standards state their policy of interaction within the document or explain whether and how their standard builds on others. In cases where I could not discern this information from documentation, a brief email questionnaire was sent.

---

[5] http://www.v-c-s.org/methodologies/what-methodology

Any interaction between standards constitutes a tie between them; this information allowed me to represent the standards as a one-mode directed network where arrows indicate who recognizes whom. Figure 2 demonstrates the network of private standards in 2014. Each node represents a different standard. The circles are private standards. The squares are public ones. The size of the nodes indicates how *many* other standards recognize them.

There are three key findings from these data. First, it is clear both visually and in terms of descriptive statistics that some standards are more important than others—in the sense that they are recognized by more standards. In the parlance of network analysis, these are "prestigious" standards: They possess a large number of incoming ties or "indegree centrality." Graphically, these are represented as the largest nodes.

Table A1 in the appendix ranks the most prestigious private standards in 2014. The VCS and ISO are the most prestigious private standards; they are recognized or used by the largest number of other private standards in the network. In addition, the most prestigious standards recognize the CDM[6]—to be a desirable private standard, one must recognize the CDM—the only global public offset standard. It appears to be a necessary condition for being an important player in the landscape of private carbon regulations.

These descriptive statistics provide a more nuanced picture of the field of private standards. There are clearly leaders, who occupy a more central position in the network than others. Moreover, there is not simply an unchecked proliferation of different rules; rather these rules have some shared content.

The landscape of the voluntary market provides a useful departure point for examining the interactions between public and private rules. Not all

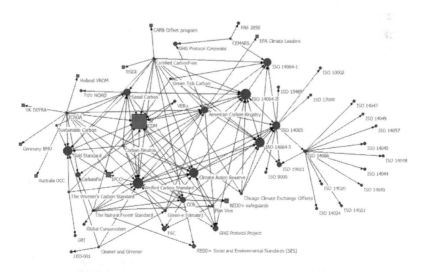

Figure 2. Network of offset standards, 2014.

---

[6]The exception is the ISO 14064 standard, which is a carbon accounting standard rather than an offset standard.

private standards are created "equal"; some are more important, as indicated by their central position in the network and by their market share. More significantly, "important" private standards are also those that interact with public rules under the CDM. Thus, despite a nominal division between the CDM and voluntary markets, there is considerable overlap in the content of rules. These observations motivate the hypotheses, which seek to explain the interactions between domestic public carbon regulations and private offset standards.

Mapping the Dependent Variable: Public/Private Interactions

What does the variation in interactions actually look like? I focus my analysis on carbon-pricing schemes that could potentially include offset policies: emissions trading schemes, carbon taxes, and an "other" category of voluntary reduction schemes. This "other" category includes offset programs, crediting schemes, and efforts at achieving carbon neutrality. In constructing the universe of cases this way, I exclude general policies on energy, agriculture, or adaptation, which do not have any scope for offsets.

Interaction with private standards occurs when governments agree to accept voluntary offsets in lieu of or in addition to government-created ones. It also occurs when governments explicitly appropriate private standards into their own rules, as characterized in Table 1. For example, Australia has a voluntary program called the "Carbon Neutral Program" that certifies products, firms, and events as carbon neutral. Participants may use the government's National Carbon Offset Standard to achieve neutrality. Alternatively, the government also accepts offsets generated and verified by the Gold Standard and the Verified Carbon Standard.[7]

As outlined previously, interactions can take a variety of forms. But the goal of this article is to conduct a systematic analysis; as such, some simplification of the nature of the interactions is necessary. I have therefore classified them into two categories: weak and strong.

Table 1. Types of Interaction among Public and Private Rules.

	Compliance Programs	Voluntary Programs
Strong interactions	Incorporate content of private standards into public ones Allow private standards in lieu of or in addition to a publicly created standard	Accept private offset standards in lieu of public ones
Weak interactions	Build on or adapt contents of private standards	Promote the use of private standards in addition to public ones Build on or adapt contents of private standards

[7] Data on file with the author.

Interactions between public and private rules are strong if public rules adopt the content of private offset standards. I note here that I use standards as shorthand for all rules governing offsets, which may include offset programs or add-on standards; I explain this decision further in the following. Thus, private rules are "imported" into public regulations that are used for compliance purposes. In another strong type of interaction, public regulations accept private offsets in lieu of or in addition to public ones—again, for compliance purposes. Weaker interactions occur when offsets created by private rules are a supplement to existing public regulations. For example, states may allow private offsets to be used in lieu of offsets created by public rules. Alternatively, they may accept them in addition to other offsets. These interactions are summarized in Table 1.

To construct the data set, I used the World Bank's report, the *State and Trends of Carbon Pricing 2014*, as a starting point for compiling an exhaustive list of all active ETS and carbon taxes. In addition, I drew from a report by the think tank Ecosystem Marketplace, which analyzes government programs involved with the voluntary carbon market (Peters-Stanley 2012). I then compared this list to other documents and Web sites that purportedly provide a comprehensive list of carbon pricing mechanisms.[8] Finally, using government documents, policy reports, and other Web sites as relevant, I determined whether these programs contained some provision for offsets.

This coding process yielded 41 countries with climate policies that could potentially include some offsetting provision; 28 of these are in the EU. Table 2 provides a list.

The fact that more than half of the sample is comprised of EU nations presents some challenges. On one hand, it suggests that the overall number of nations with climate policies is actually smaller, since the EU effectively functions as a single actor under the Kyoto Protocol. However, there is variation among EU member states on voluntary initiatives. For example, there is a voluntary trading program in northeastern Italy that promotes offsetting through local mitigation projects in agro-forestry.[9] This program is completely separate from the EU-ETS. Similarly, the Netherlands has had a carbon tax in place since 1990, well before the EU climate policy was put in place. For this reason, I consider the EU as one entity when considering compliance-based programs and as separate nations when examining voluntary programs.

Table 3 shows the 12 countries that have an offsetting program interact with one or more private standards (29% of the total).[10] These countries can

---

[8] http://www.eesi.org/files/FactSheet_Carbon_Pricing_101712.pdf; http://www.edf.org/climate/worlds-carbon-markets; https://icapcarbonaction.com/component/attach/?task=download&id=152

[9] http://www.carbomark.org/?q=en/node/8

[10] Since some of these are European nations with domestic policies distinct from the EU-wide policy, it makes sense to treat EU nations as independent observations, at least in the descriptive data. I was unable to get detailed information in English about emissions trading programs in Kyoto and Saitama in Japan. Thus, it is possible that these too contain offsetting provisions.

Table 2. Countries with Offsetting Provisions in Their Carbon Regulations (N = 41).

Australia	*Republic of Korea*
Austria	Latvia
Belgium	Lithuania
Brazil	Luxembourg
Bulgaria	Malta
Canada	Mexico
China	*Netherlands*
Costa Rica	New Zealand
Croatia	Norway
Cyprus	Poland
Czech Republic	Portugal
Denmark	Romania
Estonia	Slovakia
Finland	Slovenia
France	Spain
Germany	Sweden
Greece	*Switzerland*
Hungary	*Thailand*
Ireland	*United Kingdom*
Italy	*United States*
Japan	

Note. **Bold** indicates interactions with private standards.

Table 3. Recognition of Private Standards by Government Programs.

Country	Examples of Recognized Standards	Type of Government Program
Australia	Gold Standard, Verified Carbon Standard	Voluntary
Canada	ISO 14064-2, Climate Action Reserve, Verified Carbon Standard, GHG Protocol for Project Accounting	Mandatory
Costa Rica	Gold Standard, Verified Carbon Standard	Voluntary
Italy	Verified Carbon Standard	Voluntary
Japan	ISO 14064-2, ISO 14064-3, ISO 14065	Voluntary
Mexico	Verified Carbon Standard, Gold Standard, Plan Vivo, Climate Action Reserve	Voluntary
Netherlands	CarbonFix Standard	Voluntary
Republic of Korea	ISO 14064 series, ISO 14065	Voluntary
Switzerland	Gold Standard	Mandatory
Thailand	ISO 14064-2, ISO 14064-3	Voluntary
United Kingdom	Gold Standard; Verified Carbon Standard; the Climate, Community and Biodiversity Standards, Plan Vivo	Voluntary
United States	American Carbon Registry, Climate Action Reserve, Verified Carbon Standard, Chicago Climate Exchange, GHG Protocol for Project Accounting	Mandatory/Voluntary*

Note. *Some state-specific programs with carbon offsetting mechanisms are mandatory (for example, California), while other are voluntary (for example, Oklahoma).

all be characterized as rich, green, and free. They are developed nations, which have relatively strong environmental records and high levels of political freedom. A quick glance shows that the majority are located within

North America and Europe. The shaded rows indicate those *mandatory* programs that interact with private standards; these are strong interactions as characterized by Table 1. Although there is some interaction between public and private rules on offsets, the majority of interactions are weak, in that they do not occur for compliance-based rules.

Evaluating the Evidence

The previous section demonstrates that states that interact with private regulations tend to be rich, green, and free. Which hypotheses best explain this pattern of participation in transnational climate governance? To investigate, I evaluate the evidence among the 41 countries with policies that contain offsetting provisions. Since the N for this study is relatively small, I use a multiple methods approach (Lieberman 2005). There are three forms of evidence to evaluate the hypotheses: descriptive inference, multivariate logit analysis, and indicative qualitative evidence.

Descriptive Inference

The descriptive data demonstrate three important trends. First, for countries with emissions regulations, offsetting is a widely used policy instrument: At least 89% of the emissions trading schemes in the data set include provisions for offsets.[11] Similarly, 100% of the voluntary initiatives include offset provisions. Clearly, studying offsets is important; they are a prominent fixture of carbon pricing policies.

Second, offsets, and carbon pricing in general, are generally used in the developed world. This suggests preliminary evidence *against* H1, which posits that governments lacking in regulatory capacity will be more likely to interact with private standards. Using wealth as a rough proxy for regulatory capacity, we would expect poorer countries to interact with private standards, yet this is not the variation that we observe. Since wealth is correlated with CO_2 emissions, the observed variation provides preliminary support for H2: Carbon-intensive economies are more likely to interact with private standards.

Roughly one-third (29%) of all states with carbon pricing mechanisms interact with private standards in some way. If one treats the EU as a single entity, then the figures change. There are 14 entities with an offsetting mechanism in their policy, and 12 of them (85%) interact with private regulations.

Third and most importantly, the vast majority of these interactions are "weak," as characterized by Table 1. Private standards are used in voluntary initiatives, as opposed to mandatory regulations, and/or in addition to the use of public offset standards. Only three nations have the "strong" form of

---

[11]As noted, it is possible that Japan does not, since I could not obtain documents in English.

interaction—Canada, Switzerland, and the United States—utilizing private standards in mandatory programs.

Thus, the first key finding is that there is "blurring" of the lines between public and private authority, insofar that there are a multiple interactions between the two spheres. However, a closer look reveals that most of these are of a relatively "weak" nature.

Multivariate Analysis

The second form of evidence is a systematic examination of the relationship between the dependent variable (interaction with private carbon standards) and different operationalizations of explanatory factors as per the hypotheses. I first explain the dependent variable and then describe the other factors that I expect to influence interaction as set forth in each of the hypotheses. Table A2 in the appendix provides summary statistics of the variables used, and Table 4 presents the results of the analysis.

The dependent variable is interaction with private standards. The universe of cases is the 41 countries listed in Table 3 with carbon pricing policies. Because of the relatively small N, I treat interactions as a dichotomous variable, rather than distinguishing between weak and strong, as I do in the following qualitative analysis.

To conduct the analysis, I begin by examining each hypothesis separately, using both independent variables. Moreover, since 28 of the 41 states with offset programs are in the EU, I also include a control for EU membership in each model.

Table 4. Determinants of Interactions between Public and Private Carbon Regulations.

	Model 1	Model 2	Model 3	Model 4	Model 5
GDP Per Capita	1.74*			1.26	
	(1.05)			(1.26)	
Government effectiveness	−1.62			−1.74	−0.59
	(1.37)			(1.54)	(1.01)
CO_2 emissions per capita		0.12		0.18	0.23
		(0.09)		(0.21)	(0.22)
Fossil Fuel Exports		−0.04		−0.05	−0.04
		(0.04)		(0.06)	(0.07)
Number of NGOs (logged)			1.39**	1.35*	1.58*
			(0.64)	(0.78)	(0.74)
Number of ISO14001 firms (logged)			0.18	.1671507	.0811244
			(.31)	(.36)	(.33)
EU membership	−3.25***	−3.23***	−2.86 ***	−3.67**	−3.19***
	(0.99)	(0.98)	(1.10)	(1.64)	(1.45)
Constant	−13.99	.20	−3.15	−13.60	−3.25
	(8.61)	(0.95)	(2.45)	(11.11)	(2.87)
N	40	40	37	36	36
Log Likelihood	−15.40	−15.98	−12.45	−10.57	−11.09
LRchi^2	16.25	15.09	21.72	23.16	22.14
Prob > chi^2	0.00	0.00	0.00	0.00	0.00

Note. *$p<.01$, **$p<.05$, ***$p<.01$. Standard errors indicated in parentheses.

H1 posits that states interact with private standards because they lack the capacity to create their own rules. I operationalize capacity with two different measures. First, I use GDP per capita, with the assumption that richer countries have greater capacity to create their own rules and thus will not need to "borrow" from private rule makers. I use an additional measure of capacity, government effectiveness, which is drawn from the World Bank's Worldwide Governance Indicators. This variable measures the ability of the government to create and implement policies. Averaged from 1996–2010, government effectiveness ranges in value from −2.5 (weak) to 2.5 (strong). (For a similar approach, see Andonova, Hale, and Roger 2014). If H1 is correct, then we should expect to see a negative correlation between the variables: As capacity decreases, interactions with private regulations increase.

H2 posits that carbon-intensive economies are more likely to interact with private standards. Both per capita emissions and fossil fuel exports capture the extent to which a country's economic well-being depends on fossil fuels and thus would be negatively impacted by reductions requirements. Per capita emissions data are from the World Bank's World Development Indicators. Their emissions calculation, averaged from 1990–2014, is based on "burning of fossil fuels and the manufacture of cement," and is measured in metric tons per capita.[12] Fuel exports data are also from the World Bank's Indicators and are averaged over the same time period. They are measured as a percentage of total merchandise exports.

If H2 holds, we should expect a positive relationship between both independent variables and the dependent variable: As reliance on fossil fuels increases, there should be an increase in interaction as a way to defray political and economic costs.

To evaluate H3, the notion that private regulators themselves are driving the interactions with government, I use two measures—one for civil society and the other for firm activity. Unfortunately, there is no country-level data on the number of private regulators. As a second-best solution, I evaluate the activity of nonstate actors more generally. First, I use a count of the number of NGOs active in the country, using data drawn from Bernauer, Bohmelt, and Koubi (2013) and Andonova (2014). Second, to distinguish between NGO and firm activity, I also include a measure of the number of firms with the ISO14001 sustainability certification, also drawn from Andonova (2014).

All models include only those states that have some public carbon regulation—an ETS, a tax, or a voluntary program such as those outlined previously in the "other" category. This limits the sample to those states that can possibly choose to recognize a private standard—an N of 41. The dependent variable, whether or not there is an interaction with private regulations, is

---

[12] http://data.worldbank.org/indicator/EN.ATM.CO2E.PC

dichotomous, with a 1 assigned to all public regulations that interact with private standards.

Model 1 examines whether state capacity, measured by GDP per capita and government effectiveness, affects interactions with private regulations. If H1 were correct, we would expect the relationship to be *negative*: As per capita GDP falls, the probability of interaction rises. However, we observe the opposite relationship. Similarly, since weaker governments score negatively on the World Bank Indicators, confirmation of H1 would require a negative sign of that coefficient, which is not evident. The large standard errors for both coefficients also indicate reason for concern—an issue I return to later.

Model 2 examines the effects of fossil fuel dependency on the interaction between public and private standards. The relationship between per capita emissions and probability of interaction is positive, as we would expect, though not significant: An increase in emissions increases the likelihood of interacting with private standards. In addition, as fossil fuel exports rise, the probability of private interaction falls, which is the *opposite* of what we should expect.

Model 3 tests whether nonstate actor involvement explains interactions with private standards. Here, I find support for NGOs but *not* for firms. For each additional NGO, the odds of using private rules in public regulations increase by a factor of 1.39.[13] The very small coefficient for ISO14001 suggests that the number of ISO14001-certified firms in a country has no effect on the use of private regulations. This provides evidence debunking the notion that green firms are pushing for private regulations.

To further probe the relationships presented in each hypothesis, I also conducted trivariate logit analyses, examining each independent variable and again controlling for EU membership. In these analyses, once again, only the number of NGOs and EU membership had a statistically significant effect on the dependent variable.[14]

Model 4 presents all of the covariates. Holding all other variables constant, only the number of NGOs and EU membership increase the likelihood of interactions with private offset standards. Controlling for the other variables, each additional NGO present in a country increases the odds of interacting with private offset regulations increases by 21.3% ($p < .05$).[15] Interestingly, this runs counter to Bernauer, Bohmelt, and Koubi's (2013) assertion that there is a "democracy-civil society paradox" where the effect of NGOs on green behavior is less pronounced in democracies than in nondemocratic regimes. By contrast, these findings demonstrate that the presence of NGOs

---

[13] I use the listcoef command to generate this outcome.

[14] The results of these analyses are accessible through the replication data.

[15] I use the listcoef percent command to generate this outcome; see replication data for further detail. For ease of interpretation, this is done with the absolute number of NGOs rather than with the log.

spurs *more* green behavior, in the form of interacting with private carbon standards.

Model 4 also surprisingly shows that EU membership drastically reduces the likelihood of interaction with private standards. States within the EU are 98% less likely to interact with private standards than other states with carbon regulations. Though the EU is generally considered a climate leader, only three EU nations (Italy, the Netherlands, and the United Kingdom) interact with private carbon regulations. And since all 28 EU member states are included in the sample, this means that compared to other wealthy nations, EU is by no means a leader.

I also find robust evidence that private authority does not serve a "gap-filling" function, as many have claimed. For each point government capacity falls, the probability of interacting with private standards decreases by 91.5%. Thus, less capable governments *do not* turn to private standards to fill regulatory gaps.

To ensure that there is no multicollinearity among the variables, I examine the variance inflation factor. Table A4 (in the appendix) demonstrates that all variables are within the acceptable range. The VIF values for per capita GDP and government effectiveness are much higher than the rest. As a result of this finding, I omit per capita GDP and reexamine the VIF values (see the appendix). Here, the diagnostics indicate considerably less collinearity. As a result of this finding, Model 5 examines whether omitting the potentially (though not definitively) collinear variable changes the findings. It does not.

Clearly, the multivariate analysis is most supportive of H3: The presence of NGOs matters for whether or not states choose to interact with private offset regulations. Importantly, the same is not true for firms. For further confirmation of the strength of H3, I consider qualitative evidence for all three hypotheses in the following.

Qualitative Evidence

The quantitative evidence provides one indication that NGO presence is an important factor in interaction with private offset regulations, as posited by H3. However, I also investigate additional qualitative evidence for each of the hypotheses.

Qualitative evidence comes from two sources. I examine how variation in the dependent variable conforms or departs from the expected observable implications outlined previously. I then supplement these inferences with insights from policymakers involved with both public and private regulation. I interviewed eight people from seven different organizations involved with either public or private offsetting.

I find little support for the intrinsic explanations and relatively strong support for the role of NGOs (as opposed to firms). In general, the findings suggest that interactions between public and private rules are not driven by governments but by NGOs and civil society in both domestic and global politics. I should note, however, that these hypotheses are not mutually exclusive, so these conclusions indicate which actors have the most (rather than the sole) influence on the recognition of private authority. Certainly, governments are not irrelevant; but their preferences do not appear to be the main driver of interaction.

If H1 is correct, states recognize private authority because they lack the regulatory capacity to create their own rules. Thus, we should expect wealth to be inversely related to recognition of private offset standards. Wealthier states should have ample capacity to create and enforce their own regulations. Table 3 overwhelmingly shows that the opposite is the case: With the exception of Thailand, *only* OECD nations interact with private regulations. Rich countries, which generally have higher governmental capacity, are *most* likely to recognize private standards—contrary to expectations. However, they are also more likely to have carbon pricing schemes; thus, this observation only provides preliminary evidence for the hypothesis.

More convincingly, the majority of countries that recognize private regulations *also* have their own government-created rules. For example, the Canadian province of Alberta created an emissions trading scheme in 2007. It allows for the use of offsets and has its own standard but also interacts with private standards such as the Climate Action Reserve. The presence of its own rules clearly indicates that the provincial government does not lack capacity.

Additional evidence contravenes H1: "weak" interactions are dominant. Thus, private regulations are rarely used for compliance purposes. Instead, states interact with private regulations through voluntary programs that serve as an additional approach to mitigating climate change. Indeed, only three states— Canada, the United States, and Switzerland—recognize private regulations for compliance purposes. This is persuasive evidence that recognition of private authority is viewed as an "extra"—a set of activities that exists in addition to the "real work" of public regulation. Private authority is rarely recognized as a *sole* source of rules. Thus, there is little qualitative evidence to support the hypothesis that private authority serves as a substitute for public regulation.

The cases of strong interaction merit further investigation, given that they align with the observable implications of H1. All three states use private standards in addition to public ones, rather than in lieu of them. Switzerland allows offsets *certified by* the Gold Standard, rather than created by Gold Standard's rules. Thus, interaction with the Gold Standard is at the level of certification, rather than creation or utilization of rules. In Alberta, Canada, the emissions trading scheme draws from other rules, meaning that "[Alberta] reviews the content of these protocols when developing Alberta based protocols to ensure prior learning [sic] best practices are incorporated."[16] In this case, interaction is a type of consultation with private rules.

The strongest interaction occurs in California, which accepts offsets that are created by the Climate Action Registry and the American Carbon Registry—both private offset standards. Interestingly, the Climate Action Registry was originally the *California* Climate Action Registry (CCAR), created by the state legislature of California. The state of California was preparing to regulate emissions but was not yet ready to do so. It created CCAR as a first step, to help businesses prepare for forthcoming regulation and potentially get credits for early reduction action.[17] Creating CCAR was a way to develop capacity for future regulation. Thus, history plays an important role in explaining the strong interaction between public and private rules in the California case. Essentially, the state government delegated to a private actor, CCAR, which eventually became the Climate Action Registry. When AB 32 was passed, creating a cap and trade system in California, the legislature turned to the Climate Action Registry because of the "comfort level" with the organization and its work.[18]

This brief history of the interaction with the Climate Action Registry provides definitive evidence *against* H1. The strongest interaction between public and private rules occurs in California, precisely because the private actor *was created by the state*. The government designed CCAR, predecessor to the Climate Action Registry, to fulfill a specific regulatory role; in essence, this is a form of delegation to a private actor (Green 2014).

If H2 is correct, interactions with private standards are driven by the desire to lower costs for those participating in mandatory regulations or voluntary initiatives. To do this, they will utilize a variety of different offset standards in their policies, maximizing compatibility with other standards and expanding network effects. In particular, we should expect strong interactions with those private standards that dominate the voluntary market. These standards have the largest market share and are likely to have strong interactions with *other* private standards. In the parlance of network analysis, these are "prestigious" standards, in the sense that many other standards choose to recognize some or all of their rules. We should also expect to see linkage among different carbon markets; indeed, this would provide much stronger evidence for concerns about controlling costs.

The evidence for H2 is mixed. In 2013, the last year for which data were available, the Verified Carbon Standard and the Gold Standard were also two of the top three most widely used standards, capturing the largest share of the voluntary market (Peters-Stanley and González 2014:xiv). Governments frequently interact with these two standards, as indicated in Table 4, though through weak interactions.

---

[17]Interview, Rachel Tornek, Vice President for Programs, Climate Action Registry and Craig Ebert, Vice President for Policy, Climate Action Registry, November 24, 2015.
[18]*Ibid.*

Moreover, the network analysis demonstrates that the most prestigious standards are often those with which governments choose to interact. The Gold Standard and the VCS are among the most prestigious private standards—in the sense that they are recognized by the most other standards. All of the strong interactions are with prestigious standards: the Gold Standard, VCS, ISO 14064-2, Climate Action Reserve, and the American Climate Registry.

However, interviews revealed that these interactions were not driven by concerns about costs. One government representative explained their use of the Verified Carbon Standard: "We generally try to focus on protocol systems that are widely recognized and used internationally..."[19] But the rationale is not lowering the costs of compliance but rather "to ensure prior learning [and] best practices are incorporated."[20]

Linkages among different carbon markets would provide stronger network effects-based evidence of concerns about costs. When states officially link their markets, they increase the overall pool of credits and allowances, thereby reducing compliance costs for regulated entities. This strategy has been hailed by optimists as an important strategy for lowering the costs of expanding carbon markets (Jaffe, Ranson, and Stavins 2009). Yet there is little evidence that this logic is driving state behavior. Despite the fact that about 40 national and 20 subnational jurisdictions have a price on carbon, only two emissions trading schemes—in California and Quebec—are linked (World Bank and Ecofys 2014).

The final hypothesis is that the presence and activity of rule *makers*—that is, the private regulators themselves—rather than governments, best explain the interaction with private regulations. We should therefore expect states with large civil society sectors to be more likely to have these interactions. In addition, evidence that private rule makers are actively promoting their standards would affirm H3.

Here the qualitative variation is not terribly instructive, since most nations that recognize private regulations are relatively free. However, a difference in means test reveals that countries that recognize private standards have roughly four times more active environmental NGOs than those that do not ($p < .01$). This provides additional evidence for H3.

Stronger evidence in support of this hypothesis comes from interviews with a variety of policymakers. Australia accepts the Gold Standard in its voluntary initiative that promotes carbon neutrality—the National Carbon Offset Standard (NCOS). Ingrid Kroopman, the Assistant Director for the Carbon Neutral Program, explains this design choice:

> During the creation of the NCOS, voluntary market stakeholders were consulted ... about what if any international [carbon] units should they considered to be

---

[19] Email communication, Amanda Bambrick, Senior Offset Policy Advisor, Alberta Canada, November 26, 2015.
[20] *Ibid.*

credible for use under the NCOS. The feedback from this consultation was that ... the Gold Standard and ... the [Verified] Carbon Standard should be included.[21]

Thus, when the Australian government solicited input from private rule makers and participants in the voluntary market (voluntary market stakeholders) about what public/private interactions, if any, should be recognized, they made a strong case for the inclusion of private rules.

Thus, taken together, the descriptive inference, the quantitative and qualitative analyses, provide the most support for the extrinsic explanation of public/private interactions that private regulators—and specifically NGOs—are the main engine for interaction. Countries with more civil society activity and active private regulators are also more likely to interact with private rules. The qualitative evidence shows that private regulators have advocated for these interactions when given the opportunity to do so.

Conclusion

This article contributes to our collective understanding of domestic variation in participation in transnational climate governance. It examines a specific form of the institutionalization of private carbon offset standards: the extent to which domestic carbon regulations choose to interact with private rules.

Perhaps the most important finding is that the interactions between public and private authority, though fairly common, are generally weak. Private standards are not substituting for weak government capacity but are instead serve the interests of those who create them. The second key finding is that the presence of NGOs matters: It meaningfully and substantively affects whether states choose to recognize private offset standards. Thus, the impetus for "blurring the lines" between public and private does not come from governments or firms but rather from nonstate actors who are pushing their own regulatory agenda.

Another key finding is the order that emerges out of the apparent chaos of the voluntary carbon market. There are clear market leaders, who are also the best connected within the network of carbon rules. These leaders are most often the ones recognized by governments. Thus, governments are taking their cues from the voluntary market, in which certain actors dominate. This raises the question: What makes *these* private regulators successful?

Fortunately, the evidence indicates that the most successful private regulations are also deemed to be the "greenest," according to an independent alliance of standard setters. (Of course, this poses a problem of infinite regress, since one could legitimately ask whether they are sufficiently impartial to make such an evaluation.) This provides some reason for optimism: The blurring of public and private tends to promote strong rather than weak rules.

---

[21]Email communication, November 25, 2015.

In the end, these findings raise more questions than they answer. As I have argued elsewhere, private authority does not occur in a vacuum; public authority is always present. In some cases, however, private rule makers are able to create their own opportunities, persuading governments to use their rules in addition to public ones. But the interactions are "weak" in the sense that they are not supplanting public rules, merely complementing them. These findings indicate that the domestic politics can, under certain conditions, provide an environment hospitable to the expansion of private authority.

Acknowledgments

The author would like to thank the project organizers—Liliana Andonova, Tom Hale, and Charlie Roger—as well as Jennifer Hadden and Gerald Schneider for their comments on earlier drafts. I am grateful to Quentin Karpilow for his outstanding research assistance and to three anonymous reviewers for their comments.

References

Abbott, Kenneth W. (2012) The Transnational Regime Complex for Climate Change. *Environment and Planning C: Government and Policy* 30(4):571–590.

Abbott, Kenneth W., Jessica F. Green, and Robert O. Keohane. (2016) Organizational Ecology and Institutional Change in Global Governance. *International Organization* 70 (2):247–277.

Abbott, Kenneth W., and Duncan Snidal. (2009) The Governance Triangle: Regulatory Standards Institutions and the Shadow of the State. In *The Politics of Global Regulation*, edited by W. Mattli and N. Woods. Princeton, NJ: Princeton University Press, pp. 44–88.

Alchian, Armen A., and Harold Demsetz. (1972) Production, Information Costs and Economic Organization. *American Economic Review* 62(5):777–795.

Andonova, Liliana B. (2014) Boomerangs to Partnerships? Explaining State Participation in Transnational Partnerships for Sustainability. *Comparative Political Studies* 47(3):481–515.

Andonova, Liliana, Thomas Hale and Charles Roger. (2014) How Do Domestic Politics Condition Participation in Transnational Climate Governance? Paper Presented at the Political Economy of International Organizations conference, Princeton, NJ, January 16-18.

Andonova, Liliana B., and Marc A. Levy. (2004) Franchising Global Governance: Making Sense of the Johannesburg Type II Partnerships. *Yearbook of International Cooperation on Environment and Development 2003–04: An Independent Publication of the Fridtjof Nansen Institute, Norway*. London: Earthscan, pp. 19–31.

Bartley, Tim. (2011) Transnational Governance as the Layering of Rules: Intersections of Public and Private Standards. *Theoretical Inquiries in Law* 12(2):517–542.

Bernauer, Thomas, Tobias Böhmelt, and Vally Koubi. (2013) Is There a Democracy–Civil Society Paradox in Global Environmental Governance? *Global Environmental Politics* 13 (1):88–107.

Bernstein, Steven. (2001) *The Compromise of Liberal Environmentalism*. New York, NY: Columbia University Press.

Borzel, Tanya and Thomas Risse. (2005) Public-Private Partnerships: Effective and Legitimate Tools of Transnational Governance. In *Reconstituting Political Authority: Sovereignty,*

Effectiveness, and Legitimacy in a Transnational Order, edited by Edgar Grande and Louis W Pauly. Toronto: University of Toronto Press.

Buthe, Tim. (2008) The Globalization of Health and Safety Standards: Delegation of Regulatory Authority in the SPS Agreement of the 1994 Agreement Establishing the World Trade Organization. *Law and Contemporary Problems* 71(1):219–256.

Buthe, Tim, and Walter Mattli. (2011) *The New Global Rulers: The Privatization of Regulation in the World Economy*. Princeton, NJ: Princeton University Press.

Cashore, Benjamin, Graeme Auld, Steven Bernstein, and Constance McDermott. (2007) Can Non-State Governance "Ratchet Up" Global Environmental Standards? Lessons from the Forest Sector. *Review of European Community & International Environmental Law* 16 (2):158–172. http://doi.org/10.1111/j.1467-9388.2007.00560.x

Cashore, Benjamin, Graeme Auld, and Deanna Newsom. (2004) *Governing Through Markets: Forest Certification and the Emergence of Non-State Authority*. New Haven, CT: Yale University Press.

Eberlein, Burkard, Kenneth W. Abbott, Julia Black, Errol Meidinger, and Stepan Wood. (2014) Transnational Business Governance Interactions: Conceptualization and Framework for Analysis. *Regulation & Governance* 8(1):1–21.

Green, Jessica F. (2013) Order out of Chaos: Public and Private Rules for Managing Carbon. *Global Environmental Politics* 13(2):1–25.

Green, Jessica F. (2014) *Rethinking Private Authority: Agents and Entrepreneurs in Global Environmental Governance*. Princeton, NJ: Princeton University Press.

Green, Jessica F., and Graeme Auld. (2016) Unbundling the Regime Complex: The Effects of Private Authority. *Transnational Environmental Law*. Available on CJO. http://dx.doi.org/10.1017/S2047102516000121

Green, Jessica F., Thomas Sterner, and Gernot Wagner. (2014) A Balance of Bottom-Up and Top-Down in Linking Climate Policies. *Nature Climate Change* 4(12):1064–1067.

Gulbrandsen, Lars H. (2004) Overlapping Public and Private Governance: Can Forest Certification Fill the Gaps in the Global Forest Regime? *Global Environmental Politics* 4 (2):75–99.

Gulbrandsen, Lars H. (2014) Dynamic Governance Interactions: Evolutionary Effects of State Responses to Non-State Certification Programs. *Regulation & Governance* 8(1):74–92.

Hafner-Burton, Emilie, Miles Kahler, and Alexander Montgomery. (2009) Network Analysis for International Relations. *International Organization* 63(3):559–592.

Hadden, Jennifer. (2015) *Networks in Contention: The Divisive Politics of Climate Change*. Cambridge, UK: Cambridge University Press.

Hawkins, Darren G., David A. Lake, Daniel L. Nielson, and Michael J. Tierney. (2006) Delegation under Anarchy: States, International Organizations and Principal-Agent Theory. In *Delegation and Agency in International Organizations*, edited by D. G. Hawkins, D. A. Lake, D. L. Nielson, and M. J. Tierney. Cambridge, UK: Cambridge University Press.

Hoffmann, Matthew. (2011) *Climate Governance at the Crossroads*. Oxford: Oxford University Press.

Jaffe, Judson, Matthew Ranson, and Robert Stavins. (2009) Linking Tradable Permit Systems: A Key Element of Emerging International Climate Policy Architecture. *Ecology Law Quarterly* 36(4):789–808.

Knill, Christopher, and Dirk Lehmkuhl. (2002) Private Actors and the State: Internationalization and Changing Patterns of Governance. *Governance* 15(1):41–63.

Kollmuss, Anja, Helge Zink, and Clifford Polycarp. (2008) *Making Sense of the Voluntary Carbon Market: A Comparison of Carbon Offset Standards*. Stockholm Environment

Institute and Tricorona. Retrieved from http://assets.panda.org/downloads/vcm_report_final.pdf

Krasner, Stephen D., and Thomas Risse. (2014) External Actors, State-Building, and Service Provision in Areas of Limited Statehood: Introduction. *Governance* 27(4):545–567.

Lake, David A. (2009) *Hierarchy in International Relations*. Ithaca, NY: Cornell University Press.

Lieberman, Evan S. (2005) Nested Analysis as a Mixed-Method Strategy for Comparative Research. *American Political Science Review* 99(3):435–452.

Mattli, Walter, and Ngaire Woods. (2009) *The Politics of Global Regulation*. Princeton, NJ: Princeton University Press.

Mayer, Frederick, and Gary Gereffi. (2010) Regulation and Economic Globalization: Prospects and Limits of Private Governance. *Business & Politics* 12(3):1–25.

Oberthur, Sebastian, and Olav Schram Stokke, eds. (2011) *Managing Institutional Complexity*. Cambridge, MA: The MIT Press.

Peters-Stanley, Molly. (2012) *Bringing It Home: Taking Stock of Government Engagement with the Voluntary Carbon Market*. Washington, DC: Ecosystem Marketplace.

Peters-Stanley, Molly, and Gloria González. (2014) *Sharing the Stage: State of the Voluntary Carbon Markets 2014*. Washington, DC: Forest Trends' Ecosystem Marketplace.

Raz, Joseph. (1990) *Authority*. New York: New York University Press.

Sabel, Charles F., and David G. Victor. (2015) Governing Global Problems under Uncertainty: Making Bottom-Up Climate Policy Work. *Climatic Change* 1–13.

Sabel, Charles F., and Jonathan Zeitlin, eds. (2010) *Experimentalist Governance in the European Union: Towards a New Architecture*. Oxford: Oxford University Press.

Scott, Colin, Fabrizio Cafaggi, and Linda Senden. (2011) The Conceptual and Constitutional Challenge of Transnational Private Regulation. *Journal of Law & Society* 38(1):1–19.

Strange, Susan. (1996) *The Retreat of the State*. Cambridge, UK: Cambridge University Press.

Tarrow, Sidney G. (2004) Bridging the Quantitative-Qualitative Divide. In *Rethinking Social Inquiry: Diverse Tools, Shared Standards*, edited by H. Brady and D. Collier. Oxford: Rowman & Littlefield.

Vogel, David. (2005) *The Market for Virtue*. Washington, DC: The Brookings Institution.

Widerberg, Oscar. (2016) Mapping Institutional Complexity in the Anthropocene: A Network Approach. In *Environmental Politics and Governance in the Anthropocene: Institutions and Legitimacy in a Complex World*, edited by Philipp Pattberg and Fariborz Zelli, 81–102. New York, NY: Routledge.

World Bank and Ecofys. (2014). *State and Trends of Carbon Pricing 2015*. Washington, DC: The World Bank.

Appendix

TABLE A1. Indegree Centrality, private standards, 2014

Name	Indegree Centrality
VCS, ISO 14064-2	0.17
Climate Action Reserve, ISO 14064-3, Gold Standard	0.14
ISO 14064-1, ISO 14065	0.12
Social Carbon, American Carbon Registry	0.09

In degree centrality indicates the percentage of other standards in the network that recognize a given standard. The prestigious private standards are also the market leaders. The three market leaders are the VCS, the CAR and the Gold Standard. Collectively, they account for between 70–75% of credits sold on the voluntary market between 2009 and 2014. VCS is the most prestigious private standard, and also clear market leader. About half of all credits sold on the voluntary market are VCS credits. Similarly, the Climate Action Reserve represents between 10 and 13% of credits sold. The Gold Standard has a similar market share.

TABLE A2. Collinearity Diagnostics

Variable	VIF	SQRT VIF	Tolerance	R-Squared
GDP per capita	5.63	2.37	0.1779	0.8221
Government effectiveness	5.27	2.30	0.1897	0.8103
CO2 emissions per capita	1.82	1.35	0.5507	0.4493
Fossil fuel exports	1.18	1.09	0.8493	0.1547
Number of NGOs	1.43	1.20	0.6971	0.3029
Number of ISO 14001 firms	1.20	1.09	0.8356	0.1644
EU membership	1.36	1.16	0.7376	0.2624
Mean VIF	2.55			

TABLE A3. Independent Variables

		N	Mean	Std. Dev	Min	Max
Government Capacity						
	Gov't effectiveness	158	−.007328	.9961613	4.951988	11.03912
	GDP per capita	183	7.878316	1.519869	−2.20178	2.14615
Carbon Intensity						
	Emissions per capita	169	4.313665	6.431995	0	53.1054
	Fossil fuel exports	169	10.29731	18.91173	0	100.6055
Private Rulemakers						
	Number of NGOs	149	4.169311	6.747548	0	51.52941
	Number of ISO 14001 firms	192	1145.953	5251.068	0	55316

TABLE A4. Collinearity Diagnostics Recalculated

Variable	VIF	SQRT VIF	Tolerance	R-Squared
Government effectiveness	1.66	1.29	0.6023	0.3977
CO2 emissions per capita	1.77	1.33	0.5654	0.4346
Fossil fuel exports	1.17	1.08	0.8529	0.1471
Number of NGOs	1.40	1.18	0.7158	0.2842
Number of ISO 14001 firms	1.19	1.09	0.8381	0.1619
EU membership	1.33	1.15	0.7529	0.2471
Mean VIF	1.42			

Transnational Climate Governance Initiatives: Designed for Effective Climate Change Mitigation?

Katharina Michaelowa and Axel Michaelowa

ABSTRACT
The Paris Agreement of December 2015 set a highly ambitious target for global climate change mitigation, but it remains unclear how it will be reached, and the individual countries' pledges do not add up to the overall target. Can transnational climate governance initiatives be expected to fill the gap? We assess 109 such initiatives based on four design criteria: existence of mitigation targets; incentives for mitigation; definition of a baseline; and existence of a monitoring, reporting, and verification procedure. About half of the initiatives do not meet any of these criteria, and not even 15% satisfy three or more. Many initiatives were created only for the purpose of networking. Orchestration by national governments and international organizations increases the number of criteria met. On average, the mitigation focus of new initiatives was highest during the "heyday" of the international climate policy regime between 2005 and 2010. While mitigation-oriented entrepreneurial initiatives are generally started only in response to existing regulation, subnational governments and NGOs show some attempts to go beyond that and compensate for insufficient regulation at the national and international level. Yet, given the low overall quality assessment, transnational climate governance initiatives cannot be expected to fill the "mitigation gap."

The Paris Agreement adopted by all member countries of the United Nations Framework Convention on Climate Change (UNFCCC) in December 2015 sets a highly ambitious global target for a limitation of global warming to "well below" 2°C from preindustrial levels (UNFCCC 2015a), specifying that greenhouse gas emissions and sinks shall reach a balance in the second half of the twenty-first century. Thus massive reductions of greenhouse gas emissions are required in the next decades. However, the Agreement builds on government mitigation pledges (Nationally Determined Contributions, NDCs) that, for developing countries, largely depend on the availability of external funding. The existing pledges are estimated to imply a temperature increase of at least 2.7°C by 2100 (Ecofys et al. 2015; UNEP 2015b; UNFCCC

Color versions of one or more of the figures in the article can be found online at www.tandfonline.com/gini

2015b). While the Agreement foresees a "ratcheting up" of NDCs every five years, it remains to be seen whether this process can close the emissions gap.

The UNFCCC can be seen as being part of a larger regime complex for climate change (Keohane and Victor 2011). Hence achieving mitigation depends not only on the UNFCCC. High hopes have been put in transnational climate governance (TCG) initiatives, including subnational entities, private sector associations and individual firms, as well as NGOs. In 2014 UN Secretary-General Ban Ki-moon called a special summit inviting world leaders from finance, business, and civil society along with governments "to galvanize and catalyze climate action" (United Nations 2014). Similarly, in the run-up to the decisive 2015 UNFCCC conference in Paris, French President François Hollande underscored the important role of TCG initiatives (Hollande 2015:85).

A rich strand of academic literature exemplified by Bulkeley, Andonova, Bäckstrand, Betsill, Compagnon, Hale, Hoffmann, Newell, Paterson, Roger, and VanDeVeer (2014) examines the rise of these initiatives in recent years. However, it is unclear so far whether TCG initiatives are effective in reducing emissions (Stavins, Zou, Brewer, Conte Grand, den Elzen, Finus, Gupta, Höhne, Lee, Michaelowa, Paterson, Ramakrishna, Wen, Wiener, Winkler, Bodansky, Chan, Engels, Jaffe, Jakob, Jayaraman, Leiva, Lessmann, Newell, Olmstead, Pizer, Stowe, Vinluan 2014). Pinkse and Kolk (2009) stress the complexity of measuring outcomes. A number of papers suggest that effectiveness depends on complementarity with national and/or international regulation. Green (2013:2), for instance, describes the UNFCCC's Kyoto Protocol as a "coral reef" that attracts a number of interesting complementary initiatives. Pfeifer and Sullivan (2008) see government regulation as crucial to send signals to investors that are then reflected in a TCG initiative. Companies want to achieve their commitments in an efficient way and thus engage in TCG initiatives once national-level mitigation policy instruments have been established. Similar arguments about complementarities are made in the general literature on TCG initiatives (Berliner and Prakash 2014; Potoski and Prakash 2005) and by some of the articles in this issue. TCG initiatives may also influence government regulation, such as private carbon market standards that lead to an improvement in mandatory carbon market regulation (Hoffmann 2011). A substantial literature examines the general context in which such voluntary programs—in the area of climate change mitigation and beyond—can be successful (Baccaro and Mele 2011; Baranzini and Thalmann 2004; Berliner and Prakash 2015; Cashore, Auld, Bernstein and McDermott 2007; Darnall and Kim 2012; DeLeon and Rivera 2009; Morgenstern and Pizer 2007; Overdevest 2010; Overdevest and Zeitlin 2014).

We directly examine which contribution TCG initiatives can be expected to make to climate change mitigation. Our first contribution is the development of a specific set of criteria that can be used for that purpose covering the whole range of TCG initiatives. As it is too early for an evaluation of their effectiveness, we focus on their design and the direct mitigation benefits that can be expected thereof. In line with Koremenos, Lipson, and Snidal (2001a:767, 2001b:1079) we believe that design is highly relevant for later effectiveness and that therefore, the study of the initiatives' design already provides us with important elements for their evaluation. Our second contribution is the empirical examination of the conditions under which an initiative is more likely to fulfill these criteria. In this context, we specifically consider the initiatives' membership composition (entrepreneurial, NGOs, subnational) and their complementarity to national and international regulation. Eventually, we can shed some light on the question of whether the high expectations regarding the role of TCG initiatives for climate change mitigation can be fulfilled. Overall our results are rather sobering, but certain types of initiatives show promise in complementing existing regulation.

In principle, TCG initiatives can contribute to the ambitious target of the Paris Agreement in two ways: First, they can react to national or related international regulation by simply responding to these regulations promoting the concrete implementation of corresponding measures and thereby helping governments to reach their NDCs (or, prior to the Paris Agreement, their Kyoto targets). We refer to these initiatives as "*complementary initiatives.*" Second, they can proactively address the lack of national government ambition and thereby contribute to closing the current gap between the sum of NDCs and the mitigation needed to reach the Paris Agreement target. We refer to these initiatives as "*stand-alone initiatives.*" Despite their greater independence, stand-alone initiatives do not necessarily need to be more promising than complementary ones.

We expect these two types of initiatives to be driven by different motivations. Existing regulation may provide strong incentives for the private sector to develop innovative strategies to efficiently handle the respective requirements. This may lead to business-driven, complementary TCG initiatives. Other actors like NGOs may focus more on filling the gaps by pushing for reforms where existing regulation is lacking or appears to be insufficient. The underlying motivation should play a role for the design of these initiatives, and hence we will systematically distinguish between complementary and stand-alone initiatives when assessing whether and under which conditions they meet our key criteria for an effective mitigation-oriented institutional design. This provides important insights regarding the interaction of different institutions within the climate change regime complex and regarding the implications of this interaction for mitigation.

Our assessment of 109 initiatives started between 1990 and mid-2015 finds that less than 15% satisfy at least three of the following four criteria of a mitigation-oriented design: (1) existence of mitigation targets; (2) incentives for mitigation; (3) definition of a baseline; and (4) existence of a monitoring, reporting, and verification procedure. About half of the initiatives do not meet any of these criteria.

Through multivariate econometric analysis we show that entrepreneurial initiatives require regulation in order to have a mitigation-oriented design, while initiatives developed by subnational governments and NGOs are more likely to target mitigation beyond existing national-level policies. Overall, we conclude that the lack of mitigation ambition on the government level cannot be "made up" by mitigation achieved through transnational climate governance initiatives, as too few of the latter have a mitigation-oriented design.

Measuring the mitigation orientation of TCG initiatives

Many studies on transnational climate governance simply look at the emergence of new initiatives. An analysis of their expected or actual mitigation effectiveness is rare. This may lead to an overly optimistic picture. But how to assess the initiatives' potential to actually contribute to mitigation?

Conceptual difficulties

Measuring an initiative's mitigation contribution and thereby distinguishing effective from ineffective (or less effective) initiatives is a difficult task (Chan and Pauw 2014; Pinkse and Kolk 2009). It is rarely possible to directly observe effects of transnational initiatives or voluntary programs more generally. Exceptions are possible only when examining a single program on the basis of very detailed information of the mitigation action of its individual members. A convincing example is the analysis of the Global Compact by Berliner and Prakash (2015). Assessing the impact of a program further requires the specification of a plausible counterfactual or baseline. For instance, while we might be able to measure that emission reduction projects under the "Gold Standard" are indeed more convincing than projects that do not fulfill this standard, how do we know that these convincing projects would not have been better than other projects even without the existence of the standard? This identification problem plagues the literature of the effectiveness of international regimes more generally (see Helm and Sprinz 2000:633ff; Tetlock and Belkin 1996:3; Young 1999).

We solve this problem by focusing our analysis on the assessment of the different initiatives' institutional design. Thus, we can examine a broad range of initiatives and make them comparable with the view to a single objective, namely mitigation, the key goal of the Paris Agreement toward which TCG initiatives must contribute. From a results chain perspective, a mitigation-oriented design can be considered as an "output," the initial step toward effectiveness at the outcome or impact level. Assessing outputs is much less ambitious than assessing outcomes or impact, and it may entail the risk to overestimate success (Young 2011). Indeed the evaluation literature based on results chain frameworks typically considers the relevant outputs as a necessary but not a sufficient condition for outcomes and impact. Therefore, we look at the minimum requirements for possible effectiveness.

Admittedly, this perspective ignores unexpected or unintentional effects. Scholars from a social-constructionist school of thought discuss several theoretical mechanisms that may lead to an impact beyond initial intentions. They suggest that private initiatives, even if not initially designed for public good benefits, may eventually develop dynamics that could still yield such benefits in the long run driven by the interaction between different members within the initiative or between members and other actors such as national governments and consumers (for example Baccaro and Mele 2011; Cashore et al. 2007; Christensen, Morsing and Thyssen 2013; Haack, Schoeneborn, and Wickert 2012; Overdevest 2010; Overdevest and Zeitlin 2014). However, so far this literature tends to find only very limited empirical evidence for these processes to work in practice (Baccaro and Mele 2011; Cashore et al. 2007). Some exceptions seem to exist for specific areas and under specific conditions, such as strengthening consumer demand that induces competition between firms (Overdevest 2010; and Overdevest and Zeitlin 2014 for forestry).

We are thus rather skeptical about the significance of such positive dynamics in our context and doubt the potential of TCG initiatives without a mitigation-oriented design to develop in a way that generates significant mitigation. At least without considerable changes in external conditions (an exogenous rise in consumer demand or stronger regulation), whose effects would, however, not be confined to existing TCG initiatives, such developments seem to be rather unlikely. Therefore, we believe that a convincing mitigation-oriented design can indeed be considered as a minimum requirement for the later mitigation effectiveness of TCG initiatives.

What constitutes such a design? A potential trade-off between stringency and participation is frequently discussed in the institutional design literature (for example, Bernauer, Kalbhenn, Koubi, and Spilker 2013). The basic idea is that both stringency and broad-based participation are important, but that emphasis on the former tends to reduce the latter. Hence, the most stringent initiatives are not necessarily the most effective ones. Clearly, the optimum can neither lie at very low stringency (if there are no requirements, there will be no effect), nor at very low participation (if there are no participants, there will equally be no effect), but it must be somewhere in between. This implies that for sufficiently basic stringency criteria, enhancing stringency will lead to higher effectiveness.[1]

---

[1] Mathematically, this can be illustrated as follows. Let mitigation (M) be given by $M = x(m) \cdot m$, where m is mitigation achieved per member, and x is the number of members. x is a negative function of m. For simplicity, let it be a linear function, $x = a - bm$, with a and b being some positive parameters. Overall mitigation M can thus be rewritten as: $M = (a - bm) \cdot m$ or $M = am - bm^2$. We obtain the optimum by maximizing M over m: $M'(m) = a - 2bm = 0 => m^* = a/2b$. The optimal level of stringency is m^*. As long as stringency is below m^*, this is suboptimal even though lesser stringency increases membership. Only beyond m^*, greater stringency reduces effectiveness because the negative effect on membership overrides the positive direct effect of stringency.

The same argument can be made for the potential trade-off between stringency and the number of TCG initiatives. Having a large number of different initiatives may be beneficial for the effectiveness of the regime complex as a whole, and high stringency may limit the number of initiatives. Yet, again, the negative effect on the number of initiatives will only dominate the positive direct effect of stringency beyond a certain point.

We will hence formulate basic design criteria, which we consider necessary for any plausible effect on mitigation.

Basic design criteria for effective mitigation

Our ability to build on existing approaches in this context is very limited. To the best of our knowledge, no comprehensive classification of TCG initiatives with respect to their mitigation potential has been provided so far. UNEP (2015a) has come closest to this objective and provides a clear and credible approach, but by limiting the assessment to the analysis of mitigation targets the final indicator can be calculated only for a small subset of 15 initiatives. Similarly, Hsu, Moffat, Weinfurter, and Schwartz (2015) also focus on mitigation targets (announced either by the initiatives or by their members). While this focus on targets allows the authors to compute the potential volume of emission reductions, it ignores other pathways of climate change mitigation that are not directly quantified within the initiatives—for example, through the use of financial incentives. Research initiatives to go beyond these initial classifications are under way but not yet fully developed and applicable (Galvanizing the Groundswell of Climate Actions 2015; German Development Institute [GDI] and London School of Economics [LSE] 2015).

It appears to us that including other criteria beyond the definition of a mitigation target is essential to do justice to the different types of initiatives. As stated, financial incentives may also contribute to effective emission reductions, at times even more than the definition of targets. The Pilot Auction Facility, for example, invites project developers to participate in auctions and thereby selects and funds the most efficient mitigation projects. In addition, monitoring, reporting, and verification (MRV) devices can raise transparency and thereby create competition for best practice, at least as far as this is valued by the population. An example is the International Council of Local Environmental Initiatives (ICLEI), a city network that supports inventories of its members' emissions so that they become comparable within and across countries. This may have some effect even without the definition of targets. Finally, the definition of a baseline is important to distinguish any kind of mitigation activities from business as usual.

We hence consider four criteria that should be met for any initiative to plausibly contribute to mitigation action: the definition of a mitigation target, the introduction of financial incentives, the specification of a baseline, and the definition and use of MRV. Note that these criteria are truly basic in that we do not further specify any requirements regarding the stringency of the target, the volume of the financial incentives, or any special methodological requirements regarding the calculation of the baseline or the stringency and robustness of the MRV system. We only consider whether there is *any* mitigation target, incentive, baseline, or MRV.

We note a substantial complementarity among these criteria. In fact, a target without verification may not have any effect, no matter how ambitious the announcement. Similarly, financial incentives may not generate the expected effects if there is no monitoring—moral hazard would undermine mitigation. And the most serious monitoring may not guarantee any improvement beyond business as usual if the latter is not assessed. For any convincing initiative we would hence expect those criteria to be met simultaneously. A stand-alone initiative should ideally meet all four criteria; for complementary initiatives, either a mitigation target or a financial incentive may be sufficient to generate mitigation benefits. For instance, the target may be provided through national commitments made under the Kyoto Protocol, so that individual initiatives would not need to define such targets. However, even initiatives intended to complement rather than to substitute for domestic and international regulation are much more credible when several criteria are fulfilled.

Figure 1 presents the distribution of initiatives according to the number of criteria met. It shows that only a single initiative meets all four criteria while almost half of the initiatives do not meet any of them: 25% of the initiatives meet only one of the four criteria, 15% two, and 13% three. Given the complementarities discussed previously, we must conclude that only 13% of all 109 TCG initiatives show a design convincingly directed at climate change mitigation, and only one may be considered convincing as a stand-alone initiative. Especially since there are no requirements regarding the level

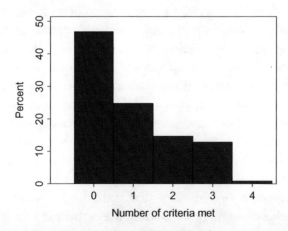

Figure 1. Share of initiatives meeting zero to four basic design criteria for effective mitigation.

Table 1. TCG initiatives by purpose.

Main purpose of TCG initiatives	Number	Share
A. Mitigation		
Networking	63	57.8%
Standards	21	19.3%
Carbon funds	9	8.3%
Technology development	4	3.7%
Other	7	6.4%
B. Adaptation	5	4.6%
Total	109	100%

of ambition underlying the individual design criteria, the overall distribution provides little justification for the high hopes expressed regarding their potential to support governments in meeting their mitigation objectives or to even go beyond that. The shares of initiatives fulfilling the individual criteria are: 46% for MRV, 27% for a baseline, 13% for incentives, and 11% for a mitigation target (see Appendix I, Table A1).

Not surprisingly, this sobering result regarding the design characteristics of TCG initiatives directly reflects their purpose. Table 1 provides an overview that illustrates this point: While most initiatives are mitigation related in principle, many focus on networking, and direct benefits for mitigation are not necessarily intended. Such initiatives may still be valuable for their respective purposes, but we expect a limited climate change mitigation benefit.

Theoretical considerations

The creation of a TCG initiative with a design encouraging effective mitigation reflects the disposition of its members to actively engage in combating climate change. However, why should a rational actor want to take any serious steps toward mitigation given that true mitigation is usually costly, and so is even the mere participation in transnational networks (see Dolšak and Prakash, 2017)?

In our theoretical discussion, we distinguish between three major groups of participants within TCG initiatives: The private sector (firms and business associations), subnational governments, and NGOs. We will discuss the incentives of each of these groups and to what extent they depend on existing regulation at the national and international level. In addition, we consider the role that national governments or international organizations may play in reinforcing the incentives for creating TCG initiatives designed for effective mitigation.

Private sector

The general literature on voluntary corporate environmental programs identifies several mechanisms that may create incentives for the private sector to participate in such initiatives. Berliner and Prakash (2014, 2015) suggest that demand for products from participating firms may be greater allowing price increases. More generally, firms can reap reputational benefits (Potoski and Prakash 2005, 2013; see also Green 2017), directly increasing their market value. However, to ensure that reputation cannot accrue from simple window dressing, considerable transparency is required. In climate change mitigation, such transparency is not easy to achieve and may depend on national and international regulation. Furthermore, public awareness often depends on national and international government action since debates about existing or upcoming regulation, notably at UNFCCC meetings, frequently spur substantial media attention (see, for example, Michaelowa and Michaelowa 2012:578; Footnote 2 also refers to additional details in the earlier discussion paper version).

Moreover, provided there is domestic regulation, membership in a TCG initiative may signal regulatory compliance to the national authorities (for example, through ISO certification of their company-internal processes) who then redirect their verification efforts toward other firms. In this case, the firms can reduce transaction costs of the verification process. This obviously hinges on the seriousness of the national verification process, including the absence of corruption (Berliner and Prakash 2014).

A similar mechanism is conceivable with respect to international regulation. For instance, to facilitate the acceptance of a project under the Kyoto Protocol's Clean Development Mechanism (CDM), which generates certified emission reductions that can be sold on the market, it may be helpful to adhere to the stricter rules of the private "Gold Standard" initiative in the first place.

Finally, firms' voluntary engagement may be based on the expectation to achieve domestic or international regulatory requirements in a more cost-efficient manner. This may be achieved by the promotion of research and development activities or by exploring first mover advantages: for example, by investing in carbon funds early on to benefit low-hanging fruits—cheap and large mitigation interventions. In these cases, participation in voluntary initiatives may make sense as soon as the regulation is expected, even if it is not yet agreed upon.

All this suggests that the private sector should have a strong incentive to respond to existing or imminent domestic and/or international greenhouse gas emissions regulation by participating in effective mitigation-oriented TCG initiatives. However, can mitigation-oriented TCG initiatives also be attractive for the private sector independently of national or international regulation?

In principle, they could if there were sufficiently high direct cobenefits—for example, through information about new and efficient technologies that can reduce production costs in the medium to long term. We expect, however, that efficient technological adjustments are already partially accounted for in business as usual scenarios and that the specific (additional) mitigation orientation of such stand-alone initiatives will thus be low, notably in comparison to initiatives created in response to existing regulation.

> H1: *Stand-alone entrepreneurial TCG initiatives do not have a mitigation-oriented design.*

> H2: *Complementary entrepreneurial initiatives (entrepreneurial initiatives responding to existing or imminent national or international regulation) have a stronger mitigation-oriented design than stand-alone initiatives.*

Subnational governments

Regarding subnational entities such as regions or cities, we assume that the profit maximizing perspective we adopted for firms can be replaced by a utility maximizing perspective based on public support or, more specifically, electoral support if countries are democracies. People in specific localities may have a direct interest in climate change mitigation that is not met by regulation at the international or domestic level. In fact, in many countries in which the populations are most vulnerable to climate change, domestic regulation has no potential to solve the problem: Because of poverty and lack of industrialization, there are hardly any local emissions that could be reduced. Transnational cooperation of subnational entities such as cities and regional governments may then provide an alternative avenue to push the agenda. The effectiveness of transnational cooperation created on this basis will, of course, depend on the willingness of high greenhouse gas emitters to also participate in such initiatives and to increase their mitigation efforts. If high emitters are not willing to make such serious efforts and this can be anticipated by developing countries, it does not make much sense for the latter to promote such initiatives either.

The key question therefore is whether people in highly emitting regions—possibly without much direct benefit from climate change mitigation—may support local or regional governments engaging in TCG initiatives. This could happen because they generally value the protection of the environment and/or care for people more directly concerned in other world regions or in later generations. Cobenefits of greenhouse gas mitigation such as reduction of health costs due to local air pollution can also provide a motivation, notably in emerging economies. This can lead to special efforts by some subnational governments to go beyond required regulation or to even try to compensate for national and international policies that are considered to be insufficient.

At the same time, the literature also suggests positive relationships between national environmental policies, national regulation, and the engagement of subnational entities (Andonova, Hale, and Roger 2014). By highlighting the role of domestic NGOs on the engagement of cities, Dolšak and Prakash (2017) also point at the link between national and subnational policy support. Moreover, arguing that domestic mitigation policy instruments may loosen the subnational units' budget constraints, Cao and Ward (2017) provide an alternative theoretical rationale for a complementary rather than stand-alone engagement of cities and regions. However, this only applies for specific national policies that provide a direct financial reward for mitigation action.

In sum, as opposed to private firms, theoretical arguments can be made for both stand-alone and complementary activities of subnational entities. We consider that notwithstanding the previous arguments, their engagement for mitigation-oriented design of TCG initiatives may be even greater for stand-alone initiatives because in many areas, regulation at higher levels will already fulfill the needs of the local constituencies. Except for the rationale based on special financial incentives provided by national governments, even in the case of complementary initiatives, the argument for local or regional governments' interests to achieve mitigation eventually hinges on either altruistic preferences of the population that may be partially offset by vested interests of local industries or on local cobenefits that tend to be relevant only up to a certain point in economic development. Beyond this point local pollutants will be reduced through the use of filters and other technical devices, while greenhouse gas emissions continue to rise. Overall, this may lead to some positive, albeit not very strong, incentives to participate in TCG initiatives with a convincing mitigation-oriented design.

> H3: *TCG initiatives based on subnational government membership have a mitigation-oriented design (albeit only weakly so).*
>
> H4: *Stand-alone TCG initiatives based on subnational government membership have a stronger mitigation-oriented design than complementary initiatives.*

NGOs

NGOs are usually assumed to be intrinsically motivated for climate change mitigation driven by environmental and distributional norms. As people self-select into different groups of actors, it is indeed plausible that NGO members have particularly strong preferences in this respect. This should induce them to promote both transnational activities complementary to existing regulatory policies and stand-alone initiatives going beyond current regulation. In order to be most effective, they might even wish to engage primarily in stand-alone activities attempting to move things ahead where government has not (yet) taken any responsibility.

However, NGOs work under budget constraints, just like any other actors considered here. Their budget is usually composed of private donations and public subsidies. This is why their activities also depend on the valuation by the general public and different levels of government. If a topic runs out of fashion, NGO resources in this area may dry up. This is why even for NGO-driven initiatives the stand-alone potential must be considered as rather limited.

It should also be noted that NGOs cannot themselves reduce emissions but only induce others to do so. As a consequence, there are no TCG initiatives only consisting of NGOs, and in the TCG initiatives where they are present, they tend to focus on consulting or knowledge sharing. While their inclusion might signal a willingness of all actors to strive for climate change mitigation, their actual influence on the design of the initiative may be limited.

> H5: *TCG initiatives with NGO membership have a mitigation-oriented design (albeit only weakly so).*

> H6: *Stand-alone TCG initiatives with NGO membership have a stronger mitigation-oriented design than complementary initiatives.*

Orchestration by international organizations and national governments

Finally, we consider international organizations and national governments that initiate and shape TCG initiatives. While "initiating" refers to the influential role as a founding member, "shaping" refers to an influence over the initiative after its creation, either directly or through funding. They are considered as the two dimensions of "orchestration," which is examined in detail by Hale and Roger (2014).

In our view, orchestration should be positively related to a design for TCG initiatives that effectively addresses mitigation. While national governments can contribute funding and establish matching national policies (for example, through the recognition of certain standards for offset credits), international organizations can provide advice or help strengthening the coordination between members. Sometimes they also host the initiatives. Thus, the initiatives are regularly exposed to the ideas developed in the organization in which they are embedded. Since some international organizations such as the World Bank have already gained considerable experience in the field of carbon market mechanisms, they could use their influence to improve the mitigation orientation in the design of TCG initiatives.

They might use their influence even more at times when their climate-related preferences are not matched by corresponding progress at the international level. As illustrated by the example of the Ban Ki-moon summit, during the pre-Paris lack of progress at the UNFCCC level, there was a clear attempt to mobilize stand-alone bottom-up initiatives. This suggests a general tendency of increased initiating and shaping activities in recent years, possibly also with an effect on the mitigation-related design of these initiatives. As a consequence, the role of orchestration might be even greater for stand-alone initiatives than for complementary ones.

> H7: *TCG initiatives orchestrated by international organizations and national governments have a mitigation-oriented design.*

H8: *For stand-alone TCG initiatives, orchestration has a stronger positive effect on mitigation-oriented design than for complementary initiatives.*

Empirical analysis

We test these hypotheses for a total of 109 initiatives. They include 65 initiatives from the Roger, Hale and Andonova (2017) data set. From the original data, 10 observations have been dropped because they either constitute subinitiatives of initiatives already taken into account, do not meet Hale and Roger's (2014) inclusion criteria for TGC initiatives (according to the latest information available on the respective Web sites), or do not provide any information at all so that not even their mere existence can be ascertained. At the same time, we update the data set by including 44 additional initiatives, mostly for the period from 2010 onwards, when the coverage of the original data set ends. To select these initiatives, we follow the original codebook used by Roger et al. (2017), based on the definitions developed in Andonova, Betsill, and Bulkeley (2009) that were first applied in Bulkeley et al. (2012, 2014).

Operationalization

Let us first define our dependent variables. Based on our four basic criteria, several indicators could be used. Given their complementarity, we would ideally have constructed an indicator variable for those initiatives that meet all four criteria. However, as this is the case only for a single initiative, we provide alternative indicators based on lower requirements. "Three criteria met" is a dummy variable taking the value of 1 if three out of the four conditions are fulfilled, and "two criteria met" is a similar measure for at least two criteria being met. For each of these, Figure 2 shows the number of initiatives by foundation year as well as the total number of initiatives created. The latter shows a peak after the entry into force of the Kyoto Protocol in 2005 and in 2014 due to the Ban Ki-moon summit.

In addition to these indicators, we use a variable for the total number of criteria met measured by adding up all criteria that are fulfilled ("sum of criteria"). Finally, we consider all the individual criteria separately. This leads to seven dependent variables that are systematically introduced in all our regression tables.

The operationalization of our explanatory variables relies partly on Roger et al. (2017) (for a discussion, see also Bulkeley et al. 2012). To distinguish the actor groups, we use the categories "entrepreneurial" (nonstate actors played the leading role in initiating the initiatives) and "transgovernmental" (only substate actors were responsible for their creation). While the definition of entrepreneurial initiatives does not exclude NGOs, in practice, this

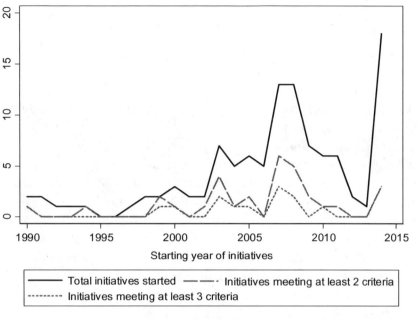

Figure 2. The development of new initiatives, overall and by number of criteria met. *Note.* The y-axis shows the number of newly created initiatives. The year 2015 is omitted due to incomplete observations.

category is dominated by the private sector (firms and business associations). To specifically analyze the role of NGOs, we code an additional indicator variable "NGO members" for TCG initiatives including NGOs. NGOs usually do not create TCG initiatives (although there are some exceptions), but they may be members in initiatives created by others and thereby able to exert some influence. Note that only the first two categories (entrepreneurial and transgovernmental) are mutually exclusive. At the same time, some initiatives do not fall in any of the categories—for example, when they are initiated by international organizations and do not have NGO membership.

For orchestration, we supplement the variables for initiating and shaping from the Roger et al. (2017) database by the additional indicator "Depends on gov.," which captures the initiation of the initiative by national governments (and in exceptional cases some other form of direct influence of government policy, without participation of the government in the initiative).

Our concept of stand-alone versus complementary initiatives is measured in relation to the existence of country targets ("Country target") representing national regulation[2] and the existence of a functional legally binding international regime ("Kyoto operational") representing international regulation. This period of effective international regulation (2005–2009) is contrasted

---

[2]Country targets have to meet some minimum stringency criteria as defined by Ecofys et al. (2014) to be counted here. See the appendix, Table A1.

with the period "Post Copenhagen" (after 2009) where it became clear that the Kyoto Protocol had no long-term future. A TCG initiative created in a country with a country target or during the period in which the Kyoto Protocol was operational is considered as complementary, otherwise as stand-alone.

We systematically control for those initiatives whose main purpose is adaptation ("Adaptation focus"), as well as for the membership structure ("Structure") of the initiative varying from 1 (centralized) to 3 (decentralized), thereby capturing the specificities of networking initiatives. In addition, we control for the initiatives' starting year ("Year") and for cases in which there is no single founding country because the initiative was set up by international organizations, the World Bank ("WB"), the European Union ("EU"), or other international organizations ("INT"). In additional analyses presented in the appendix, we further control for economic, political, and emission-related characteristics of the founding country.

Results

Tables 2–4 present the results from heteroscedasticity-consistent linear regression models (see Appendix II for a methodological discussion). In Table 2 the focus is on complementary versus stand-alone initiatives with respect to national regulation. In Table 3 the perspective shifts to international regulation. Finally, Table 4 provides some more insights in the role of orchestration. The appendix follows the same structure with a larger set of controls (see Tables A2-A4).

Throughout all models (in all tables), national governments seem to play an important role. The variable "Depends on gov." is one of the most robustly significant variables across all regressions. It increases the "sum of criteria" by more than one point and raises the probability to achieve a positive score on "two criteria met" and "three criteria met" as well as on most of the individual criteria by over 50%. A general exception is the mitigation target. This is plausible, since a country can be expected to set its mitigation target through other means, so that this is not what governments would primarily encourage TCG initiatives to do. Among the other individual criteria, the effect is the smallest (and least significant) for MRV—probably because generally, most initiatives focus on this aspect. Overall, however, this result suggests a strong effect of national government initiation and thereby provides some initial support for Hypothesis 7.

Another variable that quite robustly shows a positive association with the mitigation focus of TCG initiatives is the existence of country targets in the founding country. Regarding the coefficient estimates for the individual criteria, the effect is at times only marginally significant or not significant at all, but the

Table 2. Correlates of mitigation-related design – examining complementarity with national regulation.

	(1) Sum of criteria	(2) 2 criteria met	(3) 3 criteria met	(4) Mitigation target	(5) Incentives	(6) Baseline	(7) MRV
Depends on gov.	1.49***	0.58***	0.77***	0.00	0.62***	0.54***	0.32**
	(0.00)	(0.00)	(0.00)	(0.98)	(0.00)	(0.00)	(0.03)
Country target	1.14*	0.35*	0.45*	0.18	0.29*	0.35	0.32
	(0.07)	(0.10)	(0.06)	(0.14)	(0.07)	(0.11)	(0.44)
Entrepreneurial	-0.14**	-0.10***	0.05	0.03*	-0.05	-0.09**	-0.02
	(0.04)	(0.00)	(0.11)	(0.10)	(0.10)	(0.02)	(0.48)
Target x Entrepr.	0.37	0.20	-0.12	0.11	0.04	0.16	0.05
	(0.24)	(0.15)	(0.27)	(0.36)	(0.37)	(0.23)	(0.58)
Transgovernmental	0.39***	0.08*	0.19***	0.18***	-0.09**	0.09**	0.20***
	(0.00)	(0.07)	(0.00)	(0.00)	(0.02)	(0.03)	(0.00)
Target x Transg.	-0.65*	-0.15	-0.24***	-0.21*	0.21**	-0.16	-0.49***
	(0.07)	(0.19)	(0.00)	(0.08)	(0.05)	(0.15)	(0.01)
NGO members	0.32	0.06	0.21*	0.06	0.18***	0.09	-0.01
	(0.15)	(0.34)	(0.10)	(0.13)	(0.00)	(0.41)	(0.91)
Target x NGOs	-0.42	-0.04	-0.19	-0.11*	-0.16**	-0.10	-0.05
	(0.18)	(0.57)	(0.17)	(0.07)	(0.01)	(0.36)	(0.85)
Structure	-0.36***	-0.16**	-0.01	0.04	-0.04	-0.17**	-0.20***
	(0.00)	(0.03)	(0.80)	(0.11)	(0.46)	(0.04)	(0.00)
Adaptation focus	-0.82	-0.26	-0.21	-0.06	-0.14	-0.24	-0.38*
	(0.12)	(0.20)	(0.14)	(0.17)	(0.44)	(0.20)	(0.07)
EU	1.21***	0.36***	0.42***	0.89***	-0.16	0.35***	0.14
	(0.01)	(0.00)	(0.00)	(0.00)	(0.15)	(0.00)	(0.39)
WB	0.50	0.18	0.13	0.07	0.29	0.08	0.05
	(0.45)	(0.40)	(0.61)	(0.47)	(0.11)	(0.72)	(0.89)
INT	0.61	0.24	0.24	0.00	0.32**	0.20	0.09
	(0.30)	(0.18)	(0.27)	(0.98)	(0.04)	(0.23)	(0.82)
Year	-0.02	-0.00	-0.00	-0.00	-0.01	-0.00	-0.02**
	(0.18)	(0.82)	(0.82)	(0.92)	(0.13)	(0.99)	(0.03)
Constant	47.38	3.97	2.92	1.35	13.98	0.58	31.47**
	(0.17)	(0.81)	(0.84)	(0.93)	(0.13)	(0.97)	(0.03)
Adj. R2	0.46	0.39	0.45	0.15	0.50	0.36	0.34
N	109	109	109	109	109	109	109

Note. Linear regression models with p-values in parentheses based on robust standard errors (heteroscedasticity consistent and clustered by founding country); ***, ** and * indicate significance at the 1%-, 5%- and 10%-level respectively. Variable names are abbreviated in interaction terms: Country target → Target, Entrepreneurial → Entrepr., Transgovernmental → Transg., NGO members → NGOs.

effect on the aggregated measures "sum of criteria," "two criteria met," and "three criteria met" is always significant at least for one of these measures. This provides a first indication of relevant complementarities between effective TCG initiatives and national regulation. The complementarities that other authors in this volume find between the creation of new initiatives and government regulation hence also exist regarding the mitigation orientation of these initiatives.

Note that in Table 2 (and Table A2) the coefficient estimates and significance of this variable have to be interpreted differently than in the other tables, as the variable also enters in different interaction terms to explore complementarity with the engagement of individual actors. The coefficient of the variable itself only refers to those initiatives that are neither entrepreneurial, nor transgovernmental, nor have NGO members.

Table 2 shows that in the absence of country targets, the overall association of entrepreneurial initiatives with a mitigation-oriented design tends to be negative. Regression 2 for instance, indicates that the probability that entrepreneurial initiatives meet at least two out of our four basic criteria is 10% lower than for other initiatives. The existence of a country target does not seem to matter much in this context, as all interaction terms are insignificant. The overall negative assessment is consistent with other evaluations of voluntary agreements of companies that have been found mostly to represent business as usual (Baranzini and Thalmann 2004) or to focus on the least-costly measures that still guarantee recognition by the market (Berliner and Prakash 2015). The findings are also in line with Hypothesis 1 that expected no mitigation-oriented design for stand-alone entrepreneurial initiatives. Yet Hypothesis 2 suggested a more strongly mitigation-oriented design for complementary initiatives. At least on the basis of our proxy for national regulation, we find no evidence for this.

However, in our estimations, the negative association is not homogeneous across all criteria. Entrepreneurial initiatives seem to do relatively well regarding the specification of mitigation targets, which is the least frequently met criterion otherwise. In addition, there are individual entrepreneurial activities that score really highly, so that there is no significant effect with respect to the "three criteria met" indicator.

As opposed to entrepreneurial initiatives, in the absence of domestic regulation, transgovernmental initiatives are clearly positively associated with the initiatives' mitigation orientation. The coefficient is significant and positive for all three aggregated indicators: "sum of criteria," "two criteria met," and "three criteria met." However, if there is a domestic target, the effect is reversed. It seems that, in line with Hypothesis 4, transgovernmental actors compensate (at least partly) for a lack of regulation by generating their own, mitigation-oriented TCG initiatives. When there is a national target, they do not seem to see the requirement for their own engagement any more. We expected the stronger design in cases of missing domestic regulation, but we did expect that some (albeit weak) positive correlation would remain even when national regulation is functioning (Hypothesis 3). This cannot be observed in our data. Interestingly, with respect to the incentives-related subindicator—Regression 5—the relationship is reverse. Apparently, subnational entities engage in incentive-based initiatives in a way that complements domestic regulation. Maybe in this specific context, the intention is to financially support private companies in the subnational constituencies in meeting the requirements of national regulation.

Again in line with our theoretical argument (Hypotheses 5 and 6), initiatives including NGOs tend to show similar characteristics as transgovernmental initiatives. While the association is less clearly significant, there is evidence for a positive effect of NGO participation when there is no country target—the overall effect is significant for "three criteria met" (see Regression 3)—and primarily works through a higher share of incentive-based mechanisms (see Regression 5)—and a reversal of this effect indicated by negative coefficients of similar size when such a country target is present.

In sum, we observe that, as opposed to entrepreneurial initiatives where stand-alone initiatives are negatively associated with mitigation-oriented design, stand-alone initiatives of subnational entities and NGOs show a stronger mitigation-oriented design than complementary initiatives. This is in line with our theoretical predictions. Results are confirmed by the analysis presented in the appendix.

Table 3 presents a similar analysis with respect to international regulation. Our indicators for functional international regulation ("Kyoto operational") and the lack thereof ("Post Copenhagen") are therefore interacted with the three actor-related variables. A positive interaction term with "Kyoto operational" and a negative interaction term with "Post Copenhagen" indicate that the actors tended to initiate TCG initiatives with a relatively clear mitigation-oriented design as a complement to functioning international rules, while the reversed signs indicate a stronger mitigation-oriented design for stand-alone initiatives.

Examining entrepreneurial initiatives first, we find indications of complementarity with significant coefficients in Regressions 1 for "sum of criteria," 4 for mitigation targets, and 7 for MRV (where, however, only the negative coefficient for the interaction term with "Post Copenhagen" is significant). This provides some confirmation for our theoretical argument that private companies come up with effectively designed initiatives when rules and regulation lead them to expect that some costly action is unavoidable. While we did not find this effect with respect to domestic regulation, the effect with respect to international regulation appears quite clear. This provides support for Hypothesis 2, at least regarding the international level.

In contrast, just as in the context of national regulation, transgovernmental initiatives with a mitigation-oriented design rather tend to emerge when regulation is perceived to be lacking at the international level. While transgovernmental TCG initiatives did not stand out for particular effectiveness during the high time of the Kyoto Protocol, we find some positively significant coefficient estimates for these initiatives during the post-Copenhagen period (see Regression 1 for "sum of criteria" and Regression 4 for the definition of mitigation targets). These results indicate more stand-alone initiatives with mitigation-oriented designs when the UNFCCC process

Table 3. Correlates of mitigation-related design – examining complementarity with international regulation.

	(1) Sum of criteria	(2) 2 criteria met	(3) 3 criteria met	(4) Mitigation target	(5) Incentives	(6) Baseline	(7) MRV
Depends on gov.	1.44***	0.55***	0.70***	0.04	0.57***	0.50***	0.33*
	(0.00)	(0.00)	(0.00)	(0.47)	(0.00)	(0.00)	(0.05)
Country target	1.05*	0.35*	0.35*	0.16	0.24	0.35**	0.30
	(0.09)	(0.08)	(0.08)	(0.23)	(0.11)	(0.04)	(0.50)
Kyoto operational	-0.31	0.02	-0.21	-0.10	-0.08	-0.17	0.04
	(0.54)	(0.96)	(0.24)	(0.55)	(0.57)	(0.64)	(0.89)
Post Copenhagen	0.17	0.13	-0.03	-0.03	-0.02	0.02	0.19
	(0.78)	(0.70)	(0.89)	(0.89)	(0.93)	(0.96)	(0.63)
Entrepreneurial	-0.00	0.07	-0.13	0.11	-0.12	-0.08	0.09
	(0.99)	(0.73)	(0.32)	(0.26)	(0.25)	(0.73)	(0.56)
Kyoto x Entrepr.	0.69*	0.14	0.14	0.16*	0.14	0.29	0.10
	(0.08)	(0.40)	(0.30)	(0.07)	(0.36)	(0.21)	(0.73)
Copenh. x Entrepr.	-0.50**	-0.18	0.03	-0.21*	0.12	-0.05	-0.36**
	(0.05)	(0.28)	(0.80)	(0.09)	(0.33)	(0.82)	(0.04)
Transgovernmental	-0.93	-0.20	-0.30	-0.17	-0.05	-0.28	-0.43
	(0.13)	(0.47)	(0.32)	(0.37)	(0.77)	(0.34)	(0.17)
Kyoto x Transg.	1.32	0.35	0.57	0.16	0.24	0.50	0.43
	(0.16)	(0.34)	(0.15)	(0.39)	(0.29)	(0.25)	(0.30)
Copenh. x Transg.	1.29***	0.22	0.40	0.49***	0.04	0.28	0.48
	(0.01)	(0.34)	(0.10)	(0.00)	(0.83)	(0.22)	(0.11)
NGO members	0.16	0.15	0.04	-0.01	0.16	0.05	-0.03
	(0.73)	(0.41)	(0.87)	(0.91)	(0.23)	(0.83)	(0.90)
Kyoto x NGOs	-0.03	-0.14	0.12	0.04	-0.03	0.00	-0.05
	(0.94)	(0.58)	(0.57)	(0.81)	(0.79)	(0.99)	(0.75)
Copenh. x NGOs	-0.20	-0.14	0.01	-0.04	-0.17	-0.06	0.06
	(0.72)	(0.56)	(0.97)	(0.70)	(0.20)	(0.82)	(0.82)
Structure	-0.30	-0.14	-0.02	0.07*	-0.02	-0.16	-0.20***
	(0.12)	(0.12)	(0.79)	(0.08)	(0.77)	(0.13)	(0.00)
Adaptation focus	-0.73*	-0.24	-0.17*	-0.02	-0.13	-0.22	-0.36*
	(0.09)	(0.18)	(0.09)	(0.55)	(0.40)	(0.11)	(0.05)
EU	1.32***	0.33***	0.43***	0.99***	-0.07	0.32***	0.08
	(0.00)	(0.00)	(0.00)	(0.00)	(0.55)	(0.00)	(0.59)
WB	0.74	0.25	0.20	0.13	0.33*	0.15	0.13
	(0.23)	(0.24)	(0.35)	(0.28)	(0.07)	(0.40)	(0.74)
INT	0.88	0.27	0.32*	0.10	0.30*	0.26*	0.22
	(0.15)	(0.14)	(0.09)	(0.37)	(0.05)	(0.08)	(0.62)
Year	-0.05	-0.01	-0.01	-0.00	-0.00	-0.00	-0.03
	(0.18)	(0.64)	(0.67)	(0.80)	(0.66)	(0.79)	(0.14)
Constant	91.35	16.19	12.43	7.83	3.49	10.22	69.82
	(0.18)	(0.64)	(0.68)	(0.81)	(0.68)	(0.78)	(0.14)
Adj. R2	0.48	0.37	0.45	0.17	0.47	0.35	0.32
N	109	109	109	109	109	109	109

Note. Linear regression models with p-values in parentheses based on robust standard errors (heteroscedasticity consistent and clustered by founding country);
***, **and *indicate significance at the 1%-, 5%- and 10%-level respectively. Variable names are abbreviated in interaction terms: Kyoto operational → Kyoto, Post Copenhagen → Copenh., Entrepreneurial → Entrepr., Transgovernmental → Transg., NGO members → NGOs.

seemed to stall. The substantial effect on "sum of criteria" is strong, indicating that on average, after the Copenhagen summit, newly initiated transgovernmental TCG initiatives met over one criterion more than in earlier periods (the reference period is the period before 2005). These results are again in line with our theoretical arguments—namely, Hypothesis 4. Only for initiatives with strong NGO membership do we not find any significant effects, so that Hypothesis 6 cannot be confirmed at the international level. As before, results are generally confirmed by the regressions with further control variables in the appendix, although results for entrepreneurial initiatives are somewhat less significant, while results for transnational ones are even more significant than presented here.

We finally come back to the role of national governments' or international organizations' orchestration. As already mentioned earlier, the role of governments in getting the initiatives started has a robust positive effect on designs oriented toward effective mitigation. Beyond this, we do not find any specific effects for international organizations initiating TCG initiatives (results not shown). However, when we look at the second component of orchestration—namely, shaping or influencing the development of an initiative beyond its creation—we find a number of interesting correlations (see Table 4). In particular, the interaction term with the "Post Copenhagen" dummy is generally large, positive, and highly significant. This is consistent with an attempt of national governments and/or international organizations to compensate for the insufficiency of international regulation by supporting stand-alone TCG initiatives and thereby confirms Hypothesis 8. Only with respect to the incentive criterion, the effect is quite different (see Regression 5). It appears that in this context, shaping was relatively most successful in the period before Kyoto became operational, while other, nonshaped initiatives focused more on incentives thereafter.[3]

Given that the World Bank is a major player in the orchestration of TCG initiatives, one might imagine that the strong effect of shaping for the mitigation orientation of stand-alone initiatives is driven by the Bank's interventions. To test this, we also interact the period dummies with the dummy for the World Bank as the founding agent. It becomes clear that the increasing focus on a mitigation-oriented design in the post-Copenhagen period is not due to World Bank engagement. At the exception of the mitigation target, the association between World Bank-founded initiatives and the design criteria met was highest in the period before Kyoto became operational and lower both during the high time of the Kyoto Protocol and after the Copenhagen conference. All results are again confirmed by the corresponding, more complete regression table in the appendix.

---

[3] Given our focus on institutional design, it may be surprising to see that—at least regarding the influence of international organizations—shaping has a stronger role here than initiating, although it refers to a later period in the life of the institution. We assume that this is related to some influence the relevant organizations may have had right from the beginning, even though they did not join the initiative as a founding member.

Table 4. Correlates of mitigation-related design – examining 'shaping' in conjunction with international regulation.

	(1) Sum of criteria	(2) 2 criteria met	(3) 3 criteria met	(4) Mitigation target	(5) Incentives	(6) Baseline	(7) MRV
Depends on gov.	1.14***	0.45***	0.75***	-0.08	0.56***	0.44***	0.22
	(0.00)	(0.00)	(0.00)	(0.41)	(0.00)	(0.00)	(0.19)
Country target	0.91	0.33**	0.32	0.19**	0.22	0.28*	0.23
	(0.14)	(0.04)	(0.18)	(0.03)	(0.21)	(0.10)	(0.56)
Kyoto operational	0.10	0.02	-0.01	-0.04	0.01	0.07	0.06
	(0.77)	(0.87)	(0.89)	(0.49)	(0.89)	(0.63)	(0.82)
Post Copenhagen	0.15	0.03	0.03	-0.03	-0.03	0.07	0.14
	(0.75)	(0.88)	(0.87)	(0.83)	(0.78)	(0.71)	(0.76)
Shaping	0.12	0.01	0.13	-0.11	0.37***	0.05	-0.19
	(0.72)	(0.96)	(0.49)	(0.21)	(0.00)	(0.73)	(0.35)
Kyoto x Shaping	-0.31	0.09	-0.17	-0.01	-0.43***	0.05	0.08
	(0.62)	(0.73)	(0.39)	(0.91)	(0.00)	(0.83)	(0.81)
Copenh. x Shaping	1.64***	0.99***	-0.17	0.07	-0.41***	0.95***	1.03***
	(0.00)	(0.00)	(0.39)	(0.41)	(0.00)	(0.00)	(0.00)
Kyoto x WB	-0.98***	-0.35***	-0.36***	0.09**	-0.05	-0.76***	-0.26
	(0.00)	(0.00)	(0.00)	(0.02)	(0.38)	(0.00)	(0.14)
Copenh. x WB	-0.62**	-0.32***	0.00	-0.00	-0.01	-0.35***	-0.26
	(0.03)	(0.01)	(0.99)	(1.00)	(0.84)	(0.00)	(0.28)
Structure	-0.45***	-0.19***	-0.03	0.02	-0.02	-0.20***	-0.24***
	(0.00)	(0.00)	(0.51)	(0.44)	(0.61)	(0.01)	(0.00)
Adaptation focus	-0.78**	-0.24	-0.12	-0.13**	-0.14	-0.16*	-0.35**
	(0.04)	(0.15)	(0.15)	(0.05)	(0.41)	(0.07)	(0.04)
EU	0.90***	0.23**	0.42***	0.81***	-0.04	0.26**	-0.12
	(0.00)	(0.02)	(0.00)	(0.00)	(0.21)	(0.02)	(0.22)
WB	1.11	0.44*	0.22	0.07	0.35	0.44*	0.25
	(0.14)	(0.07)	(0.47)	(0.34)	(0.11)	(0.08)	(0.56)
INT	0.53	0.16	0.29	0.03	0.28	0.14	0.08
	(0.39)	(0.28)	(0.22)	(0.77)	(0.11)	(0.36)	(0.84)
Year	-0.03	-0.00	-0.00	0.00	-0.00	-0.00	-0.03
	(0.39)	(0.85)	(0.87)	(0.99)	(0.66)	(0.82)	(0.35)
Constant	63.71	6.67	4.86	-0.20	3.78	8.37	51.76
	(0.38)	(0.85)	(0.88)	(0.99)	(0.67)	(0.81)	(0.34)
Adj. R2	0.47	0.43	0.42	0.10	0.45	0.44	0.35
N	109	109	109	109	109	109	109

Note. Linear regression models with p-values in parentheses based on robust standard errors (heteroscedasticity consistent and clustered by founding country);
***, **and *indicate significance at the 1%-, 5%- and 10%-level respectively. Variable names are abbreviated in interaction terms: Kyoto operational → Kyoto, Post Copenhagen → Copenh.

In sum, our empirical results are largely in line with theoretical expectations. There is no evidence for any kind of stand-alone moves by private firms toward TCG initiatives with a mitigation-oriented design but some evidence for related activities in response to international regulation (in line with Hypotheses 1 and 2). In contrast, some attempts to establish mitigation-oriented stand-alone initiatives when national and international regulation is missing (or insufficient) can be observed by subnational governments (transgovernmental initiatives) and NGOs (the latter only at national level). This is in line with Hypotheses 4 and 6, while the generally positive (albeit weak) effect of these membership groups on the design of TCG initiatives cannot be observed (no support for Hypotheses 3 and 5). Moreover, Hypothesis 7 on orchestration is confirmed with respect to the initiating role of governments, and Hypothesis 8 on orchestration for stand-alone initiatives is confirmed with respect to shaping.

What does this imply in terms of the questions posed earlier? Can we expect TCG initiatives to support governments' efforts to reach their NDCs or even to go beyond that and hence contribute to closing the gap remaining between the sum of NDCs and the emission reductions necessary to remain below the 2° target as agreed in Paris? Since convincing entrepreneurial initiatives are primarily reactive to existing international regulation, it can be expected that they will also respond to the Paris Agreement and help in implementing related domestic policies in an efficient way. Transgovernmental initiatives and initiatives with NGO members may wish to go beyond that by building up mitigation-oriented stand-alone initiatives if they feel that the existing national and international regulation is not far-reaching enough. This could help to fill the remaining emissions gap. However, given the generally very weak design of TCG initiatives when it comes to the basic criteria mitigation target, incentives, baseline, and MRV, our results do not suggest that their contribution will be substantial.

Conclusions

While the Paris Agreement is a breakthrough in the multilateral climate negotiation process under the UNFCCC, its target of keeping global warming well below 2°C is not consistent with the sum of the national emission reduction pledges. Thus transnational climate governance initiatives are seen by many observers as opportunities to close this gap and to be an "add-on" to the insufficient mitigation effort of national governments. Is this really the case, or is the role of such initiatives rather a complementary one so that we can expect them to contribute to emission reduction only in combination with existing regulation at the international and domestic level? Under which conditions can these initiatives be expected to achieve any mitigation at all?

We assess 109 transnational initiatives through a simple design indicator that is determined by the existence of a mitigation target, the provision of incentives for mitigation, the specification of a baseline from which mitigation is determined, and the existence of provisions for MRV of mitigation. About half of the initiatives do not fulfill any of these basic criteria, while about 13% meet three of them. Only one initiative satisfies all four criteria. As the different criteria are complementary, meeting several of them simultaneously is necessary for a convincing design. The main purpose of most initiatives is simply some networking. This is a rather sobering result to start with and does not suggest that these initiatives will provide any significant contribution to closing the emissions gap. This is true unless—as suggested by a more social-constructionist literature—they develop some internal dynamics that drive them to become effective despite their initial design and the initial intentions of their members. We do not believe that this is very plausible in our context.

While some stand-alone mitigation-oriented initiatives can be found among transgovernmental initiatives and initiatives with NGO participation, entrepreneurial initiatives tend to show a convincing design only in response to international regulation. Indeed the few cases of effective entrepreneurial activities (meeting more than two of the criteria) can be seen as complementary to regulation under the Kyoto Protocol.

Some other variables are statistically linked to our indicators of mitigation-related design. Initiatives orchestrated by governments or international institutions focus more on incentives but are lacking mitigation targets. Generally, government support in setting up an initiative is positively linked to a mitigation-oriented design. As far as stand-alone initiatives are concerned, we find no specifically positive effect of initiation but of shaping by international organization and national governments.

In sum, the ambition of transnational climate governance initiatives is way too low to close the emissions gap under the Paris Agreement. This holds for all types of initiatives, no matter whether the key actors are private firms, subnational governments, or NGOs. In addition, the initiatives' mitigation ambition often directly depends on the willingness to mitigate resulting from the international climate negotiation process (notably for entrepreneurial initiatives). While potentially useful to improve the efficiency of the implementation of existing national policies, these initiatives cannot be expected to make up for lack of country-level mitigation ambition in the UNFCCC process.

What are the implications of these findings for policymakers?

First, national governments cannot rely on other actors to do their job. As long as they hesitate to set sufficiently ambitious emission targets at the domestic level and to define appropriate policy instruments for implementation, there is little chance that the global climate change limitation target affirmed in the Paris Agreement will be met.

Second, governments have ample choice among different policy instruments. They need to provide the incentives for others to act. Whether they do so by increasing the cost for the production or consumption of emission-intensive goods and services (for example, through taxes), or whether they provide funding to reward emission reductions (thereby increasing the opportunity cost for those actors who continue to generate high emissions), both can be designed in a way to internalize the negative externalities related to global warming. In the former case, governments can use their traditional policy instruments, while in the latter one, they can make use of approaches that have been applied within the framework of TCG initiatives. The Pilot Auction Facility, for instance, provides rewards for emission reduction projects, while the diverse carbon funds allow governments (and other actors) to directly buy emission reduction credits. These are alternative ways to provide the same kind of incentives, but what matters is the determination and clarity of the approach. We have seen that government initiation and shaping can influence the design of TCG initiatives. But in order to reach a substantial impact, the magnitude of the financial incentives must be proportionate to the severity of the problem to solve.

There will be substantial costs of mitigation commensurate with the Paris Agreement target, and the choice between alternative policy instruments will have an impact on the distribution of wealth within the society. This is another aspect that policymakers will have to consider, but its discussion goes beyond the scope of this article. Once the incentives for mitigation are set, government support for further activities like networking and information exchange can help private and nonprivate actors to achieve mitigation cost efficiently.

Acknowledgments

Replication data and programming files are available at http://dvn.iq.harvard.edu/dvn/dv/internationalinteractions. For all questions related to these files, please directly contact the authors. We would like to thank Paula Castro, Simon Hug, Ayse Kaya, Jakob Skovgaard, Detlef Sprinz, as well as the editors and three anonymous referees for extremely helpful comments and suggestions. We are also grateful for useful exchanges in the framework of the project "The Politics of Informal Governance," which was funded by the Swiss Network for International Studies (SNIS), and at the Jawaharlal Nehru Institute of Advanced Study, Jawaharlal Nehru University (New Delhi), which hosted Katharina Michaelowa during the final phase of this research. No funding was received by the authors of this paper. Work on this paper was part of the authors' contribution to SNIS funding.

References

Ai, Chunrong, and Edward Norton. (2003) Interaction Terms in Logit and Probit Models. *Economics Letters* 80(1):123–129.

Andonova, Liliana, Michele Betsill, and Harriet Bulkeley. (2009) Transnational Climate Governance. *Global Environmental Politics* 9(2):52–73.

Andonova, Liliana, Thomas Hale, and Charles Roger. (2014) How Do Domestic Politics Condition Participation In Transnational Climate Governance? Paper presented at Political Economy of International Organizations (PEIO) conference. Princeton University, Princeton, New Jersey, January 16–18. Available at www.peio.me.

Baccaro, Lucio, and Valentina Mele. (2011) For Lack of Anything Better? International Organizations and Global Corporate Codes. *Public Administration* 89:451–470.

Baranzini, Andrea, and Philippe Thalmann. (2004) *Voluntary Approaches in Climate Policy*. Cheltenham, UK: Edward Elgar.

Beck, Thorsten, George Clarke, Alberto Groff, Philip Keefer, and Patrick Walsh. (2001) New Tools in Comparative Political Economy: The Database of Political Institutions. *World Bank Economic Review* 15(1):165–176.

Berliner, Daniel, and Aseem Prakash. (2014) Public Authority and Private Rules: How Domestic Regulatory Institutions Shape the Adoption of Global Private Regimes. *International Studies Quarterly* 58(4):793–803.

Berliner, Daniel, and Aseem Prakash. (2015) "Bluewashing" the Firm?: Voluntary Regulations, Program Design and Member Compliance with the United Nations Global Compact. *Policy Studies Journal* 43(1):115–138.

Bernauer, Thomas, Anna Kalbhenn, Vally Koubi, and Gabriele Spilker. (2013) Is There a Depth versus Participation Dilemma in International Cooperation? *Review of International Organizations* 8(4):477–497.

Bulkeley, Harriet, Liliana Andonova, Karin Bäckstrand, Michele Betsill, Daniel Compagnon, Rosaleen Duffy, Ans Kolk, Matthew Hoffmann, David Levy, Peter Newell, Tori Milledge, Matthew Paterson, Philipp Pattberg, and Stacy VanDeveer. (2012) Governing Climate Change Transnationally: Assessing the Evidence from a Database of Sixty Initiatives. *Environment and Planning C: Government and Policy* 30:591–612.

Bulkeley, Harriet, Liliana Andonova, Michele M. Betsill, Daniel Compagnon, Thomas Hale, Matthew Hoffmann, Peter Newell, Matthew Paterson, Charles Roger, and Stacy VanDeveer. (2014) *Transnational Climate Governance*. Cambridge, UK: Cambridge University Press.

Cao, Xun, and Hugh Ward. (2017) Transnational Climate Governance Networks and Domestic Regulatory Action. *International Interactions* 43(1):76–102. doi: 10.1080/03050629.2016.1220162

Cashore, Benjamin, Graeme Auld, Steven Bernstein, and Constance McDermott. (2007) Can Non-State Governance "Ratchet-Up" Global Standards? Assessing Their Indirect Effects and Evolutionary Potential. *Review of European Community and International Environmental Law* 16:158–172.

Chan, Sander, and Pieter Pauw. (2014) A Global Framework for Climate Action: Orchestrating Non-State and Subnational Initiatives for More Effective Global Climate Governance. Discussion Paper 34/2014 Bonn: German Institute for Development.

Christensen, Lars, Mette Morsing, and Ole Thyssen. (2013) CSR as Aspirational Talk. *Organization* 20:372–393.

Climate Action Tracker. (2015) 2.7°C Is Not Enough—We Can Get Lower. Available at http://climateactiontracker.org/assets/publications/briefing_papers/CAT_Temp_Update_COP21.pdf

Darnall, Nicole, and Younsung Kim. (2012) Which Types of Environmental Management Systems Are Related to Greater Environmental Improvements? *Public Administration Review* 72(3):351–365.

Deleon, Peter, and Jorge E. Rivera, eds. (2009) *Voluntary Environmental Programs: A Policy Perspective*. Boulder, CO: Rowman & Littlefield.

Dolšak, Nives, and Aseem Prakash. (2017) Join the Club: How Domestic NGOs Induce Participation in the Covenant of Mayors Program. *International Interactions* 43(1):26–47. doi: 10.1080/03050629.2017.1226668

Ecofys; Climate Analytics; PIK and New Climate Institute. (2014) Climate Action Tracker. Available at http://climateactiontracker.org/countries.html.

Galvanizing the Groundswell of Climate Actions. (2015) Accelerating the Action Agenda through Robust and Credible Climate Commitments from Non-State Actors. Available at http://static1.squarespace.com/static/552be32ce4b0b269a4e2ef58/t/55aff450e4

b0e464348417ac/1437594704526/Accelerating+the+Action+Agenda+through+Robust+and+Credible+Climate+Commitments+from+Non-state+Actors+NEW.pdf.

German Development Institute (GDI) and London School of Economics (LSE). (2015) GAFCA—Global Aggregator for Climate Action. Available at http://static1.squarespace.com/static/552be32ce4b0b269a4e2ef58/t/558d8fa1e4b0cba66cbefa29/1435341166099/Introducing+GAFCA.pdf.

Green, Jessica. (2013) Order out of Chaos: Public and Private Rules for Managing Carbon. *Global Environmental Politics* 13(2):1–25.

Green, Jessica. (2017) Blurred Lines: Why Do States Recognize Private Carbon Standards? *International Interactions* 43(1):103–128. doi: 10.1080/03050629.2016.1210943

Greene, William. (2002) *Econometric Analysis*. Fifth Edition. Upper Saddle River, NJ: Prentice-Hall.

Haack, Patrick, Dennis Schoeneborn, and Christopher Wickert. (2012) Talking the Talk, Moral Entrapment, Creeping Commitment? Exploring Narrative Dynamics in Corporate Responsibility Standardization. *Organization Studies* 5(6):813–845.

Hale, Thomas, and Charles Roger. (2014) Orchestration and Transnational Climate Governance. *Review of International Organizations* 9(1):59–82.

Helm, Carsten, and Detlef Sprinz. (2000) Measuring the Effectiveness of International Environmental Regimes. *Journal of Conflict Resolution* 44(5):630–652.

Hoffmann, Matthew J. (2011) *Climate Governance at the Crossroads. Experimenting with a Global Response after Kyoto*. Oxford, UK: Oxford University Press.

Hollande, François. (2015) Speech by François Hollande at the World Summit Climate & Territories, Lyon, France, July 1–2. In *Outcomes of the Summit*: 83–87. Available at http://www.codatu.org/wp-content/uploads/Outcomes-of-the-summit1.pdf

Hsu, Angel, Andrew S. Moffat, Amy J. Weinfurter, and Jason D. Schwartz. (2015) Towards New Climate Diplomacy. *Nature Climate Change* 5(6):501–503.

Keohane, Robert O., and David G. Victor. (2011) The Regime Complex for Climate Change. *Perspectives on Politics* 9(1):7–23.

Koremenos, Barbara, Charles Lipson, and Duncan Snidal. (2001a) The Rational Design of International Institutions. *International Organization* 55(4):761–799.

Koremenos, Barbara, Charles Lipson, and Duncan Snidal. (2001b) Rational Design: Looking Back to Move Forward. *International Organization* 55(4):1051–1082.

Michaelowa, Katharina, and Axel Michaelowa. (2012) India as an emerging power in international climate negotiations. *Climate Policy* 12(5):575–590.

Morgenstern, Richard, and William Pizer, eds. (2007) *Reality Check: The Nature and Performance of Voluntary Environmental Programs in the United States, Europe, and Japan*. Washington, DC: RRF Press.

Overdevest, Christine. (2010) Comparing Forest Certification Schemes: The Case of Ratcheting Standards in the Forest Sector. *Socio-Economic Review* 8:47–76.

Overdevest, Christine, and Jonathan Zeitlin. (2014) Assembling an Experimentalist Regime: Transnational Governance Interactions in the Forest Sector. *Regulation & Governance* 8:22–48.

Pfeifer, Stephanie, and Rory Sullivan. (2008) Public Policy, Institutional Investors and Climate Change: A UK Case-Study. *Climatic Change* 89:245–262.

Pinkse, Jonatan, and Ans Kolk. (2009) *International Business and Global Climate Change*. Abingdon, UK: Routledge.

Potoski, Matthew, and Aseem Prakash. (2005) Green Clubs and Voluntary Governance: ISO 14001 and Firms' Regulatory Compliance. *American Journal of Political Science* 49(2):235–248.

Potoski, Matthew, and Aseem Prakash. (2013) Green Clubs: Collective Action and Voluntary Environmental Programs. *Annual Review of Political Science* 16:399–419.

Roger, Charles, Thomas Hale, and Liliana Andonova. (2017) Domestic Politics and Climate Governance. *International Interactions* 43(1):1–25.

Stavins, Robert, Zou Ji, Thomas Brewer, Mariana Conte Grand, Michel den Elzen, Michael Finus, Joyeeta Gupta, Niklas Höhne, Myung-Kun Lee, Axel Michaelowa, Matthew Paterson, Krishnan Ramakrishna, Wen Gang, Jonathan Wiener, Harald Winkler, Daniel Bodansky, Gabriel Chan, Anita Engels, Adam Jaffe, Michael Jakob, T. Jayaraman, Jorge Leiva, Kai Lessmann, Richard Newell, Sheila Olmstead, William Pizer, Robert Stowe, and Marlene Vinluan. (2014) International Cooperation: Agreements & Instruments. In *Climate Change 2014: Mitigation of Climate Change. Contribution of Working Group III to the Fifth Assessment Report of the Intergovernmental Panel on Climate Change*, edited by O. Edenhofer, R. Pichs-Madruga, Y. Sokona, E. Farahani, S. Kadner, K. Seyboth, A. Adler, I. Baum, S. Brunner, P. Eickemeier, B. Kriemann, J. Savolainen, S. Schlömer, C. von Stechow, T. Zwickel and J. C. Minx. Cambridge, UK: Cambridge University Press, pp. 1001–1082.

Tetlock, Philip, and Aaron Belkin, eds. (1996) *Counterfactual Thought Experiments in World Politics: Logical, Methodological, and Psychological Perspectives*. Princeton, NJ: Princeton University Press.

United Nations. (2014) UN Climate Summit 2014. Available at http://www.un.org/climate change/summit/.

United Nations Environment Programme (UNEP). (2015a) *The Emissions Gap Report 2015*. Nairobi, Kenya: Author.

United Nations Environment Programme (UNEP). (2015b) *Climate Commitments of Subnational Actors and Business: A Quantitative Assessment of their Emission Reduction Impact*. Nairobi, Kenya: Author.

United Nations Framework Convention on Climate Change (UNFCCC). (2015a) Decision on the Adoption of the Paris Agreement. Available at http://unfccc.int/files/meetings/paris_nov_2015/application/pdf/cop_auv_template_4b_new__1.pdf.

United Nations Framework Convention on Climate Change (UNFCCC). (2015b) *Synthesis Report on the Aggregate Effect of the Intended Nationally Determined Contributions, FCCC/CP/2015/7*. Bonn, Germany: Author.

World Bank. (2013) Database of Political Institutions 2012. Available at http://go.worldbank.org/2EAGGLRZ40. (update of Beck et al. 2001 from Jan. 2013).

World Resources Institute. (2015) CAIT Climate Data Explorer. Available at http://cait.wri.org/historical.

Young, Oran, ed. (1999) *The Effectiveness of International Environmental Regimes: Casual Connections and Behavioral Mechanisms*. Cambridge, MA: MIT Press.

Young, Oran. (2011) Effectiveness of International Environmental Regimes: Existing Knowledge, Cutting-Edge Themes, and Research Strategies. *Proceedings of the National Academy of Sciences* 108(50):19853–19860.

Appendix

Part I: Variable description
Part II: Methodological considerations
Part III: Complementary regression results

Appendix I: Variable description

Table A1: Descriptive statistics, sources and explanations

Variable	Obs.	Mean	Std. Dev.	Min	Max	Variable description	Sources
Sum of criteria	109	0.96	1.10	0	4	Total number of individual design criteria met	Authors
2 criteria met	109	0.28	0.45	0	1	Dummy=1 if at least 2 criteria met, otherwise=0	Authors
3 criteria met	109	0.15	0.36	0	1	Dummy=1 if at least 3 criteria met, otherwise=0	Authors
Mitigation target	109	0.11	0.31	0	1	Dummy=1 if initiative has defined a mitigation target, otherwise=0	Authors
Incentives	109	0.13	0.34	0	1	Dummy=1 if initiative provides a financial incentive for mitigation, otherwise=0	Authors
Baseline	109	0.27	0.44	0	1	Dummy=1 if initiative has specified a baseline for mitigation, otherwise= 0	Authors
MRV	109	0.46	0.50	0	1	Dummy=1 if initiative includes a MRV system, otherwise=0	Authors
Depends on gov.	109	0.15	0.36	0	1	Dummy =1 if start of initiative depended on national government action usually as a founding member, but also if initiative specifically refers to national government policies (whether in favor of climate policy or not), otherwise=0	Authors
Country target	60	0.95	0.22	0	1	Mitigation target of the founding country: no or "inadequate" target=0, otherwise=1, whereby "inadequate" is defined as: "if all governments put forward inadequate positions warming likely to exceed 3–4°C", missing for WB and INT	Ecofys et al. (2014)
Structure	109	2.33	0.93	1	3	Centralized=1, coordinated=2, decentralized=3 (networks)	Authors
Adaptation focus	109	0.05	0.21	0	1	Dummy=1 if initiative focuses primarily on adaptation, otherwise=0	Authors
Entrepreneurial	109	0.33	0.47	0	1	Dummy=1 if non-state actors played the leading role in creating the initiative (in practice, non-state actors in this context are primarily firms and business association, but in some cases also NGOs), otherwise=0	Roger et al. (2015), updated by the authors
Transgovernmental	109	0.15	0.36	0	1	Dummy=1 if only sub-state actors (cities or sub-national governments) were responsible for the creation of the initiative, otherwise=0	Roger et al. (2015), updated by the authors
NGO members	109	0.53	0.50	0	1	Dummy=1 if the initiative has NGO members, otherwise=0	Authors
Shaping	109	0.05	0.21	0	1	Dummy=1 if there was an active role of national government(s) or international organization in shaping the initiative, e.g., by influencing the initiative's rules and activities and/or by providing resources after the start of the initiative, otherwise=0.	Roger et al. (2015), updated by the authors

(Continued)

Table A1: Continued

Variable	Obs.	Mean	Std. Dev.	Min	Max	Variable description	Sources
Kyoto operational	109	0.40	0.49	0	1	Dummy=1 if 2005<=year>=2009, otherwise=0	
Post Copenhagen	109	0.31	0.47	0	1	Dummy=1 if year>2009, otherwise=0	
GCF	58	21.56	4.26	14.97	47.58	Gross capital formation (% of GDP) in founding country; missing for EU, WB and INT	World Bank (2015)
Energy efficiency	58	8.58	2.91	4.01	17.32	GDP per unit of energy use (constant 2011 PPP $ per kg of oil equivalent) in founding country; missing for EU, WB and INT	World Bank (2015)
Emissions pc	58	15.14	6.78	1.63	29.79	Total greenhouse gas emissions including forestry (tCO$_2$eq per capita) in founding country; missing for EU, WB and INT	World Resources Institute (2015)
Election year	58	0.41	0.50	0	1	Dummy=1 if start year coincides with major legislative or presidential election in the founding country, otherwise=0; missing for EU, WB and INT	Beck et al. (2001), updated by World Bank (2013) and by the authors
No of initiatives	109	8.82	5.63	1	18	Total number of initiatives started per year	Roger et al. (2015), updated by the authors
EU	109	0.02	0.13	0	1	Dummy=1 if initiative founded by the EU, otherwise=0	Authors
WB	109	0.12	0.33	0	1	Dummy=1 if initiative founded by the World Bank, otherwise=0	Authors
INT	109	0.33	0.47	0	1	Dummy=1 if initiative founded by actors from different countries (international, no lead country), otherwise=0	Authors
year	109	2007	5.88	1990	2015	Starting year of the initiative	Roger et al. (2015), updated and adjusted by the authors

Notes: "'Founding country" refers to the country in which the initiative was founded or in which the founding actor is located. However, the location of international organizations is not considered in this context (e.g., the United States does not count as a founding country for initiatives launched by the World Bank). The qualitative variable "founding country" contains separate categories for the World Bank, the EU and other international organizations (INT). Variables referring to founding countries have no observations for WB, EU and INT (at the exception of the country target that is defined for the EU). Otherwise, data are complete as missing values were imputed by linear inter- or extrapolation. In all multivariate estimations, missing values of country-related variables for WB, EU and INT were replaced by 0 to avoid considerable loss of observations. This is why all estimations also include dummy variables for these three international actors. Country characteristics always refer to the founding country and the starting year of the initiative.

When "Authors" is indicated as the data source, the data has been collected through a web search on the websites of the individual initiatives listed in the Roger et al. (2015) TCG dataset and additional initiatives added by the authors following the criteria in Roger et al. (2015).

Appendix II: Methodological considerations

As all dependent variables are categorical, a discussion of the appropriate statistical model seems of order. 'Sum of criteria' is a count variable with values between zero and four, and '2 criteria met', '3 criteria met' as well as the individual variables for each of the criteria are binary indicators. One could hence consider a Poisson or negative binomial model for 'sum of criteria' and logit or probit models for the other dependent variables. In terms of the goodness of fit statistics, Poisson seems to work fine (no indication of overdispersion). This led us to carry out a set of initial regressions using Poisson and Probit models. However, the Poisson model is conceptually problematic here because it implicitly assumes that the count of positive events (here the number of criteria met) could go towards infinity. A more appropriate alternative could hence be an ordered probit model. Based on our data, its results are similar in terms of the sign and significance of the coefficients.

However, there are a number of problems with these specifications. First, the results of non-linear models are difficult to interpret in a setting with (multiple) interaction terms. As shown by Ai and Norton (2003) for probit and logit models, not even the size and significance of interaction terms can be directly interpreted. It is obviously possible to separately compute the difference in predicted probability for any combinations of initial conditions, and hence the marginal effects. However, given that not only the dependent variables, but also the explanatory variables are mostly categorical, not all the combinations of initial conditions actually exist in the data. Moreover, depending on the dependent variable, some variable combinations perfectly determine the outcome so that they are dropped from the model along with the corresponding observations. While this is fine for the interpretation of the individual model, it leads to different specifications and different samples depending on the dependent variable thereby impeding comparisons across models. Finally, the structure of the data suggests that there might be multiple correlations between the error terms due, for instance, to the participation of the same actors in different initiatives. Binary response models are inconsistent in this case, and "robust" estimation cannot mitigate the problem (Greene 2002, p. 673f.).

To avoid these problems and to facilitate the presentation of results, we hence proceed with simple linear models in the following. The use of linear probability models has by now become very common as the only major problem, namely the occurrence of heteroscedasticity, can be easily healed through the use of robust estimators. Regarding the 'sum of criteria' an additional concern could be that the steps from one category to the next (meaning from meeting one criterion, to two, to three, to four) might not be equally 'distant' as a linear model would assume. However, these distances can be checked from the cut-offs of individual categories in the ordered probit, and the result gives us some confidence to proceed with the linear model. In all models, we use heteroscedasticity consistent error terms that are also clustered by founding country (or organization), i.e. based on the place where the initiative was founded or where the founding actor was located. We further carry out some robustness checks first by omitting the five adaptation initiatives, and second by merging the observations with 3 and 4 criteria met to a single category for the dependent variable 'sum of criteria'. Changes are minimal, so that we only report the outcomes of our main regressions here.

Appendix III: Complementary regression results

Table A2: Correlates of mitigation-related design – examining complementarity with national regulation

	(1) Sum of criteria	(2) 2 criteria met	(3) 3 criteria met	(4) Mitigation target	(5) Incentives	(6) Baseline	(7) MRV
Depends on gov.	1.66***	0.59***	0.79***	−0.05	0.65***	0.58***	0.47***
	(0.00)	(0.00)	(0.00)	(0.76)	(0.00)	(0.00)	(0.00)
Country Target	1.25**	0.38**	0.43**	0.24*	0.29**	0.37**	0.36
	(0.01)	(0.02)	(0.02)	(0.07)	(0.05)	(0.04)	(0.28)
Entrepreneurial	−0.10	−0.06**	0.07*	0.03	−0.05	−0.06*	−0.00
	(0.32)	(0.02)	(0.07)	(0.30)	(0.22)	(0.08)	(0.96)
Target x Entrepr.	0.40	0.22*	−0.13	0.08	0.04	0.19	0.10
	(0.22)	(0.09)	(0.28)	(0.51)	(0.66)	(0.17)	(0.23)
Transgovernmental	0.45***	0.10**	0.20***	0.19***	−0.09**	0.11***	0.23***
	(0.00)	(0.01)	(0.00)	(0.00)	(0.02)	(0.01)	(0.00)
Target x Transg.	−0.79**	−0.16*	−0.25***	−0.28**	0.19*	−0.17*	−0.53**
	(0.02)	(0.08)	(0.00)	(0.02)	(0.05)	(0.09)	(0.02)
NGO members	0.28	0.04	0.19	0.07*	0.18***	0.07	−0.04
	(0.24)	(0.55)	(0.15)	(0.08)	(0.00)	(0.56)	(0.71)
Target x NGOs	−0.33	−0.02	−0.15	−0.11*	−0.14*	−0.08	−0.01
	(0.38)	(0.84)	(0.33)	(0.06)	(0.06)	(0.58)	(0.98)
GCF	−0.01	0.00	−0.01**	−0.01	−0.01	0.00	0.00
	(0.57)	(0.26)	(0.04)	(0.32)	(0.25)	(0.51)	(0.98)
Energy efficiency	−0.17***	−0.07***	−0.04**	−0.01	−0.01	−0.06***	−0.08***
	(0.00)	(0.00)	(0.01)	(0.51)	(0.52)	(0.00)	(0.00)
Emissions pc	−0.06**	−0.02**	−0.01**	0.01	−0.01	−0.02**	−0.04***
	(0.02)	(0.04)	(0.03)	(0.52)	(0.31)	(0.02)	(0.01)
Election year	−0.15	−0.05	0.07	−0.15	0.02	−0.01	−0.01
	(0.68)	(0.70)	(0.54)	(0.32)	(0.82)	(0.89)	(0.88)
No of initiatives	0.01	0.01	0.01**	−0.00	−0.00	0.01	0.00
	(0.60)	(0.17)	(0.03)	(0.62)	(0.98)	(0.21)	(0.64)
Structure	−0.32***	−0.14**	−0.01	0.05	−0.04	−0.16**	−0.18***
	(0.00)	(0.02)	(0.73)	(0.13)	(0.47)	(0.04)	(0.00)
Adaptation focus	−0.81	−0.27	−0.28	−0.03	−0.15	−0.25	−0.37
	(0.22)	(0.24)	(0.11)	(0.61)	(0.48)	(0.20)	(0.14)
EU	−1.19	−0.41	−0.31	0.75***	−0.45*	−0.44	−1.04*
	(0.17)	(0.16)	(0.24)	(0.01)	(0.09)	(0.13)	(0.05)
WB	−2.03**	−0.54*	−0.62**	−0.05	−0.05	−0.69**	−1.24
	(0.05)	(0.07)	(0.03)	(0.90)	(0.87)	(0.04)	(0.10)
INT	−1.85*	−0.52*	−0.51*	−0.16	0.01	−0.58**	−1.12
	(0.06)	(0.06)	(0.07)	(0.63)	(0.98)	(0.04)	(0.12)
Year	−0.02	−0.00	−0.00	0.00	−0.01	−0.00	−0.01
	(0.50)	(0.78)	(0.65)	(0.84)	(0.17)	(0.95)	(0.22)
Constant	35.13	7.14	8.04	−4.53	12.41	2.22	25.02
	(0.46)	(0.75)	(0.64)	(0.84)	(0.16)	(0.92)	(0.18)
Adj. R2	0.48	0.41	0.46	0.16	0.48	0.37	0.36
N	109	109	109	109	109	109	109

Note: Linear regression models with p-values in parentheses based on robust standard errors (heteroscedasticity consistent and clustered by founding country).

***, ** and * indicate significance at the 1%-, 5%- and 10%-level respectively. Variable names are abbreviated in interaction terms: Country target → Target, Entrepreneurial → Entrepr., Transgovernmental → Transg., NGO members → NGOs.

Table A3: Correlates of mitigation-related design – examining complementarity with international regulation

	(1) Sum of criteria	(2) 2 criteria met	(3) 3 criteria met	(4) Mitigation target	(5) Incentives	(6) Baseline	(7) MRV
Depends on gov.	1.59***	0.56***	0.71***	−0.02	0.60***	0.52***	0.49***
	(0.00)	(0.00)	(0.00)	(0.85)	(0.00)	(0.00)	(0.00)
Country Target	1.18***	0.41**	0.35**	0.20	0.24*	0.39***	0.35
	(0.01)	(0.02)	(0.02)	(0.25)	(0.06)	(0.01)	(0.22)
Kyoto operational	−0.26	0.00	−0.20	−0.14	−0.05	−0.18	0.11
	(0.65)	(0.99)	(0.27)	(0.45)	(0.74)	(0.66)	(0.66)
Post Copenhagen	0.21	0.13	−0.01	−0.07	0.00	0.02	0.26
	(0.75)	(0.71)	(0.96)	(0.77)	(0.99)	(0.96)	(0.54)
Entrepreneurial	0.09	0.08	−0.12	0.08	−0.11	−0.06	0.18
	(0.77)	(0.66)	(0.30)	(0.50)	(0.31)	(0.81)	(0.23)
Kyoto x Entrepr.	0.76	0.22	0.14	0.18*	0.08	0.36	0.14
	(0.12)	(0.27)	(0.37)	(0.07)	(0.64)	(0.17)	(0.71)
Copenh. x Entrepr.	−0.41	−0.10	0.10	−0.21	0.11	0.04	−0.35
	(0.11)	(0.58)	(0.35)	(0.17)	(0.18)	(0.86)	(0.10)
Transgovernmental	−0.92	−0.21	−0.32	−0.15	−0.03	−0.29	−0.45
	(0.13)	(0.45)	(0.27)	(0.48)	(0.83)	(0.33)	(0.17)
Kyoto x Transg.	1.24	0.34	0.59	0.12	0.20	0.50	0.42
	(0.16)	(0.34)	(0.13)	(0.57)	(0.36)	(0.25)	(0.31)
Copenh. x Transg.	1.43**	0.31	0.45*	0.44*	0.01	0.37	0.62*
	(0.02)	(0.24)	(0.07)	(0.07)	(0.97)	(0.16)	(0.06)
NGO members	0.23	0.17	0.04	−0.02	0.17	0.06	0.02
	(0.64)	(0.38)	(0.85)	(0.91)	(0.19)	(0.80)	(0.90)
Kyoto x NGOs	−0.17	−0.20	0.10	0.07	−0.02	−0.05	−0.17
	(0.72)	(0.46)	(0.62)	(0.76)	(0.83)	(0.88)	(0.21)
Copenh. x NGOs	−0.36	−0.20	−0.01	−0.05	−0.17	−0.11	−0.03
	(0.50)	(0.40)	(0.96)	(0.73)	(0.22)	(0.69)	(0.91)
GCF	0.02	0.01*	−0.01	0.00	−0.01	0.01	0.02
	(0.26)	(0.06)	(0.35)	(0.82)	(0.26)	(0.13)	(0.33)
Energy efficiency	−0.13***	−0.06***	−0.03***	−0.00	−0.01	−0.05***	−0.06**
	(0.00)	(0.00)	(0.00)	(0.92)	(0.23)	(0.00)	(0.03)
Emissions pc	−0.05**	−0.02**	−0.01**	0.01	−0.01	−0.02*	−0.03**
	(0.02)	(0.05)	(0.02)	(0.49)	(0.14)	(0.08)	(0.02)
Election year	−0.13	−0.04	0.11	−0.17	0.01	0.00	0.03
	(0.73)	(0.77)	(0.40)	(0.34)	(0.94)	(1.00)	(0.69)
No of initiatives	0.02	0.01**	0.01**	−0.00	0.00	0.01*	0.01*
	(0.18)	(0.04)	(0.02)	(0.92)	(0.99)	(0.06)	(0.09)
Structure	−0.23	−0.11	−0.03	0.08**	−0.02	−0.13	−0.16**
	(0.17)	(0.16)	(0.70)	(0.03)	(0.74)	(0.18)	(0.03)
Adaptation focus	−0.65	−0.22	−0.24*	0.02	−0.15	−0.21	−0.31
	(0.23)	(0.29)	(0.08)	(0.62)	(0.46)	(0.16)	(0.16)
EU	−0.19	−0.14	−0.11	1.04***	−0.53*	−0.14	−0.56
	(0.80)	(0.56)	(0.55)	(0.00)	(0.09)	(0.63)	(0.40)
WB	−0.74	−0.15	−0.34	0.25	−0.18	−0.24	−0.57
	(0.38)	(0.65)	(0.17)	(0.59)	(0.64)	(0.56)	(0.49)
INT	−0.59	−0.17	−0.22	0.17	−0.18	−0.17	−0.42
	(0.49)	(0.57)	(0.36)	(0.69)	(0.62)	(0.64)	(0.60)
Year	−0.05	−0.01	−0.01	−0.00	−0.00	−0.01	−0.04
	(0.21)	(0.45)	(0.41)	(0.96)	(0.86)	(0.62)	(0.16)
Constant	102.71	26.97	26.35	2.03	2.51	19.63	78.53
	(0.20)	(0.44)	(0.40)	(0.96)	(0.84)	(0.60)	(0.15)
Adj. R2	0.49	0.40	0.46	0.17	0.45	0.37	0.35
N	109	109	109	109	109	109	109

Note: Linear regression models with p-values in parentheses based on robust standard errors (heteroscedasticity consistent and clustered by founding country);

***, ** and * indicate significance at the 1%-, 5%- and 10%-level respectively. Variable names are abbreviated in interaction terms: Kyoto operational → Kyoto, Post Copenhagen → Copenh., Entrepreneurial → Entrepr., Transgovernmental → Transg., NGO members → NGOs.

Table A4: Correlates of mitigation-related design – examining 'shaping' in conjunction with international regulation

	(1) Sum of criteria	(2) 2 criteria met	(3) 3 criteria met	(4) Mitigation target	(5) Incentives	(6) Baseline	(7) MRV
Depends on gov.	1.19***	0.40***	0.75***	−0.12	0.60***	0.41***	0.30***
	(0.00)	(0.00)	(0.00)	(0.30)	(0.00)	(0.00)	(0.01)
Country Target	1.07**	0.38***	0.32**	0.22*	0.22	0.32***	0.32
	(0.01)	(0.00)	(0.04)	(0.10)	(0.10)	(0.00)	(0.23)
Kyoto operational	0.15	0.04	0.01	−0.06	0.02	0.09	0.11
	(0.75)	(0.82)	(0.96)	(0.34)	(0.83)	(0.59)	(0.73)
Post Copenhagen	0.16	0.06	0.07	−0.07	−0.03	0.10	0.16
	(0.79)	(0.81)	(0.73)	(0.68)	(0.82)	(0.64)	(0.74)
Shaping	0.11	0.03	0.21	−0.20**	0.38***	0.09	−0.16
	(0.80)	(0.86)	(0.32)	(0.03)	(0.00)	(0.53)	(0.50)
Kyoto x Shaping	−0.73	−0.08	−0.31	0.16	−0.45***	−0.15	−0.29
	(0.32)	(0.73)	(0.27)	(0.11)	(0.01)	(0.52)	(0.42)
Copenh. x Shaping	1.77***	1.05***	−0.19	0.15*	−0.42***	0.99***	1.04***
	(0.00)	(0.00)	(0.37)	(0.09)	(0.00)	(0.00)	(0.00)
Kyoto x WB	−1.20***	−0.47***	−0.44***	0.11**	−0.06	−0.88***	−0.37*
	(0.00)	(0.00)	(0.00)	(0.03)	(0.21)	(0.00)	(0.09)
Copenh. x WB	−0.75**	−0.41***	−0.07	0.01	−0.01	−0.44***	−0.31
	(0.02)	(0.00)	(0.58)	(0.93)	(0.92)	(0.00)	(0.17)
GCF	−0.00	0.00	−0.01	−0.01	−0.01*	0.00	0.01
	(0.97)	(0.41)	(0.28)	(0.43)	(0.05)	(0.73)	(0.28)
Energy efficiency	−0.18***	−0.07***	−0.04***	−0.01	−0.02	−0.07***	−0.08***
	(0.00)	(0.00)	(0.00)	(0.65)	(0.13)	(0.00)	(0.01)
Emissions pc	−0.06**	−0.02*	−0.01**	0.01	−0.01*	−0.02**	−0.04***
	(0.02)	(0.07)	(0.01)	(0.38)	(0.06)	(0.02)	(0.01)
Election year	−0.12	−0.05	0.11	−0.16	0.04	−0.02	0.01
	(0.80)	(0.73)	(0.44)	(0.35)	(0.76)	(0.90)	(0.91)
No of initiatives	0.02	0.02***	0.01**	−0.00	0.00	0.02***	0.01
	(0.14)	(0.01)	(0.04)	(0.68)	(0.99)	(0.01)	(0.14)
Structure	−0.42***	−0.18***	−0.03	0.02	−0.02	−0.19***	−0.22***
	(0.00)	(0.00)	(0.39)	(0.34)	(0.63)	(0.00)	(0.00)
Adaptation focus	−0.82	−0.29	−0.20*	−0.08	−0.16	−0.21**	−0.37*
	(0.12)	(0.15)	(0.08)	(0.14)	(0.50)	(0.04)	(0.06)
EU	−1.65**	−0.57*	−0.31	0.66**	−0.49**	−0.64**	−1.19**
	(0.04)	(0.06)	(0.17)	(0.04)	(0.03)	(0.03)	(0.03)
WB	−1.18	−0.16	−0.45	−0.03	−0.13	−0.29	−0.73
	(0.18)	(0.56)	(0.18)	(0.94)	(0.46)	(0.32)	(0.32)
INT	−1.90**	−0.58**	−0.44	−0.10	−0.17	−0.71***	−0.91
	(0.05)	(0.03)	(0.11)	(0.77)	(0.41)	(0.01)	(0.19)
Year	−0.04	−0.01	−0.01	0.00	−0.00	−0.01	−0.03
	(0.44)	(0.56)	(0.62)	(0.82)	(0.92)	(0.54)	(0.43)
Constant	73.57	21.56	17.38	−8.41	1.80	23.71	56.47
	(0.42)	(0.54)	(0.61)	(0.82)	(0.90)	(0.52)	(0.42)
Adj. R2	0.50	0.46	0.45	0.11	0.44	0.47	0.38
N	109	109	109	109	109	109	109

Note: Linear regression models with p-values in parentheses based on robust standard errors (heteroscedasticity consistent and clustered by founding country);

***, ** and * indicate significance at the 1%-, 5%- and 10%-level respectively. Variable names are abbreviated in interaction terms: Kyoto operational → Kyoto, Post Copenhagen → Copenh.

Domestic Sources of Transnational Climate Governance

Miles Kahler

ABSTRACT

Transnational climate governance (TCG) is an example of complex governance in which national governments no longer serve as reliable gatekeepers between nonstate and subnational actors and global governance. The articles in this special issue demonstrate that TCG and complex governance do not eliminate the importance of domestic political institutions and actors in explaining national variation in engagement with TCG. Rich democracies provide the most favorable political setting for participation in TCG. National policies that favor climate change mitigation produce greater engagement with TCG on the part of nonstate and subnational actors. The same political ecology that produces favorable national policies supports TCG participation: NGO presence and activism, affluent consumers that encourage corporations to engage with TCG, subnational governments with political incentives and fiscal space to undertake cross-border activism. Although direct effects by TCG on greenhouse gas emissions may be limited, TCG may have longer-run and second-order effects that are larger, particularly if commitments are more precise and binding. Overall, TCG illustrates a complementary rather than competitive relationship between national governments and complex governance, a relationship that should be investigated in other issue areas.

Two questions have dominated debates over global governance during the past decade. First, have intergovernmental institutions (IGOs), at the center of global governance since 1945, been superseded by new modes of governance that award a more prominent place to private actors and subnational governments? Second, are the existing institutions of governance adequate for the provision of essential global public goods, such as financial stability, economic growth, conflict resolution, and mitigation of climate change? A third question, less central to these debates, links the first two: Are the new modes of governance an adequate solution to the perceived shortcomings of existing global governance institutions?

Each of these questions is particularly pertinent to collective efforts aimed at the mitigation of climate change. The recent proliferation of new modes of transnational climate governance (TCG) has been well documented (Andonova, Hale, and Roger Forthcoming). The timeline for the emergence of these new modes of climate governance matches closely the pattern in other issue areas: steady growth during the 1990s and a sharp acceleration during the first decade of the twenty-first century. Abbott and Snidal (2009), for example, find an increase in standard-setting arrangements that include a mix of governments, nongovernmental organizations (NGOs), and private corporations, beginning in the 1980s and accelerating in the 1990s and 2000s. Election monitoring has deployed a mix of both IGOs and NGOs, with the percentage of monitored elections in nonestablished democracies sharply increasing after the late 1980s. NGOs have played an increasingly prominent role since the late 1990s (Kelley 2012).

Action to mitigate climate change also parallels developments in other issue areas in its expansion of the targets for collective action. The intergovernmental organization (IGO) model, developed in the aftermath of the Great Depression and World War II, emphasized national governments as the target for new international constraints. Negotiated rules often aimed to prevent government backsliding into beggar-thy-neighbor policies, which had exacerbated economic distress during the interwar decades. To the degree that individuals, corporations, or groups were targets for global collective action and regulation, national policy, backed by international commitments, was the preferred instrument for influencing their behavior.

In the case of climate change, which involves long-term and complex strategies for mitigation and adaptation, diagnosis of the problem does not provide a clear definition of the most efficient target. For some observers, successful mitigation will require far-reaching changes in individual behavior. Others point to the importance of urbanization and cities to greenhouse gas emissions and argue for action at the subnational level. Still others aim at economic sectors and corporations that are primary greenhouse gas emitters, such as fossil fuels or transportation. In addition, there is disagreement over the efficacy of direct regulatory action versus market signals. Although one could pursue behavioral change through national governments and their regulatory policies, other mechanisms of global governance that engage these targeted actors directly may be more effective.

The emergence of complex global governance

Transnational climate governance is a species in the larger category of complex governance. Complex governance comprises modes of governance that have been given several labels: informal international lawmaking (Pauwelyn, Wessel, and Wouters 2012), private transnational organizations (Abbott, Green, and Keohane 2016), private authority (Green 2014), and networks in both the economic and security domains (Avant and Westerwinter 2016). These different formats of complex governance share three characteristics. First, national governments remain important actors in global governance, but in complex governance they are only one actor among a larger and much more heterogeneous group of participants. Private and nongovernmental actors are hardly novel actors in world politics. In complex governance arrangements, however, these transnational actors participate directly in governance through institutionalized and networked relations with subnational and national governments or other nonstate actors. In many cases of complex governance, organizations of different type (governments, IGOs, NGOs, MNCs) collaborate; homophily has weakened or disappeared. For example, the Global Fund to Fight AIDS, Tuberculosis and Malaria, a leading global health partnership, includes representatives of governments, international and regional organizations, NGOs (from North and South), foundations, and corporations on its board.

A second feature of complex governance further disrupts the image of a unitary national government that stands as a gatekeeper and monopolist between its society and international collaboration. National governments no longer interpose themselves between subnational levels of government and local actors on the one hand and global and regional governance on the other. Multilevel governance is no longer unidirectional, with demands moving from local to national to global: Levels of governance influence one another in less-predictable ways. Examples of transnational climate governance in this special issue, such as the European Covenant of Mayors, exemplify the direct participation by cities in complex global governance. At the same time, the reach of global and regional actors extends directly into subnational politics. In similar fashion, global institutions may directly "orchestrate" NGOs or partner with subnational governments (Abbott, Genschel, Snidal, and Zangl 2015). Peacebuilding and development assistance in postconflict states also illustrate this avenue of cross-border influence.

Finally, because of the reduced centrality of national governments, complex governance is more likely to be informal and less legalized. These informal arrangements, represented in this special issue, claim such labels as *covenant*, *initiative*, and *alliance*. They have captured functional domains that would once have been delegated to IGOs or claimed by national governments. In this third characteristic, complex governance parallels many intergovernmental agreements and institutions, which have also moved in the direct of informality (Vabulas and Snidal 2013).

Available data on complex governance arrangements do not permit firm conclusions regarding issue area variation. Complex governance seems to appear more often in issue areas that are new to the international agenda, however. TCG lies squarely within such an issue area; other environmental issues and global health are also new and rising global issues over the past two decades. Trade, on the other hand, is an issue area in which governments and intergovernmental agreements—global, plurilateral, regional—continue to dominate, and the direct engagement of subnational and nongovernmental actors is less significant. The relatively open organizational space in these domains may explain some of this variation: A dominant set of intergovernmental institutions is less entrenched, allowing greater latitude for complex governance.[1] In the case of climate change, a fragmented intergovernmental regime complex allowed for alternatives to emerge that were based on corporate, NGO, and local government participants. Although the WHO was an early orchestrator of nongovernmental partners, it did not maintain its central position in the global health regime complex, which opened space for nongovernmental competitors that are often better funded and more skillful at building cross-border coalitions.

An alternative explanation for variation in complex governance across issue areas derives from governance preferences of nonstate actors, particularly global corporations and international NGOs. Their preference for new modes of complex governance could be driven by perceptions that existing global governance institutions are underperforming or failing. For those who examine a lengthening agenda of old and new issues, "demand for international cooperation is growing even as supply grinds to a halt" (Hale, Held, and Young 2013:48). If formal intergovernmental institutions no longer deliver the collaborative dividends required, reform of those institutions or their supplementation with complex governance is necessary. Although it is a popular explanation for complex governance, this demand-driven substitution effect is at best incomplete. Once again, the trade regime provides a counterexample. Although it is widely regarded as a failure, the Doha round of trade negotiations at the WTO has not led to the adoption of complex governance. Rather, governments have chosen megaregional trade agreements and other intergovernmental clubs outside the WTO to pursue their preferred agenda in commercial policy.

TCG provides an ideal field for deepening understanding of complex governance and explaining why it has emerged in this particularly important issue area. TCG displays the three characteristics of complex governance enumerated earlier, characteristics it shares with such arenas as the European Union and the governance of global health. At the same time, the contributors to this special issue also refocus attention on national governments and policies, as well as the domestic politics that lie behind complex governance. Instead of assuming that national governments and characteristics have become marginalized in these new modes of governance, this special issue highlights the ways in which national politics, institutions, and policies remains important determinants—though not the sole determinants—of complex governance and its effectiveness. Although national governments may be less-effective gatekeepers in global politics and governance, they may remain prominent governors, setting boundaries and benchmarks as well as engaging as partners with an enlarged and diverse universe of actors.

---

[1]This argument follows from the analysis by Abbott et al. 2016.

Explaining the emergence of TCG

Explanations for the emergence of TCG and other forms of complex governance—to the degree that explanations have been offered for such diverse approaches to governance—have emphasized systemic or functionalist approaches. As the historical pattern of complex governance suggests, systemic variables may explain the timing of transnational governance arrangements across issue areas. Two systemic developments appear to be particularly important. The expansion of global economic integration to postcommunist and developing economies, beginning in the 1980s and accelerating in the 1990s, increased the networked or connected character of societies. Economic actors, such as multinational corporations (MNCs), as well as international nongovernmental organizations (NGOs), promoted this connectedness. The end of the Cold War, which permitted integration of postcommunist societies into the global economy, also contributed to the third wave of democratization, by ending support for many authoritarian regimes by the American and Soviet superpowers. Democracies are more likely to join international institutions, and, as the data on TCG indicates, their institutions are also more likely to encourage cross-border collaboration by corporate and NGO actors. The democratic difference in engagement with TCG was owed in part to this systemic shift toward democratic governance. As the articles in this special issue find, however, measures of international connectedness do not capture much of the variation in engagement with TCG arrangements across countries.[2] Degrees of global economic integration in particular do not seem to carry over directly to TCG participation.

A second explanation advances a model for TCG participation that emphasizes political actors that are motivated to substitute TCG for intergovernmental solutions to climate change. Conventional, intergovernmental cooperation via the Kyoto Protocol did not appear to reduce the emission of greenhouse gases quickly enough. Given the reluctance of governments to introduce a global regulatory regime that would curb those emissions, unconventional (complex) governance was advanced by nongovernmental actors and some governments (national and subnational) as an alternative.

Andonova et al. (Forthcoming) and Cao and Ward (2017) do not find, at the national level, such a straightforward substitution of transnational climate governance for activist national and global climate policies. They cannot rule out an international gridlock effect on choices made by actors to engage with TCG, however. Equally problematic for such a functionalist or pragmatic approach to TCG, however, is the uncertainty surrounding

---

[2] Andonova et al. (Forthcoming) do find a significant but small positive effect of transnational NGO networks on TCG participation.

TCG and its effectiveness as a mitigation strategy, as suggested by Michaelowa and Michaelowa (2017). Frustrated actors may choose TCG engagement as an alternative in the face of inadequate intergovernmental agreements, but, in doing so, they have not chosen TCG as a proven path to more effective mitigation of climate change.

Domestic politics and TCG: Institutional explanations

If systemic or functionalist explanations cannot fully explain national variation in TCG participation, domestic political variables become leading candidates in accounting for such variation. In their analysis of the significance of regime type on the involvement of sub- and nonstate actors in TCG, Andonova et al. (Forthcoming) deploy measures of the openness of a political system (respect for civil liberties and political rights as well as regime type). They find that "civil liberties and decentralization are strongly and robustly correlated" with higher levels of engagement in TCG (p. 30). They attribute this relationship to freedom awarded civil society and subnational actors in such polities "to engage in policy advocacy and to create programs and organizations with 'governance' aims." In other words, these nongovernmental and subnational actors are motivated to become involved in TCG initiatives, and liberal democracies are more likely to permit such involvement. Authors in the special issue confirm this finding indirectly, since their investigations of actor engagement are directed largely to rich democracies. The second finding regarding domestic political institutions is no more surprising: Countries that are federations or otherwise administratively decentralized are more likely to exhibit participation in TCG by subnational units, such as provinces, states, or cities (p. 30).

Both of these findings regarding political institutions and their association with TCG are confronted with one large anomaly: China. China is the largest authoritarian country, and it is also the only one of the five largest countries (by population) that is neither a federation nor administratively decentralized.[3] Yet China is an active participant in TCG: the only country among the 10 countries with the largest number of actors participating in TCG that is neither democratic, nor rich, nor federal. (India is the only other country among the top 10 that is not a rich, industrialized democracy.)

The Chinese anomaly is particularly important, given China's status as the leading emitter of greenhouse gases. Its institutional deviation from the norm suggests another path to TCG, which may apply to other authoritarian cases. If an authoritarian polity, such as China, embraces policies to mitigate climate change at the national level, state-encouraged participation in TCG by nonstate actors and subnational governments becomes a means of promoting and monitoring

---

[3] The United States, India, and Brazil are federations; Indonesia has, since democratization, introduced a substantial measure of decentralization in its previously centralized political system.

implementation of policies set at the national level. Hale and Roger (2012) document this dynamic in the case of TCG standards for carbon trading. In other domains of public policy, the Chinese government has used the resources and policy expertise found in transnational networks and international NGOs (INGOs) to enhance its ability to deal with health crises, such as HIV/AIDS, and to develop environmental policies (Hildebrandt and Turner 2009; Wang 2012). Note that this authoritarian route to TCG participation requires a government with a policy commitment to climate change mitigation and one that has substantial capacity to influence subnational governments and nonstate actors. China may not be alone in this capacity, but it possesses substantial levers to influence the actors engaged in TCG, levers that most democracies could not deploy, even if they were motivated to do so. Many NGOs in China are GONGOs, government-organized NGOs, dependent on national or local governments for their budgets and their ability to operate within a constrained political space. Many of the largest corporations in China that are active internationally are state-owned enterprises (SOEs), and their presence is particularly prominent in sectors important for climate change mitigation, such as energy and transportation. Finally, although provincial and local governments exercise some degree of autonomy in China's formally centralized political system, the reach of the Chinese Communist Party ensures some measure of responsiveness on the part of provincial and local officials.

Political actors and their incentives to participate in transnational climate governance

Most of the contributors to this special issue concentrate on the incentives of corporate, NGO, and subnational actors for participation in TCG. Although it is important to bear in mind China and the authoritarian route to TCG, rich democracies—which are also major greenhouse gas emitters—set an institutional stage that enables participation in governance across borders. Given that permissive political environment, why do some political actors choose to engage in TCG, given that the costs for participation are not insubstantial?

Subnational governments and TCG

Among issue areas in which complex governance has emerged, transnational climate governance is unusual in the prominent place awarded to initiatives and networks that engage subnational actors, particularly cities. Since urbanization is proceeding rapidly in many developing countries, encouraging a "green" path for cities could have major implications for the success of climate change mitigation. Political units also differ from other TCG participants in that they are either agents of national governments (the China case) or agents of electorates or electoral coalitions (in liberal democracies), or both, in systems that include administrative decentralization with national direction and funding.

Nives Dolšak and Aseem Prakash (2017) develop models of subnational participation in TCG by incorporating the incentives and disincentives of local politicians for participation. As they emphasize, participation in TCG—in this case, the Covenant of Mayors (COM) program—is not without cost. In order for a city to participate, local benefits must outweigh those costs. Benefits for politicians who promote TCG participation by their cities will be both reputational and electoral, satisfying constituencies that endorse measures to mitigate climate change domestically and internationally.

NGOs and TCG

Dolšak and Prakash (2017) pinpoint one constituency in particular that may shift the incentives of mayors and other influential urban actors in the direction of TCG participation: national endowments of domestic NGOs, as measured by an index of NGO sustainability developed by USAID. In contrast to international NGOs, which are central to those explanations of TCG participation that emphasize cross-border linkage, Dolšak and Prakash argue that domestic NGOs bestow political benefits on urban political elites, benefits that offset the costs of TCG participation. Those "excludable reputational and goodwill benefits, which have the characteristics of club goods" may include national and international visibility for participating cities and their political leaders. Most important, participation may "strengthen environmental credentials of city politicians with these vocal [NGO] constituencies" (Dolšak and Prakash 2017).

Within cities, NGOs could play at least two roles to promote TCG participation. One strategy would be persuasive, convincing municipal leaders that the Covenant of Mayors would provide informational or other benefits to their city that would offset the costs of participation. Equally likely is a model in which incumbent or opposition politicians find NGO political support and mobilization of activists important to their electoral success and trade engagement with COM for that support. Dolšak and Prakash (2017) provide indirect support for the role of NGOs in COM participation, since they do not present city-level data on participation, and their measure of NGO strength includes all domestic NGOs rather than those active in environmental issues. Cao and Ward (2017) offer valuable additional support for the claim that NGOs are an important support constituency for TCG initiatives. They discover that the number of domestic environmental NGOs are important determinants of TCG network ties.

Private corporations and TCG

Lily Hsueh (2017) scrutinizes the microfoundations of corporate participation in TCG. She aims to explain participation of a particular kind: involvement in TCG initiatives that appear both more demanding and more reliant on market mechanisms. Corporations that are rich in resources and have a prominent public profile (for example, Fortune 500 companies) engage in these initiatives. Other corporate correlates are also powerful predictors of TCG engagement: an "explicit sustainability focus" (marked by corporate social responsibility programs) and the presence of a bureaucratic proponent within corporate management. Because of their public profiles as large, multinational corporations and their concentration in sectors dependent on consumers, reputational considerations loom large. Although variables internal to the corporations predict TCG participation (Hsueh's interpretation), those same features could also be interpreted as indicators of concern about corporations' public image among affluent and environmentally conscious consumers. Reputational considerations are likely to motivate these corporate participants in TCG, which are concentrated in rich countries with liberal political economies and governance. A further motivation (underscored by the participation of fossil fuel producers less sensitive to consumer sentiment) is a wish to preempt mandatory rules that would mitigate climate change.

Nonstate actors and complex climate governance

Although the contributors to this special issue provide us with pieces of the political puzzle that explains engagement with TCG on the part of subnational and private actors, further investigation is required to determine whether the dynamics of TCG match those in other regulatory domains in which complex governance has emerged during the post-Cold War era of globalization. A similar pattern can be identified in sectors related to security and conflict (conflict diamonds and the Kimberley process), labor rights, and environmental protection in sectors other than climate change (forestry). NGOs or NGOs and their government allies promote a new agenda item in global governance, one that is often precipitated by a regulatory gap between the industrialized countries (host to most of the major INGOs) and transitional or developing countries, now deeply engaged in the global economy. The regulatory gap cannot be closed through intergovernmental negotiations because of domestic opposition within the industrialized countries, resistance from the developing country governments, and/or lack of regulatory capacity in the developing country. NGOs then turn to other political strategies, which include direct pressure on MNCs that are active in the issue area and alliances with sympathetic subnational governments in the industrialized countries. MNCs respond by participating in private or market-based regulatory initiatives that may strengthen their competitive advantage, burnish their public image, or preempt more binding public regulation. Subnational governments respond when local NGOs mobilize political support that can serve to reward or punish local political leaders. The contributions here are consistent with a dynamic model of this kind, capturing elements of that model (alliances between NGOs and subnational governments, corporations engaging with TCG initiatives). The contributors clearly argue against TCG as a substitute for climate change policy at the national level, an important issue in assessing the likely effectiveness of TCG in influencing global climate change outcomes.

The relationship of TCG and national-level policy on climate

In explaining and evaluating TCG, the relationship of these transnational arrangements to national policies toward climate change is a central concern. One could imagine that engagement with transnational networks and collaboration could be motivated by political deadlock or lack of movement on climate change at the national level. Such engagement might also distract important civil society actors from action at the national level, absorbing resources and participants who might otherwise have dedicated themselves to influencing the national political process and its outcomes. If binding international agreements negotiated by national governments are a desired outcome of climate change activism, TCG could have a net negative effect on achieving that goal.

Andonova et al. (Forthcoming) do not find such a substitution effect in the data on TCG involvement. Instead, they argue for a complementary or reinforcing relationship between active national policies on climate change and TCG involvement by subnational, corporate, and NGO actors. Climate-active governments will have incentives to encourage more transnational governance on the part of its civil society actors and subnational governments. This top-down effect could be characteristic of both liberal democratic governments, such as those in the EU, as well as authoritarian governments, such as China, which wield more direct influence over their corporate and NGO actors. The mutually reinforcing effects of national policies and TCG initiatives might also be owed to activism on the part of civil society actors, which can operate on both political fronts. The role of NGOs emphasized by Dolšak and Prakash (2017) provides a single explanation for both national governments that act to mitigate climate change *and* actors outside the national government that engage across national borders in a variety of collaborative ventures.

Using a restricted set of TCG initiatives (those without government participation at any level), Cao and Ward (2017) produce a model that allows for more precise understanding of when national policies and TCG will reinforce or substitute for one another. In Cao and Ward's model, lobbying at the national level by nonstate actors (NGOs and corporations) is at least a partial substitute for engaging with transnational networks: Both will produce equivalent, positive effects (from the point of view of the nonstate actors) in mitigating climate change. Nonstate actors will weigh the cost of lobbying for climate change policy at the national level against the costs of engaging in TCG. If national-level policies are already positive or moving in the right direction (from the point of view of these climate change activists or actors), they will have more resources to devote to building private, transnational ties and promoting TCG. At the same time, they may have less incentive to engage in TCG as an indirect means of influencing their national authorities. Cao and Ward present empirical results that support a view of national policies and transnational linkages as complements.

Their model may need refinement in order to capture more precisely the trade-off between domestic and transnational strategies on the part of different actors. For poor countries, TCG engagement may add resources that might enhance lobbying success at the national level. This reverse flow of resources or benefits from transnational networks would alter the incentives of nonstate actors, since TCG would become a profit rather than a cost center in their calculations. This redirection of domestic NGO efforts by INGOs and the resources that they provide is both an opportunity and a risk that derives from engagement with TCG.

Features of the domestic political environment also shift the balance between domestic and transnational action. As Cao and Ward (2017) describe, the marginal rate of substitution may differ systematically between categories of nonstate actors, although they do not model the calculus of corporate actors explicitly. For NGOs, TCG may be a distinct second best when compared to comprehensive national policies directed toward climate change; corporations on the other hand, may prefer less legalized and binding international arrangements when compared to national policy commitments. Another consideration is the scope of the two activities: National-level lobbying will affect one government; TCG could potentially influence many more. If an NGO (and the discussion of Cao and Ward is directed primarily to NGOs and subnational governments, not corporations) wishes to influence global climate change, the size of its country's greenhouse gas emissions should also affect the marginal rate of substitution between domestic lobbying and TCG.

Most important, is the question of whether these two alternatives—domestic political action or engagement with international networks—are in fact substitutes. The target of domestic political action—policies of national governments—is clear; the target of TCG is not. A boomerang effect (parallel to Keck and Sikkink 1998) would posit transnational action to influence a government more sympathetic to climate change action; that government would in turn influence a more recalcitrant government. Although authoritarian governments opposed to both climate change mitigation and the activities of domestic environmental NGOs may fit this model, it seems less appropriate for democratic governments that are laggards in climate change policy, such as India or Australia. The model of Cao and Ward (2017) seems to accept this underlying logic: The ultimate goal is changing the policies of national governments. Political action to deal with climate change, however, must consider a wider array of possible strategies. As described earlier, political strategies may aim to change national policy regimes, the practices of particular corporations, municipal commitments, and even the behavior of individuals. Uncertainty regarding the comparative effectiveness of these strategies complicates the calculations of nonstate actors who contemplate a binary choice between national lobbying and TCG—and complicates the model of Cao and Ward.

Transnational climate governance as a means to mitigate climate change

Interest in transnational climate governance has been spurred by hope that such initiatives could compensate for failure of mitigation through national targets or international commitments. As described earlier, the diverse universe of actors whose behavior is targeted, directly or indirectly, in such arrangements complicates an evaluation of the effectiveness of TCG. Evaluation also encounters the familiar issue of selection bias: Those who participate in the growing share of TCG initiatives that extend beyond information-sharing or networking may choose to participate in informal arrangements that require little or no behavioral change (Downs, Rocke, and Barsoom 1996). The counterfactual assumption, that behavior would have remained on a different and less ambitious trajectory in the absence of participation, is difficult to demonstrate. Finally, effectiveness may be evident only after a substantial period of TCG participation. If behavioral change were the result of socialization, such a lag would be expected.

An assessment of the effectiveness of TCG should guide actors in their decisions to devote resources to these modes of climate governance rather than alternatives. That decision will also depend on the relationship between TCG and government action to mitigate climate change at either the national or international level: Whether TCG is a substitute for government policy measures or a complement to those actions. Whatever its absolute effectiveness in changing behavior, any assessment of the usefulness of TCG as part of a larger climate change strategy will depend on its status as either a valuable second best when governments fail to act or a limited complement to more effective national and global government action.

Two contributions to this special issue emphatically support the view of TCG as a complement to government action at the international and national levels. Katarina and Axel Michaelowa (2017) evaluate TCG initiatives based on institutional design and prospective effects on behavior, rather than directly measuring its behavioral consequences. Their assessment treats the inclusion of four design features as a proxy for the likelihood that TCG will alter target behavior from an earlier trajectory, a "minimum requirement" for later mitigation effectiveness. Without these institutional components, they argue, the likelihood that TCG will change behavior is slender. Overall, only a small portion (<15%) of the universe of TCG initiatives included in their data set embody three or more of these design features; nearly half do not include any. Michaelowa and

Michaelowa conclude that existing TCG arrangements cannot fill a gap in effectiveness produced by inadequate government policies. Their finding that government orchestration and national emission targets in an initiative's founding country increase the quality of TCG lends further support to a strong claim of complementarity.

Although the direct behavioral effect of TCG on emissions may be limited, Michaelowa and Michaelowa (2017) note that TCG may have indirect and longer-run effects that may affect greenhouse gas emissions. In addition, given the recent creation of many TCG initiatives, their design features should not be regarded as fixed. Recent studies indicate that TCG initiatives of this kind could have a substantial effect on future emissions if their design incorporates more of the features described by Michaelowa and Michaelowa as well as through their effect on government policies over time. The United Nations Environment Program (UNEP), for example, has recently reviewed the mitigation commitments made by 15 nonstate climate initiatives (including TCG initiatives) and estimated that these initiatives could deliver substantial emission savings, over and above currently implemented policies, even when taking into account overlap with government pledges. As the UNEP report suggests, "these nonstate initiatives can also play a role in raising the level of ambition of governments by demonstrating what is possible with concerted action" (UNEP 2015:27). A shift in the universe of TCG arrangements toward more precise and binding commitments might have a large impact when compared to other, more conventional avenues toward mitigation of climate change. Investigating the conditions under which these more effective variants of TCG emerge represents a promising line of research.

Jessica Green (2017) describes a hierarchy between public and private in her investigation of carbon offset markets, one category of TCG. At the top of the hierarchy is a public, intergovernmental creation, the Clean Development Mechanism (CDM). Network analysis demonstrates regulatory convergence driven by this prestigious public standard. High prestige (widely recognized) private standards all reference the public CDM standard, which seems to add to their status in the private marketplace. Conversely, Green's analysis demonstrates that few public climate change frameworks recognize private regulation of carbon offsets; when recognition occurs, it is, with few exceptions, incorporated in voluntary programs. As Green describes, private regulation of carbon emissions is viewed as a supplement to, not a substitute for, the "real work" of public regulation. The countries that recognize private standards are also concentrated in the industrialized world, a feature that further undermines the view of these TCG mechanisms as substitutes for government action. Poor societies with low state regulatory capacity do not endorse private standards. In parallel with the findings of Michaelowa and Michaelowa (2017), Green finds complementarity between public and private initiatives in designing carbon offsets. Intergovernmental agreement provides an important reinforcement and reference point for TCG.

Combining positive and normative: Climate change and domestic politics

Transnational climate governance is a particularly important instance of complex governance. The contributors to this special issue illuminate the conditions under which NGOs, corporations, and subnational governments participate in complex governance, participation that has burgeoned in the past two decades. Drawing on an original and extensive data set, the authors identify domestic political variables that explain complex governance in climate change and other issue areas. They define a particular political ecology of actors and institutional settings that favor both TCG and complex governance.

One political variable appears and reappears in these accounts: NGO presence and activism. Green (2017) argues that the existence of robust private standards for carbon offsets is best explained by the supply of such standards by a population of standard setters (measured by the number of NGOs). Cao and Ward (2017) discover a similar association between environmental NGOs and participation in TCG networks. NGO political influence may also explain a large part of the variation in participation by subnational governments in TCG. Dolšak and Prakash (2017) link domestic NGOs to TCG participation by cities through a model of vote seeking by municipal officials, in which political benefits provided by NGOs offset the costs of participation in TCG initiatives.

The drivers of corporate participation in TCG and complex governance are explored less thoroughly in these articles. Corporate participation in private standard setting may be driven by NGO pressure coupled with a desire to avoid public regulatory intervention. (Michaelowa and Michaelowa [2017] provide evidence for the second motivation.) Hsueh's (2017) examination of a limited set of TCG initiatives emphasizes organizational variables as important determinants of corporate participation in TCG initiatives. Those organizational innovations, however, may reflect a response to NGO-motivated concerns among their publics and consumers. Just as the density of environmental NGOs is highest in rich countries, the corporations that engage with more stringent TCG are also most likely to be based in rich countries whose affluent consumers are attentive to corporate positions on climate change and are more likely to accept NGO-driven campaigns of pressure for corporate involvement in TCG.

The political ecology of climate change activism that lies behind TCG is most likely to be found in countries that Green (2017) describes as "rich, green, and free." Liberal democratic institutions provide the necessary environment for both the influence exercised by domestic NGOs and the open borders that permit TCG to flourish. National governments that support climate change mitigation appear to have a positive effect on participation by nonstate actors in TCG. In such circumstances, following the model of Cao and Ward (2017), resources that would be devoted to domestic lobbying in favor of climate change can be shifted to transnational governance and networks.

A domestic political ecology that supports both national (including intergovernmental) as well as transnational climate change governance is probably found in its most complete form in the European Union. Two other groups of countries are of particular interest, however. Industrialized countries with significant fossil fuel industries share many features of the positive climate change political ecology, combined with domestic political polarization and opposition to aggressive national policies to mitigate climate change. Australia, Canada, and the United States are the principal examples. Canada has the highest greenhouse gas emissions per capita in the world; Australia has recently seen the most substantial rollback of policies to deal with climate change of any industrialized country. In the United States, one of the two major political parties has become identified with positions ranging from climate change denial to efforts aiming to delay implementation of policies to mitigate climate change. Given the democratic politics of these countries and their activist NGO sectors, any contribution of TCG to a shift in their national policy positions is likely to be limited. In their introductory article, Roger, Hale, and Andonova (2017) argue that transnational engagement can lend legitimacy and resources to domestic supporters of action to arrest climate change and also diffuse best practices across national borders. For rich societies, however, well endowed with their own environmental and climate change constituencies, TCG appears unlikely to influence the balance in domestic political battles. Naming and shaming in intergovernmental forums and the long, hard work of domestic political mobilization will probably prove to be more efficacious strategies.

The largest emerging economies—China, India, Brazil, and other developing members of the G20—are a second and even more important category for successful global action on climate change. Among the top 10 emitters of greenhouse gases, five are now emerging economies, with China and India ranked first and fourth.[4] Success in arresting climate change will necessarily depend on the collaboration and contributions of these countries: Can transnational climate governance contribute to that prospect? Although these countries are participants in TCG, they have not been leaders in establishing TCG initiatives, and their involvement has not been concentrated in the strongest TCG initiatives. However, most possess some of the constituents of domestic political ecology that favor TCG. For example, the largest emerging economies have substantial populations of NGOs, and environmental NGOs among the most active. Their corporations have a

---

[4]This ranking takes the European Union as a single unit.

growing international profile and have become increasingly concerned with measures of corporate social responsibility.[5]

TCG initiatives can reinforce and broaden these trends in emerging economies by lending legitimacy and resources to NGOs and other nonstate actors that have limited capacity and by transmitting best practices to their counterparts in urban governments and corporations. In authoritarian settings, such as China or Vietnam, the ability of TCG to create or strengthen domestic constituencies for action on climate change is limited. Many governments, both democratic (India) and authoritarian (Russia, China) have recently adopted measures to reduce precisely such transnational effects by circumscribing the activities of international NGOs. The transmission of environmental best practices is more likely to succeed: The Chinese government, for example, has in the past turned to transnational actors as well as IGOs for technical assistance in several issue areas. Given institutional constraints on mobilization from below and the strong preference of emerging economies for conventional forms of international collaboration, TCG may be less effective in moving climate change policy than intergovernmental pressure (for example, climate clubs) or government responsiveness to more politically sensitive forms of environmental degradation (urban air pollution or threats to the water supply).

Transnational climate governance: How large a wager?

Cao and Ward (2017) suggest that nongovernmental actors calculate whether to devote resources to domestic lobbying or transnational networks, each viewed as a partial substitute for the other. Citizens, NGOs, corporations, and governments must make a similar calculation among even more options. Given limited resources and the pressing need to implement significant climate change mitigation measures, investments in TCG must be compared to intergovernmental negotiation and commitment or action to change national policy through domestic means. Within the sphere of TCG, choices must be made among actors whose behavior must be changed (often radically) and TCG initiatives that are more or less likely to be most effective in enacting that change.

The evidence presented in this special issue points toward an important though delimited role for TCG. Michaelowa and Michaelowa (2017) suggest that the institutional design of most existing TCG initiatives is unlikely to induce a rapid or radical shift in behavior, though a shift toward more precise and binding mitigation commitments would dramatically amplify their effects. Green and other contributors outline the importance of public benchmarks and programs, even in the design of private governance arrangements. Indeed, many of the

---

[5]In 2012 a total of 1,722 Chinese companies filed CSR reports, among them nearly one-quarter of large state-owned enterprises (Larson 2013). Large, internationally engaged Brazilian corporations have also endorsed corporate sustainability programs (Scharf 2008). The effect of these commitments on corporate practices, however, and on the large population of small and medium enterprises is unclear.

proponents of and participants in TCG seem to acknowledge that national regulatory measures are likely to be the most efficient means of inducing the large-scale changes required for climate change mitigation. The question then becomes whether and how TCG, itself a manifestation of a particular domestic political ecology, can promote, diffuse, and strengthen that ecology in order to alter national policies and strengthen intergovernmental collaboration. If TCG can create cross-border diffusion effects that not only enhance policy innovation and scientific understanding but also promote the domestic political constituencies that render TCG both more effective and less essential, complex governance in climate change will be judged a success. Any preliminary assessment of contemporary TCG and its effectiveness must be tempered by its relative novelty, with many of its governance initiatives appearing during the last decade. Its complementary and reinforcing relationship with more conventional national policy processes and intergovernmental agreements may only be recognized over time.

In addition to the important explanatory and prescriptive contributions made by this special issue to our understanding of TCG and its effects on climate change politics, the authors also advance a more precise comprehension of complex governance. Their focus on the domestic political ecology that promotes TCG, one important variant of complex governance, produces an important conclusion regarding the mutually reinforcing relationship between national governments and complex governance. Although existing research on complex governance is often framed in terms of the shortcomings of both national policy regimes and intergovernmental modes of global governance, this exploration of TCG offers a more nuanced portrait of complex governance and its sources. Not only are domestic political institutions and politics important determinants of the emergence of complex governance, national policies and intergovernmental agreements remain significant elements in the success of TCG and, arguably, other forms of complex governance. National governments may no longer be effective gatekeepers between private actors and new modes of global governance, but they remain important partners, if often silent partners, in the collective action that complex governance aims to achieve.

Acknowledgments

The author thanks Min Jung Kim for her research assistance and the editors of this special issue for their valuable comments on earlier drafts of this article. The author wishes to thank Daniel Chardell for his assistance in preparing this article.

References

Abbott, Kenneth W., Philipp Genschel, Duncan Snidal, and Bernhard Zangl. (2015) Orchestration: Global Governance through Intermediaries. In *International Organizations as*

Orchestrators, edited by Kenneth W. Abbott, Philipp Genschel, Duncan Snidal, and Bernhard Zangl. Cambridge: Cambridge University Press.

Abbott, Kenneth W., Jessica F. Green, and Robert O. Keohane. (2016) Organizational Ecology and Institutional Change in Global Governance. *International Organization* 70 (2):247–277.

Abbott, Kenneth W., and Duncan Snidal. (2009) The Governance Triangle: Regulatory Standards Institutions and the Shadow of the State. In *The Politics of Global Regulation*, edited by Walter Mattli and Ngaire Woods. Princeton, NJ: Princeton University Press.

Andonova, Liliana B., Thomas Hale, and Charles Roger. (Forthcoming) How Do Domestic Politics Condition Participation in Transnational Climate Governance? *International Studies Quarterly*.

Avant, Deborah, and Oliver Westerwinter, eds. (2016) *The New Power Politics: Networks and Transnational Security Governance*. New York: Oxford University Press.

Cao, Xun, and Hugh Ward. (2017) Transnational Climate Governance Networks and Domestic Regulatory Action. *International Interactions* 43(1):76–102. doi:10.1080/03050629.2016.1220162

Dolšak, Nives, and Aseem Prakash. (2017) Join the Club: How the Domestic NGO Sector Induces Participation in the Covenant of Mayors Program. *International Interactions* 43(1):26–47. doi:10.1080/03050629.2017.1226668

Downs, George W., David M. Rocke, and Peter N. Barsoom. (1996) Is The Good News about Compliance Good News about Cooperation? *International Organization* 50(3):379–406.

Green, Jessica F. (2014) *Rethinking Private Authority: Agents and Entrepreneurs in Global Environmental Governance*. Princeton, NJ: Princeton University Press.

Green, Jessica F. (2017) Blurred Lines: Why Do States Recognize Private Carbon Standards? *International Interactions* 43(1):103–128. doi:10.1080/03050629.2016.1210943

Hale, Thomas, David Held, and Kevin Young. (2013) *Gridlock: Why Global Cooperation Is Failing When We Need It Most*. Cambridge: Polity Press.

Hale, Thomas, and Charles Roger. (2012) Chinese Participation in Transnational Climate Governance. In *From Rule Takers to Rule Makers: The Growing Role of Chinese in Global Governance*, edited by Scott Kennedy and Suaihua Cheng. Research Center for Chinese Politics and Business (RCCPB) and International Centre for Trade and Sustainable Development (ICTSD). Available at http://www.ictsd.org/downloads/2012/10/the-growing-role-of-chinese-in-global-governance.pdf.

Hildebrandt, Timothy, and Jennifer L. Turner. (2009) Green Activism? Reassessing the Role of Environmental NGOs in China. In *State and Society Responses to Social Welfare Needs in China*, edited by Jonathan Schwartz and Shawn Shieh. London: Routledge, pp. 89–110.

Hsueh, Lily. (2017) Transnational Climate Governance and the Global 500: Examining Private Actor Participation by Firm-Level Factors and Dynamics. *International Interactions* 43(1):48–75. doi: 10.1080/03050629.2016.1223929

Keck, Margaret E., and Kathryn Sikkink. (1998) *Activists beyond Borders: Advocacy Networks in International Politics*. Ithaca, NY: Cornell University Press.

Kelley, Judith G. (2012) *Monitoring Democracy: When International Election Observation Works, and Why It Often Fails*. Princeton, NJ: Princeton University Press.

Larson, Christina. (2013, December 12) "Corporate Social Responsibility" Reports in China: Progress or Greenwashing? *Bloomberg Business*. Available at http://www.bloomberg.com/bw/articles/2013-12-12/corporate-social-responsibility-reports-in-china-progress-or-greenwashing.

Michaelowa, Katharina, and Axel Michaelowa. (2017) Transnational Climate Governance Initiatives: Designed for Effective Climate Change Mitigation? *International Interactions* 43 (1):129–155. doi: 10.1080/03050629.2017.1256110

Pauwelyn, Joost, Ramses Wessel, and Jan Wouters. (2012) An Introduction to Informal International Lawmaking. In *Informal International Lawmaking*, edited by Joost Pauwelyn, Ramses Wessel, and Jan Wouters. Oxford: Oxford University Press.

Roger, Charles, Thomas Hale, and Liliana B. Andonova. (2017) Domestic Politics and Transnational Climate Governance. *International Interactions* 43(1):1–25. doi: 10.1080/03050629.2017.1252248

Scharf, Regina. (2018) Why Brazil Leads the Region in CSR. *Americas Quarterly* 2(1):68–74.

United Nations Environment Program (UNEP). (2015) *Climate Commitments of Subnational Actors and Business: A Quantitative Assessment of Their Emission Reduction Impact.* Nairobi: Author.

Vabulas, Felicity, and Duncan Snidal. (2013) Organization without Delegation: Informal Intergovernmental Organizations (IIGOs) and the Spectrum of Intergovernmental Arrangements. *The Review of International Organizations* 8(2):193–220.

Wang, Mei-Ling. (2012) Managing HIV/AIDS: Yunnan's Government-Driven, Multi-Sector Partnership Model. *Management and Organization Review* 8(3):535–557.

Index

Note: Page numbers in *italics* refer to figures
Page numbers in **bold** refer to tables
Page numbers with "n" refer to endnotes

ABB 80
Abbott, K. W. 123
Accenture 80–1
advocacy groups 11
American Political Science Association 30
Andonova, L. B. 1, 63, 101, 183–4, 188, 193; public-private partnerships 11, 126; TGC participation 51–2, 87
Arimura, T. H. 62
Arora, S. 62
AT&T Technology and Environment Awards Program 81
Auld, G. 121, 123
authority: entrepreneurial 121; private 121, 122, 124–5
Avant, D. D. 54, 58

Bäckstrand, K. 147
BAE Systems 82
Barndt, W. T. 35
Bartley, T. 11, 123
baseline emission inventory (BEI) 32
BASF 80
BEI *see* baseline emission inventory (BEI)
Berliner, D. 149, 153–4
Bernauer, T. 135, 136
Bernstein, S. 123
Betsill, M. 147, 158
Bohmelt, T. 135
Bond, P. 35
boomerang effect 28, 189
Bulkeley, H. 5, 89, 90, 147, 158
Büthe, T. 11, 69

California Climate Action Registry (CCAR) 139
Cao, X. 41, 86, 156; TCG 15–17, 19–20, 183; TCG and NGOs 186, 188–9, 192–4
Carbon Disclosure Project (CDP) 52, 56; voluntary carbon disclosure 58–9, **68**

carbon-intensive countries 125
carbon-intensive economies 125–6
Carbon Neutral Program 130
carbon regulations, public v. private: determinants of interactions **134**
Cashore, B. 121, 123, 124
Cason, T. N. 62
CCAR *see* California Climate Action Registry (CCAR)
CDM *see* Clean Development Mechanism (CDM)
CDP *see* Carbon Disclosure Project (CDP)
Central Europe, transitional economies 28, 29
Chevron 79, 81
Cisco 81
civil liberties 15
Clean Air Act (1991) 34
Clean Development Mechanism (CDM) 119, 130, 191; Kyoto Protocol 154
Climate Action Registry 139
Climate Alliance of European Cities and Indigenous Peoples 5
climate change: and domestic politics 192–4; federal regulation on 29; TCG as mitigation 190–2
Climate, Community and Biodiversity (CCBA) standard 127, 128
climate 13: governance, developments in 17; national-level policy on 188–90; negotiations, United Nations 6
climate change mitigation 180; TCG as 190–2
climate regimes 3; implications for evolving 20–2; multilateral components of 3
Climate Solutions Hub 50
Cold War 49
COM *see* Covenant of Mayors (COM)
Compagnon, D. 147
complex climate governance, nonstate actors and 187–8

INDEX

complex global governance, emergence of 180–2
control variables: justifications **117–18**; operationalization 117, **117–18**
corporate social responsibility (CSR): comparative study 54; explicit 55, **67**; implicit 55; program 51, 56; strategy 53
Covenant of Mayors (COM) 26, 36; adoption 37; participation in 32; procedural effectiveness of 42; program 27–34, 186; share of urban population covered by **39**, **41**; urban population covered by **39**, **41**; web site 31
cross-border governance 1
CSR *see* corporate social responsibility (CSR)

Darnall, N. G. 62
De Búrca, G. 108
decision-making authority 16
delegation 124
De Leon, P. 54
Dolšak, N. 14, 16, 19–21, 26, 155, 186, 188, 192
domestic decentralization 16
domestic legislations, environmental treaties as proxy for 113, **115**
domestic lobbying: activity 90; price of 95, *95*
domestic NGOs 28, 33, 36, 37, 44
domestic policy: climate change 87; effect on equilibrium of shift in *114*; on transnational activity *92*, *94*
domestic political ecology 193
domestic politics 12, 19; climate change and 192–4; and TCG 184–5
Dorussen, H. 98
Down Jones Sustainability Index (DJSI) 54
Dupont 80

E8 6
"Earth Summit," Rio de Janeiro (1992) 6
Eastern Europe, transitional economies 28, 29
Eberlein, B. 123
Edwards, D. 62
Elander, I. 108
Energy Cities 6
entrepreneurial authority 121
environmental NGOs 36, 92, 100, 192
Environmental Performance Index (EPI) 63, 100
Environmental, Social and Governance (ESG) criteria 51, 52, 55, 61, 66
environmental treaties, as proxy for domestic legislations 113, **115**
EPI *see* Environmental Performance Index (EPI)
Espach, R. H. 11
Esty, D. C. 54
EU-ETS *see* European Union Emissions Trading Scheme (EU-ETS)
Eurasia, transitional economies 28, 29
European Union Emissions Trading Scheme (EU-ETS) 30
European Union, transitional economies 28–9

FDI 40
federal regulation, on climate change 29
Findley, M. G. 41
firms 31; "policy supporters" in 61
Forest Stewardship Council 5
Fujitsu 80

GDP 40, 101
Gerring, J. 35, 44
Gleditsch, K. S. 100
Global 500: companies 79–82; by country of origin *77*; by industry sector 76, **78**; *see also* national climate governance, and Global 500
global experimentalist governance 108
global governance, emergence of complex 180–2
governmental agencies 30
government programs, recognition of private standards **132**
gravity model 100n17
greenhouse gases (GHG): emissions 30, 44, 57, 119; mitigation, cobenefits of 155
Green, J. F. 7, 18–19, 88, 119, 123, 191–2; NGOs 17; supply/demand model 87
Gugerty, M. K. 94
Gulbrandsen, L. H. 123

Hale, T. N. 1, 11, 87, 158, 185, 193
Handfield, R. 62
Hawkins, J. 41
Hicks, R. L. 41
Hirshleifer, J. 89n2
Hoffmann, M. 5, 121, 147
HSBC Holdings 81
Hsu, A. 151
Hsueh, L. 14, 17, 19, 20, 49, 186–7, 192

IGO *see* intergovernmental organizations (IGO)
industry sector: Global 500 76, **78**
intergovernmental organizations (IGO) 179, 180
International Council of Local Environmental Initiatives (ICLEI) 151
international NGOs (INGOs) 28, 37–8, 40, 95, 185
investors, multinational companies and 11
IR theory 12

Jolley, G. J. 62

Kahler, M. 179
Katayama, H. 62
Keohane, R. O. 108, 123
Khanna, M. 62
Knill, C. 123
Kolk, A. 147
Koremenos, B. 148
Koubi, V. 135
Kyoto Protocol 108, 119, 131, 160; Clean Development Mechanism (CDM) 154; commitment 30; 1997 6, 30; 2001 17

200

INDEX

latent space model: estimates for shared TCGs **115, 116**; justification 101–3, **106**
Laufer, W. S. 33
Lee, T. 88
Lekhmuhl, D. 123
Levy, M. A. 126
Lidskog, R. 108
Lipson, C. 148
Lubin, D. A. 54

Matten, D. 54
Mattli, W. 11, 69
McDermott, C. 123
Michaelowa, A. 14, 18–19, 21, 146, 183–4, 190–1, 194
Michaelowa, K. 14, 18–19, 21, 146, 183–4, 190–1, 194
MNCs *see* multinational corporations (MNCs)
Moffat, A. S. 151
monitoring, reporting, and verification (MRV) 151, 152
Moon, J. 54
Moreno, C. 35
multilevel mixed-effects models 51–2, 64, **68, 84**
multinational companies, and investors 11
multinational corporations (MNCs) 49–51, 53, 55, 183, 187; retail 57–8
multivariate analysis 134–7

National Carbon Offset Standard (NCOS) 140
national policy: on climate 188–90; private rules into 124–6
Nationally Determined Contributions (NDCs) 146
NAZCA *see* Non-State Actor Zone for Climate Action (NAZCA)
NCOS *see* National Carbon Offset Standard (NCOS)
Newell, P. 147
Newsome, D. 121
NGOs *see* nongovernmental organizations (NGOs)
Nielson, D. L. 41
nongovernmental organizations (NGOs) 16, 156–7; domestic 28, 33, 37, 44; environmental 36, 92, 100; international 28, 37–8, 40, 95; role 26, 28; and TCG 186; in transitional economies 34–6; transnational 28
nonstate actors: and complex climate governance 187–8; institutions mediate participation by 15–17; preference and strategies of 13–15
Non-State Actor Zone for Climate Action (NAZCA) 52, 56; voluntary climate action 57–8, **67**

offset standards, network of *129*
OMV Group 81
Ostrom, E. 3, 30, 90

Paris Agreement (2015) 3, 21, 120, 146, 149, 168
Parks, B. 41
Paterson, M. 147
Petrobras 79
Pfeifer, S. 147
Pinkse, J. 147
policy supporter 61; firm-level variables **77**
political liberties 15
postpurchase dissonance 31
Potoski, M. 11, 90
Powers, R. M. 41
Prakash, A. 11, 14, 16, 19–21, 26; corporate environmental policies 53, 90; investment costs 94; private sector 153–5; TCG 186, 188, 192
private authority 121; emergence of 122; recognition of 124–5
private corporations, and TCG 186–7
private regulations, states' recognition of 119–21
private rules into national policy 124–6
public v. private carbon regulations, determinants of interactions **134**
public/private interactions **130**; definitions and theory 121–3; mapping the dependent variable 130–3

resource mobilization theories, of social movements 91
Responsible Care program 32
Rio de Janeiro 89; "Earth Summit" (1992) 6
Rivera, J. 54
Roberts, T. 41
Roger, C. B. 1, 11, 69, 87, 193; TCG 43, 63, 185; TCG database 9, 56, 158–9
Rolls-Royce 82

Sabel, C. 108
Schwartz, J. D. 151
SEAP *see* Sustainable Energy Action Plans (SEAP)
Shandong Energy Group 79
shared TCGs 98–9, **115, 116**; latent space model estimates for **115, 116**; negative binomial estimation for **117**
shirking problem 33
Siemens 80
Snidal, D. 148, 180
social capital 35
social movements, resource mobilization theories of 91
Sodexo 58
SOEs *see* state-owned enterprises (SOEs)
state-dyadic level, individual organization to 96–8
state-owned enterprises (SOEs) 185
Strand, R. 54
strategic rationality, theoretical model for 112–13
subnational actors: institutions' mediation of participation 15–17; preference and strategies 13–15

INDEX

subnational authorities 16
subnational entities, transnational cooperation of 155
subnational governments, and TCG 185–6
Sullivan, R. 147
sustainability, commitment to **77–8**
Sustainable Energy Action Plans (SEAP) 32

TCG *see* transnational climate governance (TCG)
3M 80, 81
Tierney, M. J. 41
transformational leaders 54
transgovernmental initiatives 16
transgovernmental networks 1
transitional economies: Eastern and Central Europe 28, 29; Eurasia 28, 29; European Union 28–9; NGOs in 34–6
transnational activity, domestic policy on *92*, 94
transnational actors 17–18
transnational advocacy networks 15
transnational climate governance (TCG) 2; activities (1990–2010) *8*; actor composition (1990–2010) *8*; as climate change mitigation 190–2; cross-national patterns of participation (2012) *10*; domestic politics and 184–5; emergence of 183–4; initiatives 3–5, 9, 13, 14, 21, 194; interaction with formal regulations and policy 17–19; mapping the world of 4–9; and national-level climate policy 188–90; as network 88–90, 99; NGOs and 186; participation in 2, 9, 16–17, 55; political actors and participation incentives 185; private corporations and 186–7; rise of (1990–2010) 7; subnational governments and 185–6; theoretical approach to 10–13; *see also* shared TCGs
transnational climate governance, and Global 500 56, **65–8**, 67–70; CDP, voluntary carbon disclosure 58–9, **68**; country-level covariates 63–4, **78–9**; data and models 59; dependent variables 60; firm-level covariates 60–3, **77–8**; model specifications 64; NAZCA, voluntary climate action 57–8, **67**
transnational climate governance (TCG) initiatives 3–5, 9, 13, 14, 21; creation of 153; by purpose 153
transnational climate governance (TCG) initiatives, measuring mitigation orientation of 149, 160–7; conceptual difficulties 149–51; design criteria for effective mitigation 151–3; NGOs 156–7; operationalization 158–60;

orchestration by international organizations and national governments 157–8; private sector 153–5; subnational governments 155–6
transnational entrepreneurs 13
transnational networks 18
transnational NGOs 28

UNFCCC *see* United Nations Framework Convention on Climate Change (UNFCCC)
United Nations: climate negotiations 6
United Nations Environment Program (UNEP) 191
United Nations Framework Convention on Climate Change (UNFCCC) 49–50, 57, 146, 147
United Nations Global Compact (2001) 30
United States Environmental Protection Agency 30
urban populations, in cities with submitted action plans **43**
U.S. Agency for International Development 34
USAID 186

van de Meene, S. 88
VanDeVeer, S. 147
variable operationalization 36; domestic controls 38; independent variable 36–7; international controls 37–8
Verified Carbon Standard (VCS) 127–9, 140
Vogel, D. 123
voluntary carbon disclosure *see under* Carbon Disclosure Project
voluntary climate action **67**; corporate 57; NAZCA 57–8
voluntary programs 33–4; participation in 27, 32

Wal-Mart Stores, Inc. 57–8
Ward, H. 15, 16–17, 19, 20, 41, 86; alternative theoretical rationale 156; conflict between countries 98; NGOs and TCG 186, 188–90, 192–3, 194
Ward, M. D. 100
Weinfurter, A. J. 151
Widerberg, O. 88
Wilson, S. E. 41
Woolsworth 81
World Business Council on Sustainable Development 128
World Development Indicators 36
World Economic Forum: SlimCity program 89
world politics, implications for study of 19–20